SOLID

AN INDESTRUCTIBLE FOUNDATION
FOR NEW CHRISTIANS

JOHN MYER

gospel Outfitters

COLUMBUS, OHIO

Gospeloutfitters.com

Solid
Published by Gospel Outfitters. P.O. Box 604, Worthington,
OH 43085-0604.

Unless otherwise indicated, all scripture quotations used in
this book are from the *New King James Version* (NKJV) © 1979,
1980, 1982 by Thomas Nelson, Inc. Used by permission.

Scripture quotations identified NASB are from the *New American
Standard Bible,* copyright © 1960, 1962, 1963, 1971, 1972, 1973,
1975, 1977, 1995 by the Lockman Foundation. Used by
permission.

Library of Congress Control Number: 2005935204

ISBN: 0-9765284-2-8

Printed in the United States of America

CONTENTS

ACKNOWLEDGMENTS

WITH THANKS...

No book is a one man show. Aside from the author, there are influences from the past and help from the present that all play a part in producing it. As for the past, I would like to acknowledge the input of the many Christians who have brought me spiritual profit, from Martin Luther to Charles Spurgeon to Watchman Nee (including a list of names before, after, and in between theirs). Though they are too numerous to mention here, they have all, in some ways, left an enduring impression upon me. Therefore, I do not wish to pretend that I have invented the wheel in this book. The ministries of others are also to be credited.

As for the present, there are those who have greatly participated in producing this work. Thanks go to my wife, Aleisha, who gave me total support during the time of its writing along with many helpful suggestions. Also, to Ian Best, who, though he was in law school at the time, managed to edit a large portion of the manuscript. There are other players in the *Solid* saga who deserve mention: Todd and Rachel Burroughs (for their special encouragement), Sarah Chang and Heather Tropp (for photos), Tim Button (for being the boy on the rock), Tom McNaughton and Nigel Tomes (for editorial considerations), all the folks whose stories I wrote about (but whose names I have mostly changed), and last but not least, everyone who kept asking me, "How's the book coming?"

THE WINDS AND WAVES ARE COMING

The winds and waves are coming; it's only a matter of time. Jesus said,

> "Everyone who hears these words of Mine, and acts upon them, may be compared to a wise man, who built his house upon the rock. And the rain descended and the floods came, and the winds blew, and burst against that house; and yet it did not fall, for it had been founded upon the rock.
> And everyone who hears these words of Mine, and does not act upon them, will be like a foolish man, who built his house upon the sand. And the rain descended, and the floods came, and the winds blew, and burst against that house; and it fell, and great was its fall." (Matt. 7:24-27 NASB)

The key thought that crops up in these verses is *when*, not *if*. It is *when* the floods came, not *if* they came. It is *when* the winds blew, not *if* they blew. Trials, it seems, are all but guaranteed. Every man's "house"—his life—will face the onslaught of wind and wave.

Yet, according to the Lord's word, some failed to build their house on the rock. When the inevitable storm hit, what they had constructed collapsed with a catastrophic bang— "*great* was its fall."

But others were wiser and buit on the rock. The storm hit their house too, yet it remained. Take note that it survived, but not because God diverted trouble away from it. That house weathered the winds and waves without the benefit of a force field or some other special blessing. It endured because of its *foundation*. The storm unleashed the same fury on it but couldn't overcome the rock upon which it sat. This should lead us to the conclusion that foundation is a critical matter in the Christian life.

Trials don't miraculously bypass people because they go to church or because they've made a profession of faith. Crisis situations can afflict anyone, *especially* the Christian who has just started off in the faith. When that happens, it's important to be firmly footed on something stable and trustworthy.

Most of us place the utmost confidence in feelings of some kind; in other words, feelings of being saved, or feelings of being loved by God. During various trials, we look to these sensations for reassurance. But the feelings that we hope will rescue us are fragile and fickle. Consider the human condition: just eating a few doughnuts results in a burst of joy that lasts twenty minutes. Then for an hour after that, we alternate between needing a nap and needing to yell at somebody. All it took was a few sweets and a few minutes to go from earth to heaven to hell. Many Christians have tried to build their faith on such emotional sensations, but found that irate moods and the blues and other feelings swept in and demolished everything.

Others have tried to found their Christian life upon their success in changing themselves. All was well until they just had to smoke that cigarette or they finally cracked and shouted profanity at the office "jerk." Overcome with disappointment, they wonder if they should even bother following Christ anymore. Their foundation of self-improvement turned out to be a layer of thin ice which, when they tried to stand on it, gave way underneath them.

That is not to say that Christians should be void of feelings or positive change—only that the foundational aspect of our faith must be something solid, static, and unchangeable. If we go on to build up a Christian life that rests upon sugar highs, personal accomplishments, or moods, then we have built upon sand. The first crisis that strikes will wash our faith away.

Anyone who wishes to continue following the Lord had better have an indestructible foundation. It should be invulnerable to disappointment, failure, depression, and doubt. Since we often slip into bouts of spiritual laziness, it must be able to suffer neglect. And since some others, including Satan himself, will hate our new faith, our foundation should be capable of withstanding attack. This is not all. From the positive angle, "you are God's *building*" (1 Cor. 3:9), therefore He wants to do a work of eternal significance in your life. An activity of that caliber needs a permanent foundation, one that is not here today and gone tomorrow.

The requirements of being eternal, invulnerable, and indestructible disqualify everything in the created universe as candidates for the believer's foundation. Only one thing is left—*the rock*. The Lord told us that the "wise man...built his house upon *the rock*" (Matt. 7:24 NASB). Then, He defined the rock as "these words of mine" (Matt. 7:26 NASB). They are the only indestuctible platform on which to plant our feet. As Jesus said, "heaven and earth will pass away, but My words will by no means pass away" (Mark 13:31).

These same words are the basis for all the teachings in this book. Even so, none of the concepts presented in the upcoming pages have been cultivated in a theological bubble, separated from real life. The joys and struggles of new Christians whom I have worked with or observed over the years have shaped the very soul of this work. Lumped together with them are the various challenges from my own early Christian life as well. All such stories and experiences have been valuable to me in the writing of *Solid*. Though I may not always identify them in the text, they are at least silently there, adding the ingredient of firsthand experience.

The scope of this book deals with matters at the entry level of the Christian life—the fundamentals of salvation. Obviously, I hope new Christians will receive a strong introduction to these truths, but I realize that some readers may not necessarily fit the category of "Christian" at all. They will not yet have a clearly defined relationship with Christ. In those cases I hope that their reading will enable them to grasp the great potential of God's salvation. Then, maybe they could begin to understand why so many of us make a joyful noise over Jesus Christ. And maybe, just maybe, they would end up making that joyful noise over Him as well.

There are also potential readers of this book who will fit the description of "Christian," but no longer of *"new* Christian." They, too, may find help in these pages. Sheer time in the faith does not automatically mean clarity. Some truths, even foundational ones, can escape a believer's attention for years. They remain fuzzy due to all sorts of reasons. In that case, I hope that this book would be a crystallizing, clarifying, refocusing experience for them.

Finally, some Christian readers will already be conversant with everything in *Solid* simply because they themselves are solid. What possible profit could they get from reading this self-proclaimed beginner's guide? Perhaps the benefits would be more related to enjoyment than to education. Seasoned believers never tire of touring their faith. The sights of salvation are always thrilling, regardless of the vantage point from which they are viewed. A trip through this book for some then might be like a visit to the divine "Grand Canyon" all over again.

I believe there is something for everyone in *Solid*. As you journey through its contents, I hope above all else that the grace of the Lord Jesus Christ will be with you.

IT HAPPENED TO ME

I don't have a harrowing pre-salvation story to tell. My past didn't include riding with an outlaw motorcycle gang or being a member in a satanic cult group. I didn't play lead guitar for a wild rock and roll band. Nor was I an alcoholic or a drug addict. Compared to others, my story is not very dramatic. Before becoming a Christian I was just another young, indifferent guy whose main pursuit in life was to have fun. Philosophically speaking, I was not an atheist or agnostic. I had been raised in central Louisiana, in towns with names like "Ball," and "Pineville." These were places where belief in God was a given, kind of like belief in George Washington. But that type of faith, bred by southern culture, friends, and family, was basically impotent toward me.

At that time, I would rather have read the phone book

than the Bible, and to me, prayer was an exercise of talking to thin air. My feelings toward church weren't any better. I found it incredible that such a short block of time once a week could inflict so much boredom. I endured it the same way I did spinach and all the other things I had been told were good for me.

The Christian package seemed like something a person might want after they were done living. Maybe it would appeal to very old people, or young folks that had nothing else going for them. I decided to keep it at bay, visiting God at church once a week, but never allowing Him to visit me at home. Life just seemed too much fun to spoil with a bunch of serious "beliefs."

But reality has a way of catching up to people. It caught me when I left home to join the Army at age seventeen.
I had imagined the military as a big camping trip, where men ran around with guns. Instead, as an Army Private, I spent most of my time running around with a mop. I did floors, windows, and toilets. I shined boots, marched, and took orders from everyone. I was homesick in the worst kind of way and stationed more than three thousand miles away from my family.

Then the Army transferred me to Germany. That raised the reality quotient in my life higher than it had been before. Now an entire country surrounded me whose language I could not understand and whose culture was unfamiliar. My workplace was called "the rock," a small mountain where the winter was positively inhuman. It was located close to the boundary of a communist country, which meant everyone in my unit lived under the gloom of a potential World War III. There was no escaping. I still had years left to serve on my tour of duty, and my warm, peaceful little Louisiana home was on the other side of the world. A simple visit there would have meant a thousand dollars and a seventeen-hour plane flight.

When the gritty reality of life had begun to feel miserable and I had sunk to a new pessimistic low, one more thing happened. A long-distance relationship that I had worked hard to maintain fell apart. That was the last straw. It was

April 1984, about nine o'clock at night. I took a walk out onto a deserted field and yelled up at the sky, at God, blaming Him for everything. While I was at it, I brought up all the other disappointments in my life that I felt were His fault. My monologue went on and on, severely bitter, but genuine. In fact, I had never been so honest with God.

Then something happened. As I continued my complaints, naming events where I felt God had let me down, a sense of shame began to smother my anger. I had laid my life on the table, and for the first time, taken a close, honest look at what was there. It was embarrassing. There were years of moral indiscretions and misplaced priorities. My many problems started to look like the result of my own stupidity and not divine incompetence. I realized that I was tasting the bitter fruit of a life without God, and it was all my fault.

The sky was quiet that night. No voice came booming out of the clouds. But somehow, in the space of less than fifteen minutes, a quiet transformation occurred within me, driving the angry wind out of my sail. My long cold war against God subsided, and for the first time, I felt warm and green toward Jesus Christ. A springtime had entered my heart. The prospect of a relationship with Christ no longer seemed awkward or embarrassing. He had suddenly ceased being a distant, murky figure from my childhood religion, and began to blaze with a reality that I had never known.

My heart swarmed with feelings. I was sorry. I was happy. I was broken. I was whole. I was conquered. I was victorious. Yet with all of this going on inside, I still did not understand it. My Bible literacy was on par with my knowledge of rocket science.

The only thing that I had as a knowledge base, were the opinions of Army buddies, and none of those were favorable toward Jesus experiences. According to them, Christ was for men who couldn't cope with women problems or ill health or bad habits. He was a crutch that weak fellows sometimes used to straighten out their messed-up lives. As soon as things got better, they predicted, the Jesus "crutch" would go right back in the closet. That theory made the Christian experience look like nothing more than a placebo. It also made me wonder if I was just another person using a religious experience to get through a crisis.

Other attitudes around me were just as skeptical. For instance, earlier some fellows I knew had laughed at a girl who had decared she was a Christian. After making a big deal of telling everyone she had changed and would no longer drink and run around, she got tired of being good and went back to her old ways. The whole thing made Christ look like a novelty that would wear off. I had to admit that a lot of interests had marched in and out of my life. I had gotten involved with them, thrown money at them, poured time into them, and just as quickly gotten back out of them.

I wondered if Christ was going to be just another one of those things. The very thought of it provoked me to hide any evidence of my new relationship with God. No matter how things turned out, I didn't want to be laughed at like that girl who had lost her faith. I started zipping up a Bible under my coat and reading it when no one was looking. It was my attempt to try on the Christian faith like underwear.

Since that time in 1984, a lot of things have changed. I've been out of the Army so long that I've nearly forgotten all of its drill, ceremony, and jargon. That whole personal era simply faded with the passing of years. Also, my marital status changed. The carefree young bachelor's world I once inhabited gave way to marriage and domestication. Even my twenty-eight inch waist (sadly) changed into something heftier. Now in the middle of all this flux, the item I would have identified as the most fragile and most likely to collapse—my fledgling involvement with Christ—never did go quietly into the night. The opposite happened. As I continued to explore the Bible, pray, and receive the input of other Christians, Christ seemed to impress Himself even more upon my deepest sentiments. He never returned to the closet. It was a case of the "crutch" throwing the closet away. Christ became so real that moving on and forgetting about Him seemed out of the question.

Knowing what I know today, I can look back on that April night and identify what happened to me—I was saved by

faith in Jesus Christ. The entire scene had fallen far short
of a polished religious event. Somewhere though, in the
midst of my crying, complaining, and repenting, faith in
Christ was there, and God saw it.

IT HAPPENED TO YOU, TOO

Now I'm going to tell your story. I'm going to relate how
you were saved—not the details, because I obviously don't
know them—but your story, nonetheless. Every person who
has truly been saved has been saved the same way. It's like
being born. The details might vary, but every human birth
comes from the same process of male and female
reproductive substances coming together. No one gets
creative with this one and finds an alternate route, like
growing out of a watermelon patch. We are all products of
the same biological process.

Salvation also comes by means of one *spiritual* process:
faith in Jesus Christ. We might hear a thousand different
stories about how people came to Christ, but regardless of
the particular circumstances surrounding each, all were
saved by faith in Him. No one is saved by an alternate route.
For instance, no one is saved because he was such a good
person or because he was born into a Christian family.
Christians are no more brought forth by those things than
storks bring forth babies. The Bible says a man is only
justified before God "by *faith* in Jesus Christ" (Gal. 2:16),
and this is exactly how I know your story. The scriptures
tell me that through believing in Jesus, I have been saved
and so have you.

Not only have we all been saved the same way, but even
more, we've all received the same *kind* of salvation, one of
like quality. Jude spoke of it as "our *common* salvation" (Jude
3)—salvation that all believers commonly share. No one can
claim that upon believing in Jesus he received a higher
quality of salvation than did others. Neither can anyone
complain that when he believed, he received a substandard
one. The apostles referred to the believers as "those who

have received a faith of the *same kind* as ours" (2 Pet. 1:1). Christians might differ in maturity and in gifts for service, but the salvation they initially receive is identical in value with that of even the mightiest apostles.

The way of salvation and the quality of salvation are the same from one believer to the next. Also, the *contents* of our salvation are the same. God does not deliver an economy package to one and a luxury package to another. Most Christians are not aware that when they believed in Christ, they automatically received specific items, whether they asked for them or not. In this sense, believing in Christ is similar to swallowing a multi-vitamin. The ingredients are listed on the label with words like "pantothenic acid," "chromium," and "selenium." You don't know what those things are, you don't know why you need them, and you don't even know what would happen to your health without them. But somewhere in that freckle-sized vitamin is a thing or two you definitely think you need, like Vitamin C, or Vitamin B-12, so you do the smart thing, which is to swallow the pill.

We all came to Jesus looking for ingredients we thought we needed. Some of us were lonely and drawn to Him because of His love. Others experienced tragedy and came to Him for comfort. Some, feeling empty, came to Him for meaning. Others were haunted by guilt and saw in Him a cure for sins. A few curious souls were drawn to Him by the allure of discovery. Regardless, we believed in Christ, embraced Him, and received Him. We "swallowed the vitamin." According to us, we believed in order to get what we wanted. In actuality, we believed and got things we never asked for, never thought we needed, and never even knew existed. As Peter said, "His divine power *has* given to us *all things* that pertain to life and godliness" (2 Pet. 1:3).

The moment we believed in Christ, we received Him and were completely outfitted with everything we needed for salvation. In view of the whole New Testament this amounts to six basic ingredients:

> *The forgiveness of sins*
> *Deliverance from hell*

Jesus Christ
The Holy Spirit
A new birth with the eternal life of God
A position as a child of God

These items are the sum and substance of salvation. The day you received them was the most notable day of your life; you just might not have realized it at the time. Make no mistake about it, what happened to us when we believed in Jesus eclipses anything else in our previous life story.

WHERE CHRISTIANS GO WRONG

Many new Christians get off to a bad start, simply by neglecting their good start. They have been forgiven of their sins and have been saved from hell. They have received a new birth, have Christ living in them, and are now called "sons of God." But they don't know what any of that means. They might not be aware of the new rights or privileges that belong to them, nor do they seek to find out. Instead, from the very beginning, these Christians learn to major in the minors. That means they begin to pay a lot of attention to religious "stuff"—concerns, activities, pursuits, and questions that make no contribution to any true spiritual growth. That is why the initial experience of meeting Christ turns into a dead-end street for them. As they "cool off," the idea of following Christ has all the excitement of following the mailman. In a sad sense, the honeymoon sours before the marriage even begins.

As I write this, I'm reminded of Jay, a fellow who turned up in a Bible study I was conducting awhile ago. Jay had only recently been saved when he joined us. His enthusiasm for Christ had not been explosive, but after a month of fellowship in our homes, his interest was on the rise.

It looked like that in time, Jay would grow into a very healthy Christian. But then something happened. One day as he listened to a Christian radio program, he was introduced to a subject that hooked him. It was a topic of minor dispute among Christians—certainly nothing to do with Christian orthodoxy. Yet Jay was affected and then distracted by it to the point that his already weak passion for Christ began to grow even weaker. He stopped exploring his faith, even though he still hardly knew anything about it. Jay only seemed excited when he could talk about the new religious issue he had shouldered, or even better, if he could argue about it. Christ became tired and disinteresting to him, like a movie he had already seen many times. I wish I could say that I was able to help him, but I wasn't. Jay eventually disappeared, and I haven't seen him in years.

I also wish I could say that his case was unique. But again, I can't. I have seen plenty of new Christians get prematurely involved in things that eventually claimed precedence over their foundation. Not one of these people whom I know of had a faith that developed healthily. There are simply no shortcuts. If we don't develop a sound introductory knowledge of Christ and His salvation, it's hard to imagine how they could rank anywhere on our priority list. It's no great spiritual secret, either. Anyone would agree that you can't love someone you don't know, and you can't appreciate something you don't understand.

In Revelation chapter 5, a thunderous roar of praise surrounds Christ—

> "The voice of many angels around the throne, the living creatures, and of the elders; and the number of them was ten thousand times ten thousand, and thousands of thousands, saying with a loud voice: 'Worthy is the lamb who was slain to receive power and riches and wisdom, and strength and honor and glory and blessing!" (Rev. 5:11-12)

Could our voices join that throng, also shouting "Worthy is the lamb!"? It all depends upon our foundational understanding of Him and what He has done for us.

1

THE UNIQUE SAVIOR

Some time ago, a survey quizzed random groups of people, asking them to name one character from the Bible. The majority responded with what seemed to them the most obvious name of all.

No, not Jesus.

Moses.

Apparently where a lot of folks are concerned, the central figure of the Bible is the man who gave the Ten Commandments. At first this sounds like nothing of any real consequence. However, it does make a statement about God. For if *the* man of the Bible is Moses, whose entire life revolved around Old Testament law, then *the* God of the Bible must be a God of law. Once people view the Lord this way, seeing Him primarily as rule maker, giver, and enforcer, it leads to a further assumption. Namely, that a relationship with Him means following hundreds of regulations.

Of course, people who go down that road will soon run into trouble. They will begin to find that they are not very good at keeping the rules. Though God has said many times "Thou *Shalt*," they will find themselves saying "I *can't*." A relationship with God of that kind, founded upon behavioral performance, will be full of trying, failing, and then trying harder. Most people can only take so much of that. Finally, throwing up their hands in frustration and walking away, they will conclude that a relationship with God is too "high maintenance" for the common mortal. The endeavor might have been stimulating at first, but like a fad diet, it just wasn't going to last for long. The Bible says that "as many as are of the works of the Law are under a *curse*" (Gal. 3:10 NASB). And that is exactly how they will feel as their every attempt to obey God and be a better person seems to fall flat.

Because of human weaknesses, any attempt to build a relationship with a law-giving God is futile. The closer we get to Him and His commandments, the more we see how we've failed to keep them and the trouble we're in as a result. God's law cannot save anyone. It only educates men as to why they deserve to be condemned.

Some find the concept of God as Supreme Legislator and Judge too legalistic. They prefer the apparently kinder, more benign Creator of Genesis chapter one, who, as a back-to-nature Spirit, only presides over forests and trout streams. "Just give me that," they say. "Simple spirituality with no hassles."

But there are definite limitations in having only a creator. We can witness crashing waterfalls and starry nights. We can bathe in one magnificent sunset after another. None of these, however, addresses the fact that there are some very ugly things both within us at the personal level and in the world at large. After an exhilarating walk on the beach, we must go home and deal with the hurtful things of life, many of which we have brought on ourselves. And if that isn't enough, the nightly news provides a panorama of awful things others have done. There's not much that God can do about any of it as long as He is limited to the role of Creator. The power to make sea scapes and song birds cannot repair the gross darkness of the human heart. It could only succeed in engineering nice scenery for us to look at as we perish.

Men need a Savior, and thankfully, God has risen to that need. The Apostle Paul certainly understood this. In his first letter to Timothy, he wrote of *"God our Savior..."* (1 Tim. 1:1). In the very next chapter, he again wrote about *"God* our *Savior,* who desires all men to be saved and to come to the knowledge of the truth" (1 Tim. 2:4). The thought surfaces yet again in his letter to Titus, as he wrote of *"...God* our *Savior..."* (Titus 2:10) and that "the kindness and the love of *God* our *Savior* toward man appeared" (Titus 3:4).

Of course the role of Savior is not an easy one. Real salvation involves straightening out the serious mess of the human situation, while at the same time bestowing the most profound blessings. Only God is qualified to shoulder those tasks. A true Savior could not be anyone less than Him. However, we live in a world bursting at the seams with persons, philosophies, methodologies, and worldviews, all purporting to be God, or to at least be able to introduce us to Him. These clamour for attention, promising to solve the issues of human life. Under such confusing circumstances, if God were not specific about how to relate to Him as the Savior, it would leave us all in a quandry. We would be like little children wandering the worst parts of a major city at night with instructions to "find someone to save you." Many of us would find something all right, but it would not be salvation. God, therefore, must somehow help the human race to know how to find Him, the authentic Savior, so that we can receive an authentic salvation. In other words, God must grant us a point of connectivity.

This is exactly where Jesus comes in. The literal meaning of the name Jesus is "Jehovah Saves." God did many things in the Old Testament under His chief name, Jehovah, but when He moved to save men in the New Testament, He did it as "Jehovah Saves." That name is the unique place of attachment to Him as the Savior.

God did not tell us to believe only in Himself

for salvation. He never said, "Believe in God and you shall be saved." Instead, He gave us the specific name of Jesus. The Bible says, "...there is salvation in no one else; for there is no other *name* under heaven that has been given among men, by which we must be *saved*" (Acts 4:12 NASB). Besides Jesus, there is no other name, whether Peter, or Mary, or Buddha, or Mohammed, or Confucius. The phrase "No other name" eliminates all other options. It means that no additional name, whether angelic, human, or divine has been vested with the power of salvation. God has not exalted anyone else before the human race as an object of faith:

> "At the *name of Jesus,* every knee should bow, of those in heaven, and of those on earth, and of those under the earth, and...every tongue should confess that *Jesus Christ* is Lord..." (Phil. 2:10-11)

Now the entrance into salvation has been marked for all to see. Even Jesus Himself pointed it out when He said, "I am the way, the truth, and the life. No one comes to the Father except through Me" (John 14:6). Today some people do imagine that they can have Jehovah without having Jehovah Saves. They like to talk about "the big man upstairs" and "the good Lord" being in their lives, while wanting nothing to do with Jesus. But "Whoever denies the Son does not have the Father either; he who acknowledges the Son has the Father also" (1 John 2:23).

Consider the picture that the Holy Trinity[1] presents to us. There the Son is inseparably connected to the Father and the Spirit. The Father delights in the Son (Matt. 3:17), the Father is in the Son and the Son is in Him (John 14:10), the Father's work is the Son's work (John 5:17, 14:10), the Father is known by knowing the Son (John 8:19), the Father is always with the Son (John 8:19), whoever has seen the

---

[1]For a short commentary on the subject of the Holy Trinity, see Appendix 1.

Son has seen the Father (John 14:9), and the Son is the image of the invisible God (Col. 1:15) and the fullness of the godhead bodily (Col. 2:9). Finally, while every knee bows in the name of Jesus and confesses that He is Lord, it is "to the glory of God the Father" (Phil. 2:11). God therefore desires "...that *all* should honor the Son just as they honor the Father. He who does not honor the Son does not honor the Father who sent Him" (John 5:23).

As for the Spirit, He and the name of the Lord Jesus are so connected that they jointly wash, sanctify, and justify the believers (1 Cor. 6:11). It is only in the Spirit that one is capable of giving the highest honors to Jesus since "no one can say that *Jesus is Lord* except by the *Holy Spirit*"(1 Cor. 12:3). Furthermore, the Lord Jesus told us that the function of the Spirit is to "teach you all things, and bring to your remembrance all things that *I* said to you" (John 14:26).

The Spirit does not have His own private revelation and teaching agenda. He makes known whatever the Son has spoken. As Jesus said, "He will glorify *Me*..." (John 16:14).

God is not looking for some kind of polite, deferential respect to be paid to Jesus. In a world of perishing people, only the most serious of honors must be given to "Jehovah Saves." This is a continuing theme that runs throughout the New Testament. Consider one instance that occurred on a mountaintop where Jesus had taken three of His disciples.

> "He was transfigured before them. His face shone like the sun, and His clothes became as white as the light. And behold, Moses and Elijah appeared to them, talking with Him." (Matt. 17:1-2)

When Peter saw such distinguished visitors as Moses and Elijah, he was no longer quite sure where to put Jesus. Should it have been a higher or lower place? What proportion of honor was Jesus to be given now, in the presence of these other two great men of God? Peter's idea was to do what was most fair and equitable—to treat all three of them as equals. That was why he offered to build each of them a tabernacle (Matt. 17:4). The mortal mind always lowers Christ in order to be respectful and inclusive of everyone else. It's the best way to avoid offending other mortal minds. However, this arrangement that seemed so reasonable to men brought an immediate protest from God.

> "While he [Peter] was still speaking, behold, a bright cloud overshadowed them; and suddenly a voice came out of the cloud, saying, 'This is My beloved Son, in whom I am well pleased. Hear *Him!*'" (Matt. 17:5)

This sudden interruption from the Father was meant to correct Peter and the rest of the disciples. God never intended any man, no matter how great, to share equal honors with His Son. The command to "Hear Him" should have helped the disciples refocus their divided attention on Christ alone. But if they had still missed the point, there was an additional hint for them: "...When they had lifted up their eyes, they saw no one but Jesus *only*" (Matt. 17:8). The removal of Moses and Elijah from the scene should have strengthened the lesson that none can compare with Christ. It is not that others are higher, equal, or lower than Him; the fact is, they are nowhere to be found in comparison to Him! When eyes are lifted, the divine intention is that there should be "no one but Jesus only."

Yes, other figures have risen up throughout history, claiming to have found different ways to God. But Jesus said, "Most assuredly, I say to you, he who does not enter the sheepfold by *the door,* but climbs up some other way, the same is a thief and a robber" (John 10:1). Thus the Lord warned very clearly about those who led others in a quest for forgiveness, eternal life, peace, and joy, without leading them through the right entrance. He went on to say, "*I* am the door. If anyone enters by *Me,* he will be saved" (John 10:9). An authentic, biblical salvation only awaits one who enters through *the* door, not just *any* door.

God could not have demonstrated more clearly that Christ is the doorway into salvation. He marked it by showing a man who, during His time on earth healed the sick, raised the dead, commanded the demons to flee, controlled the weather, walked on water, and spoke mysteries hidden from the very beginning of the world. As if that were not enough, when this man died the earth shook, the sun was eclipsed, rocks split open, and dead people walked through the streets of the city. The greatest demonstration occurred when this dead man resurrected from the grave, was seen by over five hundred eye-witnesses and finally in a public display, ascended to heaven. Truly, the gateway of salvation has been divinely marked, lit, and announced with trumpets.

God "desires all men to be saved" (1 Tim. 2:4), but only He is capable of being the Savior. This is why He stands on the world's horizon and says, "Look to Me, and be saved, all you ends of the earth! For I am God and there is no other" (Isa. 45:22). Many millions throughout the centuries have listened to that command. They lifted their eyes and found a most compelling sight, for they saw Jehovah who created the world, but at the same time Jehovah Saves who rescues those who live in it. They saw Jehovah who gave the law, while seeing Jehovah Saves who rescues those who have broken it. So, they (and we) have come to Him. As Jesus said, "I, if I am lifted up from the earth, will draw all peoples to myself" (John 12:32). And being drawn, we have found far more than a religious figure, a philosophy, or a lifestyle. We have discovered a glorious and complete salvation.

2

FORGIVENESS OF SINS

SAVED FROM WHAT?

Christians use the word "saved" in a way that can sound puzzling to their non-Christian neighbors. We speak of such-and-such a person as being *saved,* or about this or that person who is not *saved* yet. We are sad over those who died *unsaved,* and sometimes ask people "Are you *saved?*" The word itself may not make sense to the general public when used that way. Most folks associate being "saved" with a life or death situation, like when an infant is rescued from a burning house, or a heart attack victim revived with CPR. The average person, then, would think of "saved" as resferring to someone or something that was kept from death, loss, waste, or damage. Since most don't see themselves as being in such imminent danger, they are "okay."

Salvation does not apply to them, and they don't need to apply for it.

I often run headlong into this attitude. During mission trips I meet people who politely turn down gospel literature, saying, "Please keep it and give it to someone who really needs it." Behind that apparently noble, selfless concern for "those who really need it" is the attitude that *"I* don't need it." And some honestly believe that is true. Perhaps they would agree with the poet Robert Browning—"God's in His heaven, all's right with the world."

Scripture however, doesn't agree with such a rosy "weather report." In fact, the Bible is full of an urgency to demonstrate why all is *not* well with us. Out of the eight thousand verses comprising the New Testament, it only takes the first twenty-one of them to identify why we need to be saved. We are told that "JESUS...will save His people from their *sins"* (Matt. 1:21). Salvation then, is not introduced along with the problem of being overweight, unemployed, or any other dilemma human beings have ways of working out on their own. The salvation of Jesus deals with sins, and rest assured, they are not the simple "oops" in behavior that we usually think. They are deadly. The Lord Jesus once told a group of hardened religious hypocrites, "You will die in your sins" (John 8:24). Chill finality was in those words, and even if we don't know what dying in sins really means, somehow we know from the Lord's solemn statement that it must be very, very bad.

WHAT IS A SIN?

The word "sin" literally means to mis-aim, to miss the mark, like an archer who misses a bullseye. When David sinned, he said to God, "Against...*you only* have I sinned" (Ps. 51:4). This means that the mark, the bullseye David missed was God Himself. In principle, all sin is ultimately against Him, no matter who else is directly affected. Other biblical examples support this, such as in Genesis 39:9, where Joseph had been tempted by a married woman to commit adultery with her. Although it would have been an offense against her husband, Joseph said, "How then can I do this great wickedness and sin against *God?*"

The problem is not that we disappoint our parents or run afoul of cultural norms or fail to live up to our personal best. Sin means that in either deeds, words, or attitudes we fail to match God. And since the Bible presents the standard of God in written form for all to see, no one can claim ignorance as an excuse. Anyone can read or at least hear about what God expects of us in scripture. It takes a lot of the guesswork out of knowing what counts as sin.[1]

WHY GOD HATES SIN

In the Bible, God expresses His hatred for sin in the strongest possible way, comparing it to gangrene (2 Tim. 2:16-17 NASB), the plague (1 Kings 8:38-39), corruption (2 Tim. 3:8), the polluted blood of afterbirth (Eze. 16:5-6), the vomit of dogs (2 Pet. 2:22a), the mud of a pig wallow (2 Pet. 2:22b), the grave (Matt. 23:27-28), and poison (Rom. 3:13).

The human feeling toward sin is, of course, much friendlier. For the most part, we tend to think of our sins as innocent mischief, blunders and small weaknesses that we shouldn't lose sleep over. We also wonder why sins are so foul in the sight of God and why He seems to overreact toward them.

---

[1]Some Bible teachers have rightly pointed out that there is a difference between "sin" (singular) and "sins" (plural). Sin (singular) has to do with our sinful nature, while sins (plural) refer to the deeds that come out of that nature. For the purpose of keeping our study brief and general, I have chosen to blur the distinction between the two as the Bible sometimes does (John 1:29). Therefore, where it is possible, I will refer to "sin" and "sins" interchangeably.

SINS SAY, "NO ONE IS IN CHARGE—EXCEPT ME!"

In order to answer why God hates sin, we need some basic understanding. First of all, since God created the universe, He is the legal owner of it. That means He has the full right to make every rule that governs it. Whoever disagrees with that arrangement needs to realize that this universe is someone else's property. It is not ours simply because we live in it. As a teenage boy, I frequently had to face this issue. My family had rules governing the use of the telephone, bedtimes, treatment of other family members, and curfew. If I argued too much with my parents over any one of those items, they would nicely remind me that I was living in their home. The human race often needs this kind of reminder. We don't typically have a keen awareness that the ground we stand on or the air we breathe legally belongs to the One who made them. Whenever that is the case—when we don't realize that we are on someone else's property —it becomes hard for us to feel any sense of obligation to the owner. The Bible clears up any such confusion by telling us, "All things came into being by Him, and apart from Him nothing came into being that has come into being" (John 1:3 NASB). Since this is the case, "heaven and the highest heavens belong to the Lord your God, also the earth with all that is in it" (Deut. 10:14). God's moral requirements upon us are therefore perfectly legal.

Now this is exactly where sin is a problem, because "...sin is lawlessness" (1 John 3:4)—the very absence of the law of God. Sinful acts are indulgences that reject God's regulation. They make the statement that there is no law in the universe, and that no one is in charge, except the sinner, who lives however he pleases. This is a blatant disregard of God's rightful authority. It says that the Lord's rule can safely be set aside and replaced with whatever standard the sinner likes. That could never be a suitable arrangement. The Bible says, "Your throne, O God, is forever and ever; a scepter of righteousness is the scepter of Your kingdom. You have loved righteousness and *hated* lawlessness" (Heb. 1:8-9a). Thus, God could never have a relaxed attitude toward sins because they are violations of His righteous government.

SINS ARE THE UGLY OPPOSITE OF GOD

The seriousness of sin goes beyond just breaking rules. It literally offends every quality in God. Sins are the contradiction of God. They do not come from God. They do not look like God. They do not agree with what is in God. For instance, some sins, like murder, oppose the love of God, others, like lies, oppose the truth of God. Sins of adultery and sexual immorality offend His purity. Sins of filthy talk and blasphemy oppose His holiness. Sins of rage oppose His mercy; those of hard-heartedness contradict His compassion. Sins of injustice deny His righteousness. Sin defies each and every moral perfection in God. There is no possibility of His ever having a relationship with sin or tolerating the darkness of it. As the Bible says, "God is light and in Him is no darkness at all" (1 John 1:5), and "what fellowship has light with darkness?" (2 Cor. 6:14 NASB).

SIN HAS DESTROYED HUMANITY

The Lord hates sin even more because it ruined His most beloved work of creation. Scripture tells us that "God created man in His own image" (Gen. 1:27). Adam was literally an earth-bound photograph of His Creator. In terms of status, he was higher than anything on earth and only "a little lower than the angels" (Ps. 8:5). However, when Adam disobeyed God in the garden of Eden, he ate the wrong fruit and literally "swallowed" sin. From that time forward, sin began dwelling in his body (Rom. 6:6, 7:17-18). The man who had been only a little lower than the angels fell to a level lower than the devil. Rather than having authority over all the earth, as God meant for him (Gen. 1:26), he became "a slave to sin" (John 8:34).

Now human beings are defaced masterpieces, hardly expressing the One who made them. They habitually participate in sinful lusts: "then when lust has conceived, it gives birth to sin; and when sin is accomplished, it brings

31

forth death" (James 1:15 NASB). And this is what sinful people now display—death. In many pathetic ways, they look like they were made in the image of the devil, not of God. This sad condition steadily declines just as it is written, "Evil men...will grow worse and worse" (2 Tim. 3:13). God is not indifferent toward the disease that disfigures His crowning creation. He hates the sin that ruins us.

SINS TURN MEN AGAINST GOD

An even more harmful dimension of sin is the way it turns us against our own Maker. In the beginning man was neither afraid nor ashamed to approach Him. Then, sin came along and he literally hid from God (Gen. 3:8). The prospect of seeing the Lord's face or even hearing His voice became frightening, embarrassing, and awkward for Adam. This was the first step in an irreversible downward spiral. God had wanted a loving relationship with the man and woman He had created, but sin made it impossible. In fact, as people indulge in sin, hatred for God grows in them. That is why the Bible says, "You...were alienated and enemies in your mind *by* wicked works" (Col. 1:21).

Ginger was a young girl who was raised in a Christian home. Being offended with mistakes made by some people in the church, she decided to leave and go out into the world to "have some fun" for a while. Ginger had no idea what she was getting into. The more sins she committed, the harder her heart grew, the farther she got from God, and the less she found herself caring about it. At first she kept a distant respect for the things of God, but as time passed she grew cynical toward them, and eventually mocked them. God didn't have to do anything against her. Ginger's hatred for God increased as a result of *her* doing things against *Him*. Today, after almost a decade of godless living, it is difficult to even mention the word "God" around Ginger, without provoking her to anger and cursing. Evil works affected her exactly the way the Bible said they would; they made her an enemy of God.

All sinners feel an animosity toward the Lord.

"They say to God, 'depart from us'" (Job 21:14). They said of Christ, "Away with Him! Away with Him! Crucify Him!" (John 19:15) and they "always resist the Holy Spirit" (Acts 7:51). In the presence of such negativity, love for God is out of the question. That is why the Lord finds sin repulsive. It spoils any possibility of a sweet, harmonious relationship between Himself and man.

SIN TURNS MEN AGAINST ONE ANOTHER

God is not the only target of sin-inspired hatred. Men also turn their energies against one another. The result is that "the earth is filled with violence through them" (Gen. 6:13). From the very first murder, God told Cain, "Your brother's blood cries out to me from the ground" (Gen. 4:10). This one cry has now increased to millions. It is a gruesome chorus of brothers (according to God's creation), mauling and killing each other. Imagine what would happen if our own children were to turn on one another in a murderous rage. No words could express the grief that we would feel over it. Likewise, none can express what God feels as humanity follows a course of mutual destruction. And lying at the root of all the gore and mindless slaughter is sin, once again justifiably hated by God.

SINS TAKE MEN INTO DESTRUCTION

The tragedy of sin peaks with where it ultimately takes mankind. Throughout the sinner's brief time on earth, his quality of life is constantly derailed, as the Bible says, "There is no peace...for the wicked" (Isa. 48:22). Even so, the worst is not now. It is in the future. Beyond the grave lies the wrath of a God that hates sin and will judge it without mercy. The sinner knows this and lives with an intuitive dread that he must someday answer for all the evil things he has done. He has a "certain terrifying expectation of judgment, and the fury of a fire which will consume the adversaries" (Heb. 10:27 NASB). Although strictly speaking, it is sin that God hates and not the sinner, sin saturates the sinner like a

33

gasoline-soaked rag. As the fire of judgment deals with one, it will unavoidably deal with the other.

When sin is viewed through the lens of biblical truth, it begins to look less like mischief and more like something insidious. We find that God isn't upset over some trivial mistakes. He doesn't need to "lighten up." Sin *is* that serious.

THE EASE OF ACCUMULATING SINS

The phrase "sinned through ignorance" is often repeated in the book of Leviticus. It suggests that people are capable of sinning even when they don't set out to purposely do it. Sin comes almost as naturally to us as blinking our eyes. In fact, by the time the average person is twenty years old, he has "naturally" sinned so many times that he may have forgotten most of all that he has ever done wrong. He tends to remember only those things that were very bad, that scraped the bottom of the moral barrel. The rest exist as ill-defined memories, a cloud of guilt composed of numerous, tiny indiscretions that cannot be counted. If he is honest, he must agree that "My iniquities...are more than the hairs of my head" (Ps. 40:12).

Sin is truly extensive. It has a variety of expressions similar to the way that cars have makes and dogs have breeds. Being so multi-branched, it easily accumulates in the human experience. For instance, we all generally agree that lying is wrong, however, it is still wildly popular even among those who claim to tell the truth. Lies can come packaged in a lot of ways. There are lies that dispense with words and just use looks or actions or body language. There is lying with the best intentions (to help someone), lying with evil intentions (to destroy someone), little white lies (that couldn't hurt a fly), big black lies (that need a lot of little ones to prop it up), lying with the truth (for the *really* skillful liar), lying with untruth (for amateurs), and even lying to yourself. Given all the possibilities, it is likely that a man could condemn another man for being a liar, yet be a champion liar himself.

We could illustrate the same thing with stealing. While most folks consider the label of "thief" insulting, they may have often fit the description. There's "intelligent" stealing (like computer hacking and illegal downloads), "fair" stealing ("they don't pay me enough here, anyway"), white-collar stealing (like expense account fraud), non-tangible stealing (coming to work late, leaving early, playing computer games at the office), violent stealing (like mugging), "necessity" stealing ("It's okay because I need this but can't afford it"), big stealing (burglary, bank robbery), and small stealing (shoplifting penny candy, taking office supplies home). Theft is not just the domain of low-class bad guys. Once we factor in cheating on taxes, pirating free cable television, using postage stamps more than once, and a hundred other scenarios, it will be hard to find anyone who has not been involved in some form of thievery.

Related studies on things like greed, hatred, and selfishness would only further confirm that human beings are very good at sin in all its varied forms, even when they aren't aware that they're committing it.

WHO IS A SINNER?
SURELY NOT *ME!*

"Scott, would you like to pray with me?" I asked. The young man sitting next to me nodded. I had just shared the gospel with him, and he seemed to have believed in the Lord.

"I don't know how to pray," he said.

"That's okay," I told him, "You can just copy what I say."

Scott dutifully closed his eyes. I began to pray, "Lord Jesus, thank You."

He repeated what I said, doing his best to be genuine.

I continued, "Lord, I know that I'm a sinner."

Scott was silent. He wouldn't say that part. I glanced over at him and saw a look of disagreement on his face.

"I ain't a sinner," he said, matter-of-factly.

Maybe if I had worded the prayer differently, if I had

said, "Lord, I know I've made mistakes" or "I'm sorry for the bad stuff I've done," then maybe Scott wouldn't have hesitated to pray it. But I had mentioned the word *sin*. Scott didn't want to be implicated with sin in any way. He knew instinctively, like a lot of people do, that sin is worse than a little errant behavior. Sin means you're in trouble with God. Scott's response was typical—to deny it.

But denial only makes things worse. When a person denies that he has sinned, he makes shocking statements both about God and about himself. The Bible tells us, "If we say that we have not sinned, we make Him [God] a *liar*" (1 John 1:10). A refusal to recognize our involvement in sin basically says that God has lied about us, that He has falsely pronounced us sinners, when we are, in fact, innocent.

Denying that we have sinned also reveals something about our inward condition—"If we say that we have no sin, we deceive ourselves and the truth is not in us" (1 John 1:8). When a person is void of truth he does not know what sin is, nor does he have a personal awareness of what is light or darkness. That is why he can say, "I have no sin." Without truth he has no healthy moral orientation, no sense of righteousness or unrighteousness. His inward compass is broken; the needle never points to "true north," but only lines up with majority opinions. Pontius Pilate was this kind of person. He asked Jesus, "What is truth?" (John 19:38). That question meant he was obviously a stranger to it. All that Pilate had was "mob truth"—popular opinion. That was why He yielded to the crowd's murderous cries and wrongly condemned Jesus. Like Pilate, all who are without truth are also without the healthy realization of sin. As a result, they might admit to a lot of things—that they are only human, that they are not perfect, or that they make mistakes—but they will never admit to *sin*.

Regardless of what anybody feels about himself, the Bible acts like a giant slingblade, hacking the entire human race down to the same height. Romans 3:23 says, "*All* have sinned and fall short of the glory of God." Romans 3:10-12 also says, "...there is none righteous, no, not one...All have turned aside...there is none who does good, no, not one." When we

say *mistake*, the Bible says *sin*. Where we say *some* have
sinned, the Bible says *all* have sinned. And finally, though
we might agree that *all* have sinned, there is the final step
of acknowledging that *I* have sinned. That is the hardest
for men to do, yet the logic is inescapable; *all* includes *me*.
All includes *you*. With one swoop of the blade, the words *all*
and *sinned* make every single human life a story of
transgressions against God.

The biggest proof that men have sinned is that they "fall
short of the glory of God." The Lord Jesus is the only
exception. He never sinned, so He never fell short of God's
glory. The Gospel of Matthew tells us that "He was
transfigured...His face shown like the sun and His garments
became white as the light" (17:2). Though it was hidden
within Him during His time on earth, at that moment glory
burst out of Him in a display that the disciples saw
and never forgot.

Since the Lord Jesus could be in glory, this was certainly
a proof that He was not a sinner. The question is, can any
other person do that? If a man says he has not sinned, then
that means he has not fallen short of the glory of God. He
should be able to demonstrate the divine glory at will, like
Jesus. But no sinner can do so. Try it yourself, and for
further proof, challenge ten thousand others to try as well.
It will quickly become clear that all have sinned.

Who Is A Sinner? Surely Not *Them!*

Now, how about the good people? You probably know a
few of them—saintly souls that are sensitive, caring, and
selfless. Certainly we have sinned, but what about them?
Is it fair if they are mowed down to the same height as those
who are evil? If the good are condemned with the bad, then
God's judgment is tyrannical, indifferent, and just plain
wrong.

We ask God, "What about the *good* people?" but in light
of Romans 3:12, God would ask back, "*What* good people?

Where? Who?" When the Bible says, "there is *none* who does good," it is not condemning those that do good, it is saying that those who do good don't exist. We can't deny that there are many exemplary acts of service, kindness, and self-sacrifice in the world today. The problem is that the goodness contained in them is not sufficient to merit salvation. From God's perspective, human beings are sinful to the point that even their works of goodness are stained with evil. We do not see this because the dirty parts tend to be hidden from human observation, like a shiny piece of fruit full of worms.

How many good works, for instance, are secretly riddled with pride, with secret agendas, or with hopes of self-gain? How many are tainted with manipulation? Are good works done indiscriminately toward all without favoritism or preference? We think of ourselves as humble, yet we condemn the proud. We help the poor, but despise the rich. Truly, "The heart is deceitful above all things, and desperately wicked; who can know it?" (Jer. 17:9). When it comes to the complexity of motives, human beings are terribly naïve. We see a touching, commendable work from a distance and assume that it is purely good.

Appearances can confuse us to the point that we doubt the accuracy of God's judgment. But God is not limited as we are, to surface observations. His vision is far more piercing and precise. Nothing, even in the deepest part of the human subconciousness, can hide from His gaze. Psalm 139:1-4 says,

> "O LORD, You have searched me and know me...You understand my thought afar off...and are acquainted with all my ways. For there is not a word on my tongue, but behold, O LORD, You know it altogether."

Verses like these are the reason God is called *omniscient* (all knowing). Not only does He know the count of the hairs on our heads (Matt. 10:30), but He also knows what goes on in our heads—all the way down to the most secret recesses of our heart. In short, He knows us better than we know ourselves.

As it stands, "there is no creature hidden from His sight, but all things are naked and open to the eyes of Him" (Heb. 4:13). Equipped with this unlimited knowledge, the Lord surveys not only the weak and the failing but the heroes of our race, and His assessment remains unchanged: "there is none who does good; there is not so much as one."

WHAT DO WE DO NOW?

When people finally face the seriousness of sin and the fact that they are sinners, they usually try to do something about it—fix it, or cure it, or somehow wash it off of their souls. This can lead to some bizarre situations. One major newspaper reported the story of a woman who had volunteered to be buried alive. For a period of twenty-four hours after assistants covered her, she was to breathe through a tube that ran from her mouth to the air above ground. But no one took into account that even a few feet of soil is extremely heavy...and soundproof. As a result, no one knew that she was suffocating, nor did they hear her pathetic dirt-choked screams. She died. Her death became all the more tragic in light of why she had undergone the whole affair to begin with: the poor woman had only wanted to be cleansed of her sins. Some religious group had convinced her that the weird ritual would successfully do just that.

Throughout history, people have submitted to all kinds of extremes in the hope of erasing their sins. They beat themselves, starved themselves, and donated large amounts of money. They withdrew from society and lived in caves. Some followed phony religious leaders who offered cures for sin through strange ceremonies. And when the dust settled, their sins were still there, as indelible as ever.

The majority of us have chosen a more sane, recognizable route of dealing with the sin problem. We simply try to outnumber evil deeds with good ones. The hope, of course, is that on Judgment Day the scale would tip in favor of the good. But from God's perspective, the human goodness that we seek to multiply is laced with evil as well. The prophet Isaiah testified to this when he said, "all our righteousnesses are as filthy rags" (Isa. 64:6). This is why scripture never instructs us even once to believe in ourselves.

After every effort to anull our sins, we will find that there are still stains upon us that resist being laundered out. We should therefore give our hopeless cases into the hands of Jesus, for only *"He* will save His people from their sins" (Matt. 1:21).

WHY GOD DOESN'T JUST FORGIVE AND FORGET

Nothing is too hard for the Lord, but that doesn't mean everything has always been easy for Him, either. Witness the scene in the garden, on the night before His crucifixion. Luke tells us that "Being in *agony,* He prayed more earnestly. Then His sweat became like great drops of blood falling down to the ground" (22:44). The cause of His distress was the work that He was about to undertake to deal with our sins. It would be neither light nor pleasant.

There was no way around what He had to do. Jesus prayed, "Father, if it is possible, let this cup pass from Me; nevertheless, not as I will, but as you will" (Matt. 26:39). The Father had answered His prayers before, sometimes audibly (John 12:28), but the heavens were ominously quiet that night. The silence seemed to say that it would not be possible for Him to avoid the wretched sufferings that were only hours away. His path was to lead unerringly to the cross. The only way the problem of sin could be solved was through an act of ultimate sacrifice.

Why did the Lord Jesus need to *die* in order to take away sins? Why didn't God simply forgive and forget about them? From our perspective, dealing with sins is just that simple. We wonder why God couldn't be so simple.

The problem is that there is a difference in attitude between a sinner and a righteous God. All a sinner cares about is being forgiven. God, on the other hand, is concerned with *how* forgiveness is given. Due to His love He longs to forgive us, but He will not do it in a loose, careless way.

When a man breaks the law, he has to pay for it. That is a principle of justice which always holds true. So, when a man sins against God and breaks His spiritual, moral law, then as the government in this universe, God must hold him responsible. This is a serious thing. Ezekiel 18:4 says, "The soul who sins shall die." Hebrews 9:22 adds that "without shedding of blood, there is no forgiveness" (NASB). This stern penalty exhibits how grave a matter that sin is in the universe.

God cannot pardon a sinner by pretending that sin was never committed. Neither can He arbitrarily excuse a sinner in the name of loving him. That would be illegal. Still, it's very common for people to hope that God will make exceptions. They think that as God looks at them on Judgment Day and listens to their pleas, their self-defenses, their stories, and their reasons, He will somehow go soft on them. Since such things occasionally work in human courtrooms, they think, perhaps it will work with God. But that strategy amounts to hoping that God will violate His righteous standard. It is not a very reasonable expectation, and it is safe to say that it will never happen.

Imagine what would occur if a judge acquitted a criminal out of love or pity for him. An action like that would be protested for weeks. It would be in the news. It would be on the talk shows. That judge would become a joke. The public would label him as prejudiced, crooked, and partial. God is being watched in all of His dealings with men. Those observing Him are also quite ready to accuse Him of wrongdoing. For instance, there was a time when Satan suspected God of personal bias. An Old Testament man, Job, seemed too well protected, so the devil said to God, "Have You not made a hedge around him?" (Job 1:10). Even the godly, though they do not accuse the Lord, are ready to remind Him of His commitment to righteousness. That is why we find Abraham saying to God, "Shall not the judge of all the earth do *right?*" (Gen. 18:25). There are too many eyes watching how God deals with sins for Him to simply dismiss the issue and just let "bygones be bygones."

However, whether God is watched or not, the Bible assures us that He *cannot* be unrighteous even in the smallest particular. First John 1:5 says, "In Him is no darkness at all," and Hebrews 6:18 tells us that "it is impossible for God to lie." God's own moral absolutes mean that He must punish sins in a righteous way, without partiality, completely uninfluenced by His love, pity, or mercy.

If He did not judge in such a way, it would be catastrophic. The Bible tells us that God's throne, from which He upholds and rules the entire universe, sits on a foundation of righteousness (Ps. 89:14). If He were to do one thing unrighteous, then that righteous foundation would be compromised. The throne sitting upon it would fall, and then the universe upheld by it would collapse. God *must* "judge the world in righteousness" (Ps. 9:8), which means He cannot forgive sin lightly.

GOD ON DEATH ROW

Thankfully, where God's righteousness would not allow Him to pardon us, neither would His love allow Him to sit idly by while we perished. Love drove God to deal with our sins, not by dismissing them, but by way of an unprecedented personal commitment. John 3:16 says,

> "God so loved the world that He gave His only begotten Son, that whoever believes in Him should not perish but have everlasting life."

He would go farther, however, than delivering up His Beloved, for at the same time as God gave His cherished Son to the world, He came into it Himself. John 1:1 says, "In the beginning was the Word and the Word was with God and the Word was God." John 1:14 says, "the Word became flesh...". The two phrases *the word was God* and *the word became flesh* combine to tell us that when the Son of God came, it was actually God Himself coming to earth in a body of flesh and blood. For the very first time, the Creator of the universe was anchored to the surface of this troubled planet.

In Jesus Christ, God became so much a man that He was able to live among our race without being a freakish phenomenon. He was born, He ate, He drank, and He slept. He grew and matured as other humans. In Him, God set aside the privelidges of immortality and heavenly rank— He *"emptied* Himself, taking the form of a bond-servant, and being made in the likeness of men" (Phil. 2:7 NASB). He chose a blue-collar profession, was restricted to one place at a time, could feel pain, and could even bleed and die. As the Christian writer G. Campbell Morgan, pointed out, "there came into existence a Person in all points human, in all essentials divine" (77).

Philippians 2:8 says, "being found in appearance as a man, He *humbled* Himself" and truly it was a humbling experience. God had become flesh. When the Bible mentions it in the physical sense, "flesh" refers to something mortal and weak. When it is used to describe morality, "flesh" refers to darkness, evil, and lust. It was the *flesh* that caused God to flood the earth (Gen. 6:3) since all *flesh* had corrupted His way (Gen. 6:12). Paul the apostle said that nothing good lived in his *flesh* (Rom. 7:18) and that the *flesh* cannot please God (Rom. 8:8). Yet, the Word became *flesh*.

Now this should not be taken to mean that Jesus was sinful. Had He been a sinner, then He Himself would have needed a savior. The Bible tells us instead that He came "in the *likeness* of sinful flesh" (Rom. 8:3) and that He was "tempted in all things as we are, yet *without* sin" (Heb. 4:15 NASB). One sinful man cannot die for another sinful man. In the same way, if two boys are sitting in a mudhole, neither one can make the other clean. A sacrifice for sin must itself be above sin. We find this principle in the Old Testament. There, even though death for sins was symbolic, the animal sacrifices involved had to be completely free from any kind of blemish (Ex. 12:5, Lev. 1:3,10). In accordance with this ideal, the New Testament presents the real sacrifice of the Lord Jesus as "a lamb without blemish and without spot" (1 Pet. 1:19). He was qualified to die for us because He was personally sinless.

But there is still a problem. Even if a truly guiltless man volunteered to die for another man's crime, it would be a questionable arrangement, for the guilty party would escape without punishment. Worse yet, an innocent person would be punished. A scenario like this was attempted in recent times. A young American was arrested in the Far East for vandalism and was sentenced to a public whipping. When pleas for forgiveness didn't work, the boy's father came forward, offering to take the punishment in his son's place. The authorities declined. They wanted the body of the guilty person beaten, not a noble, loving volunteer. Probably any other government would have ruled likewise.

The Lord Jesus' death for us on the cross is not quite the same as the simple one-for-one trade that says, "I'll die for your wrongdoings so that you can go free." An arrangement of that nature would create the legal and ethical complications mentioned above. Instead, the Lord took our place in a much more profound sense than we realize. Look back at the phrase "the Word became flesh" (John 1:14). Strictly speaking, John 1:14 does not tell us the Word became a man (although that is included), but that He became *flesh*. Flesh is the comprehensive realm of all mankind. It includes all of us and we are all part of it. So, when God became flesh, He became *us*. He became you and me. Yes, He took your place, but He took your place as *you*. What eventually hung on the cross was not an innocent replacement but the sinner, with every evil act that would ever be commited.

No doubt Christ was personally sinless, but He was "handcuffed" to the flesh that was under God's wrath and condemnation. There was no escape. Once conceived in Mary's womb, the "handcuffing" had already occurred. There was no turning back, no changing His mind. It was too late. The process of becoming flesh was irreversible, and from then on it would sweep Him toward a cross that loomed a mere thirty-three years away. The great judge of all had become the condemned defendant. He was God on death row.

PAID IN FULL

A favorite theme of religious oil paintings is Jesus in the garden. He is usually pictured as serene, composed, and with face illuminated by a ray of light. This is not, however, the garden scene of the gospels. There, we do not find a Christ superbly composed, but in the throes of struggle and sorrow and unimaginable pressure. The words and phrases the Bible uses to describe Him there are quite telling: *horror, awestruck, distressed, sorrowful,* and *agony.*

Some have pointed out that others have died deaths for their faith with more composure. They bravely marched out into arenas with lions or were burned as they sang hymns to God. Why then did the Lord shed tears and pray that there might be another way? Because He was about to die a death no human being has ever experienced or would ever experience. This does not refer to crucifixion. Certainly that form of capital punishment was one of the most brutal ever invented by man. But something worse awaited Him, and He knew it. What lay ahead was much more dreadful than the insults, the spitting, the stripping, the beating, and the Roman spikes. Golgotha, the place of His crucifixion, was ground zero—the very spot where the judgment of God was poised, ready to come thundering down. There, divine wrath would explode upon the sins of men. It would not come as in the days of Noah, when the earth had been covered in water. This time judgment was due to cover only one man, Jesus. The sinless One who had become us, was about to receive our punishment.

In order to truly stand in our place and take the punishment we would have received for our sins, the Lord Jesus could not expect preferential treatment from God. The judgment of the cross would have to be without mercy; the wrath suffered there would need to be comprehensive and thorough. The human being is a composition of three parts—

spirit, soul, and body (1 Thess. 5:23), all of which have been affected in some way by sin. So in order for God's judgment to completely fall upon sin in all its forms, it would have to blast all the way through the body, soul, and spirit of Jesus.

We human beings have a "body of sin" (Rom. 6:6). Our hands have been used for violent, immoral things, and our feet for carrying us where we should not go. So, the hands and feet of Jesus were made to suffer. The Psalms prophetically speak of this. Psalm 22:16 says, "They pierced *my* hands and my feet," referring to Christ being nailed to the cross. The tongue of man has lied, has cursed, and has gossiped. It has been used to utter filth of every kind. Because of this, on the cross, His tongue was made to suffer, as Psalm 22:15 says, *"My* tongue clings to my jaws." Even our heads, with eyes that see the wrong things, and ears that hear the wrong things, were punished in Him— "...the soldiers twisted a crown of thorns and put it on *His* head" (John 19:2). Finally, a Roman spear was driven through His side (John 19:34) and ruptured His heart. That was the final blow to the sinful human body.

Judgment, however, was not limited to the Lord's body. Sin goes deeper than skin and bone. It has worked its way into the sinner's very soul—his mind, emotion, and will. One result of this is that human beings are full of pride. The sinner's ego is so inflated that he must struggle to be humble, and if he finally achieves some outward humility, he quickly becomes proud of that as well. The punishment of the cross, therefore, had to strip away all pride. In Mark 15:24 we are told that the Lord's clothing was taken from him and gambled away. He was left hanging in His underwear if not completely naked, on display for all to see and to mock. It was humiliation of the most painful kind. Shame was the hallmark of the cross. Though it didn't stop the Lord from dying for us, nonetheless it was powerfully present. That day the punishment that was due the proud human soul fell on Christ. God "covered Him with *shame"* (Psalm 89:45).

The soul of man has also found excitement and happiness with sin. When we enjoy the temporary pleasure of it, we feel exhilarated. It doesn't matter if the pleasure is cheap or illegal or immoral. People have become so addicted to such thrills, that a slogan was spawned: "If it feels good, do it!" Since our souls have thoroughly enjoyed sin, the soul on the cross had to be made to feel the sorrow of it. Several times the Lord disclosed His inward condition while drawing closer to death—"Now my *soul* is *troubled*" (John 12:27) and "My *soul* is exceedingly *sorrowful,* even to death" (Matt. 26:38). The cross punished man's happiness with sin by afflicting the Lord's soul. He was made to enter the depths of grief until *"He* poured out *His* soul unto death" (Isa. 53:12).

But sin has influenced more than just the body and the soul. The human spirit has been affected as well. Everyone has a human spirit (1 Cor. 2:11). This is the deepest recess of our being, the part meant to contact God and experience union with Him (John 4:24; 1 Cor. 6:17). In the sinner, this part is deadened, separating him from God. The Lord Jesus, therefore, was made to bear the consequences of that separation. He Himself had never known a moment apart from the Father. He testified that "I am not alone, but I am with the Father who sent me" (John 8:16) and "He who sent me is with me" (John 8:29). Yet on the cross there was an interuption in the fellowship between Himself and God, leading to His cry, "My God, My God, why have you *forsaken* Me?" (Matt. 27:46). At that moment He bore the burden of the sinner's alienation. He was made "sin for us" (2 Cor. 5:17) and in His spirit felt the hopelessness of being rejected by God as something unclean. Christ became "a *curse* for us" (Gal. 3:13) and that, perhaps, most clearly signified the depths of the abandonment He suffered. In scripture the cursed are those who perish in the lake of fire (Matt. 25:41). The Lord Jesus, therefore, had to bear the horror of that torment so that He "might taste death for everyone" (Heb. 2:9 NASB). Truly, He was *you* and *me* on the cross that day, absorbing the wrath that we righteously deserved.

When at last Jesus cried, "It is finished" (John 19:30), that meant divine justice had been satisfied. In Him, man's sinful body, soul, and spirit had been punished until even God could go no further. Judgment had been exhausted, and the price for sin had been paid in full. There was no place for sin to hide. The Lord Jesus had offered His body, soul, and spirit—every part of His human being—to God for judgment. Anything hidden inside the sinner was exposed and punished.

AFTER THE TWISTER

Experts measure the destructiveness of a tornado in coded talk, speaking of them as F-2s or F-3s and occasionally, an F-5, the worst of all. However the most destructive twister ever was off the scale. Nobody can measure it. This monster came and went and didn't touch anyone. That's because it lit on Christ. In a manner of speaking, there was roaring and pounding and debris flying around like shrapnel; we just weren't hit with it. There was destruction. There was death. We just didn't feel it. Christ "bore our sins in His own body on the tree" (1 Pet. 2:24) and the storm raged in Him. Not only did we miss it having been born two thousand years after the fact, but those standing there that day at the cross missed it as well. Certainly they all witnessed indications that something was happening. As we are told, "darkness fell upon all the land" (Matt. 27:45 NASB) and "the earth quaked and the rocks were split" (Matt. 27:51), but these things only increased the bewilderment of the onlookers. No one could see the twisting, crashing fury of God descend upon Christ. The storm had been so perfectly contained in Him that not a hair on anyone's head had been blown out of place. At the end of the day, sin had been completely penalized without anyone feeling a thing.

HOW *THE* PAYMENT
BECOMES *YOUR* PAYMENT

Though Christ died on behalf of every human being, His work is not automatically credited to everyone's account.

We must each *receive* it. Consider a vaccine developed in a lab. The medicine has potential life-saving power for all men, women, and children, but it will not be effective toward any of them until they each roll up their sleeves and receive the immunization. In today's world people still die of bubonic plague and other diseases although cures exist for them. The vaccines have long been discovered but cannot save anyone while they are sitting on a shelf.

The cross of Christ is the cure for the human sin situation, but until people receive it by believing in Him, it remains little other than a cure sitting on the pages of the New Testament. It has no power to individually deal with our sins until we place our faith in Christ. Acts 13:38-39 says, "Through this man [Jesus] is preached to you the forgiveness of sins; and by Him everyone who *believes* is justified..."

When you believed in the Lord Jesus, you were forgiven of all your offenses against God. The Lord's payment for sin on the cross became *your* personal payment for it. The resulting forgiveness was so strong that you were *justified,* aquitted, excused as though you had never committed a sin at all. The distance between you and God immediately closed up and now "You who once were far off have been made near by the blood of Christ" (Eph. 2:13). This new blessed proximity to God is another reason why the scriptures say, *"Blessed* are those whose lawless deeds have been forgiven, and whose sins have been covered; *Blessed* is the man whose sin the Lord will not take into account" (Rom. 4:7-8 NASB).

God has even furnished "a receipt" to show that our debt of sin has been paid off—the resurrection of the Lord Jesus from the dead. Many men have claimed to be something or to accomplish something for God but when they died, they disappeared. The grave swallowed them and their deeds and they were never seen again. Were they lying or self-deceived? No one knows, because they vanished from this world, never to return. Had the Lord Jesus died and remained in the grave like all those other men, we would have wondered about Him, too. He had spoken of shedding His blood "for many for forgiveness of sins" (Matt. 26:28 NASB).

Yet without verification, we would question whether He was succesful in doing it.

Basically, we need a receipt of payment from beyond the grave. Thankfully, God has provided one. According to Romans 4:25, The Lord Jesus "was delivered up because of our offenses." That means He was delivered to death because of our sins. Then it says, "He was raised because of our justification" (Rom. 4:25). He was not raised so that we *would* be justified; He was raised *because* of our justification. *Because* the Lord's work on the cross effectively justified the believer, God raised Him from the grave. That demonstrated His acceptance of Christ's payment for our sins. In essence, the resurrection of Christ was a receipt marked "paid in full."

The power of a receipt can do wonders for your peace of mind. I'm reminded of the time my wife and I decided to get a new couch. The only thing we could afford, though, were used ones. That meant they either smelled like pets, were stained, or had already experienced years of kids jumping on them. It was going to be that or a local furniture company's "one year same as cash" offer. We chose the latter. The deal was that you had one year, interest free, to pay off the couch. However, if you forgot to make your payments even one second after the twelve-month period elapsed, it was bad news. You suddenly owed the unpaid balance on the couch, plus interest compounded from the day you bought it. I faithfully made payments up until the ten-month mark, and then went ahead and paid the whole thing off. I wrote the check for a triple payment, put it in the mailbox, and walked away feeling satisfied that I was finally the legal owner of the couch. But after about a month and a half, I began to get nervous. The payment deadline was coming up, and although the check had been sent I hadn't received any acknowledgment of it from the creditor. I began to harbor a few nagging doubts that maybe the check had been lost. From my standpoint, the day it had been mailed, it disappeared. I had no way of seeing it as it was processed through postal machines and traveled on trucks to its destination. I certainly had no way of knowing when the company mailroom received the letter, opened it, and then credited it to my account. It was not until a receipt was sent back to me and I had studied it closely, that I finally concluded that I no longer owed anything. I had peace. I stashed the receipt somewhere convenient in case the issue ever came into question again.

Similarly, we can know the effectiveness of the Lord's payment for sin by looking at His resurrection. Today you are not only told to believe that Christ paid for your sins, you are told to "believe in your heart that God has raised Him from the dead" (Rom. 10:9)—which is the *receipt* of His payment for sin.

The Lord's cross so effectively quenched the storming wrath of God, that the Bible insists repeatedly that He never needs to die again—"Christ...suffered *once* for sins, the just for the unjust..." (1 Pet. 3:18). "Once" means His death never needs to be repeated. After two thousand, ten thousand, or one hundred thousand years, it will never grow weak or fail.

When this present age has been brought to a close, all the believers have been glorified, and death has been swallowed up in victory (1 Cor. 15:54), what will the believers see when they look at the throne of God? They will see "the throne of God and of the *Lamb*" (Rev. 22:1). The Lamb will sit upon the throne as an eternal reminder of sin's payment in the endless ages to come. It is remarkable that the Lord Jesus was called the Lamb of God twice in the Old Testament (Isa. 53:7, Jer. 11:19), three times in the Gospels and Acts (John 1:29, 36; Acts 8:32), and once in the Epistles (1 Pet. 1:19), but in the book of Revelation, the book of eternity, He is called the "Lamb of God" twenty-eight times! In a future that stretches forward without limit, no one will ever forget that being saved was a matter secured on a forsaken hill long ago, and that work will stand forever.

Reference Notes

Morgan, G. Campbell. *The Crises of the Christ.* Westwood: Revell, 1903.

3

DELIVERANCE FROM HELL

THE CERTAINTY OF JUDGMENT

Years ago I found a parking ticket, all nice and neon orange, tucked under the windshield wiper of my car. I was irritated. I felt it wasn't fair. I had always tried to park legally, so why should I be penalized over an innocent mistake? Besides, I had just quit my job to become a full-time gospel preacher; I couldn't afford the fifteen-dollar fine. I thought about writing a formal letter of protest but there wasn't much to protest. I was guilty. Case closed. I hate to admit this but the thought crossed my mind to just drop the ticket on the ground and forget about it. Maybe if the annoying little slip of paper was out of sight it would forever be out of mind. Yet the voice of reason haunted me.

Go ahead, it said, *throw the ticket on the ground, stomp it, shred it, turn it into a paper airplane and fly it away, but don't ever forget, there's a copy at City Hall.* I got the point. Sooner or later, if the ticket remained unpaid, something would happen, something *had* to happen. That's the way tickets work. If you don't pay them, something will happen to you. For a while, sometimes for a very *long* while, nothing will happen. You can go on carelessly parking wherever you want, racking up a small fortune in fines and laughing about it. Then, some tiny mistake or technicality occurs and you're caught and slapped with a fine you can't possibly afford.

Most people choose to deal with sin just like I was tempted to deal with the parking ticket—by ignoring it. It is as though refusing to think about the problem of sin will, in some mysterious way, solve it. But if there are consequences attached to ignoring parking tickets, then sins, transgressions against God's government, certainly must carry them as well. Sins can be buried, banished, excused, and renamed, but they will not disappear. The Bible assures us that God "has appointed a day in which He will judge the world in righteousness" (Acts 17:31). A definite time has been scheduled when all sin and all sinners will be funneled into judgment.

The terror of that day not only lies in the fact that it will definitely happen, but that many sins, especially those that seemed to have disappeared from view, will suddenly reappear for examination. That includes the tiny sins, the forgotten sins, and even the ones that were committed in private, away from public view. Paul calls it "the day when God will judge the secrets of men" (Rom. 2:16). It is a time when "there is nothing covered that will not be revealed, and hidden that will not be known" (Matt. 10:26). The book of Revelation goes on to describe the scene: "...I saw the dead, the great and the small, standing before the throne." Perhaps even at that final moment some will hope that their sins have been lost in the shuffle. But then the verse goes on to say "books were opened..and the dead were judged from the things which were written in the books, according to their deeds" (Rev. 20:12 NASB). These opened documents are detailed historical records containing all the sins of men. During the final judgment, they will suddenly be opened as legal evidence. It will then become painfully clear that sins were indelibly documented before God and that ignoring them was a foolish strategy, if not suicidal. Men will find out the hard way that you can ignore the lawgiver, but not the judge.

SIN'S ULTIMATE PENALTY

Sin is the most expensive thing in the universe. We know this from two terse phrases: "The soul who sins shall *die*" (Eze. 18:4) and "the wages of sin is *death*" (Rom. 6:23). The Bible does not spell out any further particulars like what kind of sin or how many sins result in death. Apparently, *any* sin can cause the soul to perish. Human society punishes wrongdoing according to how much damage one man has done to another. There is one penalty for perjury and another for murder. However, from the spiritual perspective, sin's penalty is the same. It always results in death, regardless of the details.

We were warned of this from the very beginning. In the Garden of Eden God told Adam about the consequences of sin—"You shall surely *die*" (Gen 2:17). Adam chose to discount that warning. The sin he eventually committed, at least from the human perspective, was no big deal. It was neither murder nor some gross indecency but only a simple act of disobedience, almost innocent compared to things we hear of people doing today. Regardless, death was the result. Adam's spirit was instantly deadened, severing His relationship with God. At the same moment, his body lost its immortality and became destined for physical death.

Being the father of the human race, this "package" of death and corruption was what he would pass down to all of us. Now if the full extent of our problem was a dead spirit and a dying body, perhaps we could have tolerated it.

We might have been able to put up with a miserable, sin-wracked existence as long as we could look forward to a death that would relieve us of our earthly sufferings. But the Bible speaks of a second death—one that exists beyond the grave. Injury, sickness or old age might be the first death, however "the lake of fire...is the *second* death" (Rev. 20:14).

No biblical topic provokes the modern mind more than the lake of fire, which is also commonly called "hell." Liberal thinkers view it as a relic of some past unenlightened time. The very mention of the subject reminds them of ignorance, fear, threats, and ranting red-neck preachers. Hell has been judged intolerable by our society. In the name of political correctness, we desperately struggle to preserve the illusion that everyone is correct and on an equal footing with God, regardless of what they believe. The Bible does not square with such sentiments. It tells us that in the end, some people will be found wrong, terribly wrong, fatally wrong, and eternity will not be the peaceful bliss they had imagined.

Hell is a reality. It is not a concept invented by religious fanatics for coercing people into the Christian faith. Some might certainly use the subject that way, but they didn't invent it. The lake of fire is patently biblical. It springs from divine revelation, not religious manipulation.

The prophet Isaiah was the first to explicitly speak of a place where the wicked go, where "their worm does not die, and their fire is not quenched" (Isa. 66:24). In the New Testament, John the Baptist continued the thought, calling it a judgment of "unquenchable fire" (Matt. 3:12). Then, the Lord Jesus Himself, the sweet, loving Savior of mankind and "friend of sinners," went on to speak more about hell than any other person in the Bible. He called it "everlasting fire" (Matt. 25:41), "everlasting punishment" (Matt. 25:46), a place where both soul and body are destroyed (Matt. 10:28), and a "furnace of fire" where there will be "wailing and gnashing of teeth" (Matt. 13:42). His descriptions of that place bore the stamp of authority, not mere opinion. No doubt, His role as the Savior of the human race and His great love for us pressed Him to speak of hell frequently, like someone warning that a bridge is out up ahead.

When the apostles later spoke of hell, they also treated it as an otherworldly reality. Paul had been granted access to the spiritual realm in visions of the third heaven and paradise (2 Cor. 12:2,4). Having seen those sights, he warned that "the wrath of God comes upon the sons of disobedience" (Eph. 5:6). The Apostle Peter spoke of hell simply but ominously as "destruction" (2 Pet. 2:1), and Jude called it "the vengeance of eternal fire" (v. 7). Finally, John saw a "lake of fire and brimstone" (Rev. 20:10) and said that "anyone not found written in the Book of Life was cast into the lake of fire" (Rev. 20:15).

All of the scriptural evidence reminds us that although we might wish some people would be more tactful in their presentation of the matter, hell is not superstitious scare-mongering. We cannot discard the truth because of the excesses of some religious folks. In fact, to judge the teaching of hell as untrue is to suggest that the apostles, the prophets and the Lord Jesus were either lying about it or they were simply ignorant of spiritual things. A conclusion like that, of course, would be ridiculous in the extreme.

HELL IS MORE THAN A METAPHOR

"Divorce is hell."

"War is hell."

"I couldn't go to hell after I die, because I've already been through it here on earth."

This is what people often think. To them, hell is anything difficult or unpleasant. It might be a chronic illness or a disagreeable boss, or a nasty toothache. It might be having to stay on your diet or needing to sit through another accounting class. Thus hell and its sufferings are often viewed as mere metaphor. Some find comfort in this, as though biblical symbolism is not to be taken seriously. They think that as long as the fire of hell might only be symbolic, then maybe its terrors have been inflated and shouldn't be so feared after all. Scripture, however, does not treat hell as an allegory of life's headaches. The Bible speaks of it as an actual place that can be seen by eyewitnesses. God said, "Then shall they go forth and *look* upon the corpses of the men who have transgressed against Me. For their worm does not die and their fire is not quenched..." (Isa. 66:24). The people in this verse don't go forth and look at a figure of speech. They go forth and see the bodies of sinners in a fire that never dies out.

Even if God selected flames as only being representative of hell's torments, we should treat it with the utmost respect. One Christian scholar, G. H. Lang, addressed the issue this way:

> "You would like to ask whether I think the lake of fire...is literal, material fire, or whether this is a figure of speech only...I...ask you to solemnly remember that if it be a figure only, it is a figure of something real and actual; and that inasmuch as God never exaggerates, the reality will not be less awful than the figure, and may be more so. God has selected the most awful figure the realm of nature provides, for what can be thought of as more terrible than being cast into and abiding in the torments of a lake of fire. And if the figure employed be so intensely dreadful, what shall the reality be? (23)

Regardless of the view, it is impossible to understate the threat of hell. The Son of God did not die a painful, traumatic, humiliating death on the cross to save us from an exaggerated danger. His literal sufferings rescued us from much more than a metaphorical damnation.

THE INCREDIBLE WRATH OF GOD

As long as a man chooses to ignore his sin or explain it away, or vindicate himself, the Bible tells him, "You are storing up *wrath* for yourself in the day of wrath" (Rom. 2:5 NASB). Modern attitudes recoil from that thought.

The preferred way of thinking about God is that He has no wrath to inflict. Yet when the Bible tells us to think of Him, it says, "Consider...the kindness *and* severity of God" (Rom. 11:22). It presents a whole God, not some version with the "objectionable" parts edited out. When men hold onto God's kindness while rejecting His severity, they always end up with a parody of Him—an all-powerful being who dumbly smiles at both the innocent and the monstrously evil. This "god" has no sense of justice, equity, or outrage, only a lobotomized goodness that cannot bear to say or do anything negative. But the scriptures assure us that the severity of God is every bit as real as His kindness. He is far from being a tiger with no teeth.

The Lord Jesus somberly warned that "if your right hand causes you to sin, cut it off and cast it from you; for it is more profitable for you that one of your members perish, than for your whole body to be cast into hell" (Matt. 5:30). The point of His statement was that anything is better than facing the wrath of God...*anything*. This sentiment can be seen found in other passages as well. For instance, the Lord Jesus said of Judas Iscariot, "It would have been good for that man if he had never been born" (Mark 14:21). And this severity is not a threat limited to flesh and blood alone. Even the demons dread the coming wrath of God. They fearfully asked Christ, "Have you come here to *torment* us before the time?" (Matt. 8:29). Thousands of years before the time of judgment, these wicked spirits, who are much more powerful than men, trembled at the Lord's coming wrath. Even more incredible, they recognized Jesus as the one who would wield it.

It seems amazing that He, the sweet Lamb of God, could be feared in such a way, after all, a lamb is such an approachable creature—so innocent and gentle. But there will be a time when another side of the Lamb will be seen, when not only the demons but also the entire world will shake with fear at Him. They will say "to the mountains and rocks, 'Fall on us and hide us from the face of Him who sits on the throne and from *the wrath of the lamb*; for the great day of His wrath has come, and who is able to stand?" (Rev. 6:16-17).

Apart from the descriptions and teachings in the Bible, divine wrath is largely unknown to human beings. Moses asked God, "Who knows the power of your anger?" (Ps. 90:11). The answer is that no one knows it yet. We have no idea what the unlimited anger of an all-powerful Being feels like. We have never known it. The prophet Isaiah sums it up this way:

> "Wail, for the day of the Lord is at hand! It will come as destruction from the Almighty. Therefore all hands will be limp, every man's heart will melt, and they will be afraid. Pangs and sorrows will take hold of them; they will be in pain as a woman in childbirth; They will be amazed at one another; their faces will be like flames. Behold, the day of the LORD comes, cruel, with both wrath and fierce anger; to lay the land desolate; and He will destroy its sinners from it. For the stars of heaven and their constellations will not give their light; the sun will be darkened in its going forth, and the moon will not cause its light to shine. I will punish the world for its evil, and the wicked for their iniquity; I will halt the arrogance of the proud, and will lay low the haughtiness of the terrible...therefore I will shake the heavens, and the earth will move out of her place, in the wrath of the Lord of hosts and in the day of His fierce anger." (13:6-11, 13)

The prophet Nahum adds, "Who can stand before His indignation? Who can endure the burning of His anger? His wrath is poured out like fire, and the rocks are broken up by Him" (Nah. 1:6 NASB). The world we presently live in is one where God largely restrains His anger, where He generously "causes His sun to rise on the evil and the good, and sends rain on the righteous and unrighteous" (Matt. 5:45 NASB).

Today, God does good by giving you "rain from heaven and fruitful seasons, filling your hearts with food and gladness," even if you have not honored Him or worshiped Him (Acts 14:17). Though bad things do happen on this earth, wrath has not yet arrived. As Paul said, "the wrath of God *comes*" (Eph. 5:6). We certainly see brief glimpses of it occurring in the Bible, yet men have never yet experienced it to the fullest extent. Even when that fearsome anger devastated entire nations like Israel, Egypt, and Assyria, there were still promises of His mercy in their future. But when the final day of wrath occurs and the lake of fire appears, the Bible nowhere hints of mercy. God never promises reprieve or restoration for the sinner. Instead, He says of the condemned person that "he...shall...drink of the wine of the wrath of God, which is poured out *full strength* into the cup of His indignation. He shall be tormented with fire and brimstone in the presence of the holy angels and in the presence of the Lamb. And the smoke of their torment goes up *forever and ever...*" (Rev. 14:10-11).

THE LAKE OF FIRE IS PHYSICAL, MENTAL, AND SPIRITUAL

A strange habit that human beings have developed is to make light of their lost condition and where it will take them. Many cartoons and comedy sketches use hell for their material. Most of us have heard some variation on these kinds of jokes—"Three men went to hell. They could choose between a red door, a blue door, or a yellow door. The devil asked them which door they would prefer..." And then there are many who say they would rather go to hell, since the sinners, not the saints really know how to have fun. Why sit on a cloud and play a boring harp in heaven when you could party with the wild crowd down below? People hold onto these unfortunate perversions of truth until they are numbed to the urgency of their own situation.

The fact is, divine wrath is no joke. It is penetrating and far reaching. It is capable of penalizing the sinner in every part of his being, physical and non-physical. For instance, Jesus warned of the whole *body* being cast into hell (Matt. 5:30). This is a shocking and unfamiliar thought to many people. The typical idea is that after a person dies, his soul and spirit leave his body and stay separated from it. However, the dead do not remain in a disembodied state forever. At some time in the future, "all who are in the graves will hear His [Jesus'] voice and come forth" (John 5:28-29a). Thus, the bodies of the dead will be raised—"those who have done good to the resurrection of life, and those who have done evil, to the resurrection of condemnation" (John 5:29b). At that point, all three parts of the dead person—his spirit, soul, and body—will be rejoined. He will stand before God as a complete being once again in order to receive judgment and enter eternity.

For the wicked, this is bad news, beginning with the torment he will physically suffer. That is why, when the Lord speaks of being cast into hell, He doesn't first talk about minds or emotions going there, but bodily members such as hands and feet and eyes (Matt. 18:8-9). There is no need here to elaborate on the pain we experience when fire touches skin. If you need a graphic example, then go visit a burn ward in any area hospital and multiply what you see by infinity. As I said before, this is no joke.

We are further warned that God "is able to destroy both *soul* and body in hell" (Matt. 10:28). This destruction of mind, emotion, and will, however, does not mean that the lost dematerialize and then blissfully lose consciousness. The fire will not bring a loss of existence, only a loss of *quality* of existence. That means complete ruination. As an example, I'm reminded of our family car, a Lincoln Continental, which was used in turn by three kids. By the time it had gone through me and my brother and had been passed on to my sister, it made awful noises, bounced like a waterbed, and did weird things when you tried to use any of its electrical features. For years the Lincoln had suffered abuse from being alternately treated like a dragster and then a tractor. My frustrated dad summed it all up when he fumed, "That car has been destroyed!" He obviously did not mean that it had ceased to exist, but that it had been ruined. A once expensive luxury car had become a piece of junk, which we later sold for two hundred dollars.

Similarly, the destruction of a soul in hell does not mean

that it vanishes out of existence, but that it loses all quality of life. From the mental standpoint, the condemned person is painfully aware of his torments; he is not in a fuzzy dream-like state. Emotionally he feels utter despair, since there will be no relief, no hope, no deliverance forever. On top of this there is also the experience of abject humiliation—"shame and everlasting contempt" (Dan. 12:2). Hell is the place of ultimate indignity for the lost. In the Bible, one of the most dishonorable things that could happen to a person after death was to have his body eaten by scavengers (see 2 Sam. 21:9-10; 2 Kings 9:35-36). In hell, the sinner has a body that is both eaten and burned, but not consumed—"Their worm does not die, and their fire is not quenched" (Isa. 66:24). Therefore, the sinner's pathetic state lasts as an eternal spectacle for all to see, and it brings him never ending disgrace.

Hell not only punishes the body and soul, it penalizes the human spirit as well. The Lord will tell those whom He sends to the lake of fire to "Depart from Me" (Matt. 25:41). They will suffer the consequence of endless separation from God. It will be a spiritual suffering, a grueling loneliness, as they are shut out from the presence of God and rejected by Him as something filthy. God will not have anything to do with anyone thrown into hell. Whatever is in that place is truly lost. He is finished with it forever.

Hell is not the continuation of sin after death, a place for people to keep "having fun." It is where sinners lose all quality of life on every level. There is no mention of any activity there except for "the wailing and gnashing of teeth" (Matt. 13:42). Even the devil cannot treat it as a playground, but along with his followers will be "cast into the lake of fire and brimstone, where...they will be *tormented* day and night forever and ever" (Rev. 20:10). No one in hell plays or rules or conducts any business because "the smoke of their torment ascends forever and ever; and they have no rest day or night" (Rev. 14:11).

WHY HELL IS NECESSARY –
IT IS THE UNIVERSAL "TRASH CAN"

We might wonder why there has to be a hell at all, since it seems like such a black spot on Christian teaching. Many people are "turned off" by it and question God on the grounds of why He would allow such a place, let alone engineer it. Why does hell need to exist? That is like asking why some country homes have an ugly fifty-five gallon drum in their backyards. There is certainly no aesthetic reason involved, since it is rusted, charred black on the inside and smells of ashes. Yet, without that ugly barrel, garbage and other useless items would pile up like a mountain all over the property.

Even the universe needs a trash barrel. That is the basic function of the lake of fire. It is a place to throw things that are useless and hopelessly spoiled. But what are those useless items? If you quickly answer "bad people," then technically, you're wrong. Hell was never meant for people at all. According to the Lord Jesus, it was "prepared for the devil and his angels"(Matt. 25:41).

And for good reasons. These evil beings are a blight on the entire universe. The devil is a trouble-making spirit who is always "going to and fro on the earth and walking back and forth on it" (Job 1:7). He busies himself "seeking whom he may devour" (1 Pet. 5:8) and uses all his power "to steal and kill and destroy" (John 10:10). As the biggest liar of all, he "deceives the whole world" (Rev. 12:9). That includes slandering God (Gen. 3:5) and trying to snatch away any speck of spiritual truth that has found its way into the human heart (Matt. 13:3-4, 18-19). Though he is one of the most intelligent created beings, neither he nor his angels have any morality, restraint, or pity. Satan is not capable of being another way nor would he ever want to be. Even at the end of the Bible, there is not the slightest hint that he will ever be sorry for all the cruelty he brought into this universe. After being imprisoned for one thousand years in "the bottomless pit" (Rev. 20:3) as an interim punishment, he will eventually prove to be incapable of rehabilitation.

We are told, "Satan will be released from his prison," but rather than repent, he "will go out to deceive the nations" (Rev. 20:7-8), confirming at last that he is a hopeless case.

God desires to bring in "new heavens and a new earth, in which righteousness dwells" (2 Pet. 3:13), but while the devil roams about, there is no possibility of such a thing. What is to be done with a being who only wants evil, who does not desire mercy for himself because he is too proud, who does not want forgiveness because he feels that he is not wrong? There is only one suitable place for him—the lake of fire. The lake of fire is both necessary and just. As it imprisons and punishes the devil forever, it provides deliverance for the rest of the universe from his damaging presence.

Hell should have been a terror only to that group of rebel angels and their leader, but something went terribly wrong. In the Garden of Eden, man made a decision to follow the devil. The result was not only that he got into sin, but that sin got into him. The effect has reached down to the present, where each of us should have noticed by now that "sin...dwells in me" (Rom. 7:20). Proof of it can be seen in the way we lived our lives—"you once walked according to the course of this world, according to the prince of the power of the air, the spirit who now works in the sons of disobedience" (Eph. 2:2). Walking according to the prince of the power of the air means to behave according to the devil. It is to sin just as the devil sins, to react the way the devil reacts, and to like what the devil likes. The sinner's behavior is a photocopy of Satan's. We think it is "only human" to hate someone to the point that we rejoice when they suffer catastrophe. We tell ourselves it is "only human" to vent anger with profanity, violence, or hurtful words. We assure ourselves that it is "only human" when we seek to satisfy lawless addictions and lusts. Perhaps we would all be surprised to find out how little anything human is involved with those things. The evil urges, drives, and passions rising up from within us come from the sin in our flesh, which is linked to a *non-human* source—Satan.

In fact, this connection is so close that when Satan is finally judged and punished, the sinner who is linked to him will suffer the same fate. Being attached to the devil is similar to being chained to a giant log that is rushing down river. The fast-moving log is headed over a huge waterfall where it will crash on the rocks below. Whoever is joined to it will share its doom. Similarly, men end up in hell because they remain yoked to the unique evil one who is going there. That is why the Lord will one day not only condemn the devil but some human beings as well. He will tell them, "Depart from me, you cursed, into the everlasting fire prepared for the devil and his angels" (Matt. 25:41).

As long as people remain joined to Satan, then by default, they are also part of the problem in this universe. For even if new heavens and a new earth appeared, the sinner would be a black smudge upon them. He would be bored with a righteous and peaceful earth. If God transferred him to the heavens, he would not be happy there either, because he would miss his worldly amusements and sinful delights. As with the devil, there are not many options left concerning what to do with this kind of person. Since neither heaven nor earth is suitable for him, and since he is not good for them, that only leaves the "trash can"—the lake of fire. Hell eventually protects the earth not only from Satan, but also from the evil men attached to him.

HELL ENSURES THAT JUSTICE WILL BE DONE

The people of God might "sing of mercy and justice" (Ps. 101:1), but "evil men do not understand justice" (Prov. 28:5). In fact, sinners strongly object to the concept of hell. Some of them challenge it based upon the beloved uncle who died without being a Christian. Surely, they say, such a wonderful person could never go into the lake of fire. Men always seem to side with other sinful men against the Lord's judgment. Their endless arguments appeal to human reason and emotion while manifesting a heart of rebellion toward God. When we justify what the Lord condemns, it is our way of saying, "I am fairer, more loving, and more compassionate than God." It does not occur to us how much our human judgment has been warped by sin.

The objections continue. "How about infants that die?" "What about people that never heard the gospel?" "How about the mentally incompetent?" These questions indicate that we suspect God is incapable of fair judgment. We tend to think of hell as being populated with innocent people or at least full of those whose punishment is greater than their crimes. But as the sinner feigns concern about whether God might somehow be unfair, he forgets that the Judge of all is "a God of truth and without injustice" (Deut. 32:4). The Lord will never punish anyone in error or in excess. Human beings should not waste time with "concerns" over whether He is fair. Instead, they should worry about their own sinful condition and the precious short time that they have left to be saved. The sinner who questions the appropriateness of hell is nothing more than a condemned criminal critiquing the hangman's noose. He can pontificate on the unfairness of the rope being too stiff, the gallows being too high, and the executioner being too unloving, but his arguments will not help him a bit. All the lobbying on earth will not grant him a stay of execution.

Far from being unjust, the lake of fire guarantees that at long last justice will be served. Even evil men find it unbearable to live in a world where there is no penalty for wrongdoing. Horrid deeds leave us with the conviction that something ought to be done—no, *must* be done about them. As long as there are unsettled cases that cry out for reckoning, we feel dissatisfaction, a cosmic incompleteness. The lake of fire provides an answer to the dilemma of unfulfilled justice. It is the "long arm of the law" that fully and satisfactorily penalizes all wrongs. Hell's existence promises that although evil might have often escaped punishment in our world, it will eventually be apprehended and dealt with.

In the eighties, Israeli authorities discovered that the infamous Josef Mengele, the Nazi "Angel of Death," had been secretly living in South America. During World War II the German doctor had performed many gruesome medical experiments upon Jewish subjects. After the war he managed to evade the authorities and an almost certain death sentence for crimes against humanity. Mengele successfully avoided capture for decades. When his whereabouts finally became known, he would never stand trial for his role in the Holocaust. Mengele would neither see the hangman's noose nor the firing the squad. As it turned out, he would not even serve five minutes in jail. For by the time the "Angel of Death" was located, he had already died. Apparently he had drowned during a leisurely swim at the beach. One rabbi publicly lamented that the accident had enabled the slippery fugitive to escape justice forever. But if Mengele had been caught, what punishment would have been a just retribution for his crimes? No one can calculate the extent of the suffering that the man caused, not only upon his victims, but also in the lives of the victims' relatives. What about the nightmarish dramas that play through the minds of Holocaust survivors, sometimes on a daily basis? What is a just recompense for those kinds of psychological scars? Taking it all into consideration, perhaps the electric chair is no longer sufficient. Is there something, anything, that can penalize the monstrosity of the sin? Yes. It is the lake of fire. Where the first death failed to punish Mengele, the second death will succeed. The disappointed rabbi was mistaken. Mengele did not escape anything. His death only moved him one step closer to final justice.

Most people applaud the concept of justice fairly and equally distributed. But those who do, need to realize that they themselves are sinners. Hell is not a place exclusively reserved for the loathsome. Kindly old grandparents, ladies and gentlemen, and the multitude of others who have never had their faces on "Wanted" posters, must also confront God's condemnation for unpaid sin. This does not mean that wrath is a one-size-fits-all proposition. Certain sins invite "greater condemnation" (Matt. 23:14). Some sinners will find it "more tolerable...in the day of judgment" (Matt. 11:24) than others will. Even hell has levels of punishment according to the crimes. The point is if we indulge in the satisfaction that the sins of monsters will be penalized, it must be balanced with the knowledge that the sins of nice guys require wrath as well.

THE WAY OUT

The Lord Jesus said, "Unless you believe that I am He, you shall die in your sins" (John 8:24 NASB). Many wrongly understand Jesus to mean, "If you do not believe in Me, God will send you to hell." Looking at it that way gives the impression that God condemns some men out of revenge. Since they reject His Son, He "gets back" at them by casting them into the lake of fire. This is wrong. God does not make any man perish in hell. Long before people shun Jesus they are already lost. Their native condition is sin. They are born in it and will die in it unless someone steps in to save them. This is like a brick dropped off of a tall building. The brick's natural status is free fall. No one needs to make it hit the ground. As long as its descent goes uninterrupted, it will eventually land there. If sometime before impact a net breaks its fall, we can say that the brick was saved. But if the net is not allowed to enter the picture—if it is rejected, then the brick will continue on its default course to the ground. Sinners are also in a state of free fall. Condemnation is upon them, and apart from an intervention by the Savior, condemnation will be their future. This is why we are told, "he who disobeys the Son shall not see life, but the wrath of God *abides* on him" (John 3:36). The wrath of God is neither reckoned to him on the day he refuses Jesus, nor is it imposed upon him at the day of judgment; it silently rides him from the day he is born. It is his beginning proposition. And until he allows the salvation of Christ to interfere, it will remain there.

The Lord Jesus has certainly done His part to interrupt our fall. On the cross, He literally absorbed the punishment that belonged to all of us. "He bore the sin of many" (Isa. 53:12). He was "smitten by God and afflicted...He was wounded for our transgressions, He was bruised for our iniquities...the Lord has laid on Him the iniquity of us *all*" (Isa. 53:4-6). It is very difficult to imagine what this looked like. The Bible does describe the condemned in hell, where "their worm does not die and their fire is not quenched" (Isa. 66:24), where there is "the wailing and gnashing of teeth" (Matt. 13:42). However, it does not portray what it looked like for *one* man to bear the condemnation of *all*. The depths of such suffering are too grand for the human mind. It would mean taking the penalty of hell fire that belongs to each sinner, multiplying it by the number of sinners (billions), and then concentrating all of it upon Jesus as He hung on the cross.

A billion-fold torment must have been His while He hung there, yet He only disclosed the agony by saying, "I thirst!" (John 19:28). That little phrase gave us a portal into what was happening to Him as He died. Thirst is the condition of those who are condemned under God's judgment. The Gospel of Luke tells us about a rich man who cried out from Hades for someone "to dip the tip of his finger in water and cool my tongue; for I am tormented in this flame" (Luke 16:24). Essentially, the parched Savior was saying the same thing from the cross. That day, hell was on a hill named Calvary.

Whoever believes in Jesus Christ today, then, will find that his sins are gone—nowhere to be found. This is because he has received "the Lamb of God who takes *away* the sin of the world" (John 1:29). One of the results of this blessed reality is that divine anger has disappeared as well. When transgressions are no longer in the picture, wrath vanishes too. Anne Ross Cousin, a hymn writer of the nineteenth century, put it well when she wrote,

> Jehovah bade His sword awake,
> O Christ, it woke 'gainst Thee!
> Thy blood the flaming blade must slake;
> Thy heart its sheath must be—
> All for my sake, my peace to make;
> Now sleeps that sword for me.

So many advance warnings exists about the wrath to come, that it is amazing anyone would still perish. Notification of God's judgment has been in the Bible for thousands of years. It has been preached and taught in every setting from country church buildings to gigantic, high-profile events. Glimmers of it show up in movies, music, television, and even on placards at football games. Innumerable common folk—born-again relatives, coworkers, strangers, and friends—have testified concerning it down through the ages. With so many red flags waving, no one will be able to legitimately say in the end that God's wrath was unforeseen.

His exercised fury is always the last step after protracted warnings, patience, and restraint. During Noah's time, He pronounced the world as corrupt and declared, "I will destroy man whom I have created from the face of the earth" (Gen. 6:7). Then He granted one hundred and twenty years before the destruction actually came (Gen. 6:3). The Bible shows how that it took six days for God to create the world, but it took Him seven days to destroy the evil city of Jericho (Josh. 6:15, 20). He is "slow to anger" (Nah. 1:3), warning sinners, testifying to them, and inviting them to repent and turn to Christ. As one classic Christian writer said, "He speaks before He strikes and speaks that He may not strike" (Charnock 488). Unfortunately, sinners interpret this to mean that they have plenty of time to continue in their sins. They even reach the conclusion that since God's wrath is not everywhere apparent, then nothing at all will happen to them. Thus the very beneficiaries of God's patience often misunderstand and abuse it. A delay in judgment is meant to provide the opportunity to receive Christ, not a reason to become indifferent. God is "longsuffering toward us, not willing that any should perish, but that all should come to repentance" (2 Pet. 3:9). He has given His Son to us as the way out of condemnation. Those who choose to ignore this "exit" only have themselves to blame when the building burns down with them inside.

GETTING OFF OF THE TITANIC

In 1912, the Titanic docked for a short time in both France and Ireland before beginning its ill-fated voyage across the Atlantic Ocean. Some passengers must have gotten off on those stops. Maybe they were common workers who had only used the ship for a quick taxi ride from one port to another. Whatever the case, when they departed the Titanic, they were quite unaware that something of the gravest importance had silently and imperceptibly changed for them—their *destiny*. Stepping off that ship automatically meant that they had missed something horrible.

When you received Christ, something also changed for you that you couldn't see. It was a shift in *destiny*. This is the hardest kind of change to appreciate because it involves a matter in the future that will now no longer take place. Sometimes only a special disclosure can help us to understand such things. This was the idea behind Charles Dicken's *A Christmas Carol*. The main character, Ebenezer Scrooge, was shown what his future would have been had he continued to live as he did. The American film classic *It's A Wonderful Life* did the same thing by demonstrating to its main character what would have happened had he not been born. It was all a peek behind the curtain of possibility, a powerful means of compelling the characters to change their attitudes and have a new outlook on life.

That is the reason why we have spent so much time here at present, exploring the lake of fire. To some, studying hell may seem as morbid as studying the gas chamber. Christian teachers nervously avoid the topic or suggest that it is too shallow to merit any attention. Yet, without this somber biblical truth you might never properly appreciate "getting off the Titanic." You might never know what you missed and how significant was that moment of faith in Jesus Christ. The believer has "passed from death into life" (John 5:24). Having realized this himself, the Apostle Paul's celebratory praise was that the Lord Jesus had "delivered us from so great a death...in whom we trust that He will still deliver us" (2 Cor. 1:10).

"No hope" is a label describing those who are apart from Christ (1 Thess. 4:13; Eph. 2:12), but for those who are joined to Him through faith, it is another story. The Bible promises that "whoever believes in Him should not perish" (John 3:16) and that "We will be saved from wrath through Him" (Rom. 5:9). The future for us is no longer a dark, frightening question mark. Now we can triumphantly say, "O Lord, I will praise You; though You were angry with me, Your anger is turned away, and You comfort Me" (Isa. 12:1).

Reference Notes

Charnock, Stephen. *The Existence and Attributes of God.* Grand
    Rapids: Baker, 1996.
Lang, G.H. *The Sinner's Future.* Miami Springs: Schoettle
    Publishing, 1988.

4

WHAT IS SALVATION?

RECEIVING JESUS

WHAT SHOULD WE DO WITH JESUS?

They call it the dead room, and it ranks in the Guinness Book of World Records as the quietest place on earth. A full 99.8 percent of reflected sound is eliminated inside of it, meaning you could shout at the top of your lungs and the words would vanish almost as quickly as they came out of your mouth. This test room, created by Bell labs, is an audio black hole. A human being would find its crushing sense of isolation and silence unbearable. Within minutes his own pulse would pound inside his skull like a trip hammer—that is, if it could be heard over the ringing in his ears.

There is just such a dead room at the core of human

beings—a place of intense silence, inward loneliness, and void. We can hardly bear to live with it. That is why the human experience ends up being one long hunt to find the item that might fill the empty space with melody, sound, life, and presence.

Everyone looks for it in a different way. For instance, there are some people who indulge in low things like drugs, various forms of immorality and general base living. Satisfaction, they believe, is to be found in the "dumpster." Others take the route of crass materialism. Happiness to them is a matter of the next expensive toy and keeping up with the Joneses. And, of course, there are those who are headed up the ladder of personal achievements. They are convinced that fulfillment lies in becoming other peoples' idols.

What has been overlooked in every case is that the missing component is not an "it," but a *Him*—Christ. This might not sound like much of a revelation to folks who have already sampled the platter of life. "Jesus...yeah, right," they say, "I tried religion already and it didn't work." Very often during their search for meaning, people do come across the Lord in some way, shape, or form. The problem is that they have no idea what to do with Him.

There are signs of this general ignorance everywhere. Not knowing any better, people do all kinds of things with Jesus. They hang Him on the wall, they glue Him to the dashboards of their cars, and they ask Him to grant victories at sporting events. They study His life, memorize and recite His prayer, quote His words, and use His life as a behavioral model.

Yet, after all that, Jesus often doesn't seem to "work." For instance, statistics would probably confirm that houses with Jesus paintings on the wall are no more exempt from burning down than those without them. Car crashes still occur even when a plastic Jesus is inside one of the vehicles. There have been defeats for sports teams despite the fact that their prayer for a win included the formulaic "in Jesus' name we pray." And finally, plenty of people have learned the facts of "the Jesus story" without being able or willing to change their evil lifestyles.

Those who are disillusioned by these failures need to stop for a moment and answer a very basic question. Since "God...gave His only begotten Son" (John 3:16), what are we *supposed* to do with Him? In the middle of borrowing Him for so many things, it might never have dawned on us to ask.

The Lord Jesus came down from heaven as the unique missing piece to fit the incomplete puzzle of humanity. His coming should have made perfect sense to the world since He fit the void within it. But things didn't work out that way. "He was in the world, and the world was made through Him, and the world *did not know Him*" (John 1:10). This is true irony. A Person was among us, and though He was the source of the very planet underneath our feet, most of us failed to detect it. "The missing piece" went unrecognized.

This was the case even when the Lord "came to His own" (John 1:11)—the Jewish people. In the Old Testament, He had called them, "*My* people" (Ex. 3:7, 5:1) and provided them with detailed prophecies that described His future coming. The Jews, above all other peoples, should have recognized Him but when He came, "His own *did not receive* Him" (John 1:11). Instead they tried to use Christ for a lot of other things. Crowds came to Him for every reason from curiosity to healing and since the Lord Jesus was so kind, He allowed it. People could get what they wanted from Him and then leave, without any interest beyond the few surface things He did for them. In fact, after He had fed five thousand of "His own" with bread and fish, some began to follow Him just because of that one free lunch.

But the Lord did not want a movement of hangers-on who were hoping to use Him. The interaction He longed to have with human beings was something on a much deeper level. He wanted them to *receive* Him. He said to the crowd, "You seek Me...because you ate of the loaves and were filled. Do not work for the food which perishes, but for the food which endures unto eternal life" (John 6:26-27 NASB). Then Jesus identified that mysterious food: "*I am* the bread of life" (John 6:35).

This self-description is very significant, because bread

is a food product and food is supposed to be received. In fact, nothing in our world can be received more deeply and intimately than food. It enters our mouths for chewing, enters our stomachs for filling, and then enters the process of digestion to become part of our very make-up. Without a doubt, food is the closest, most intimate thing to us in the world. And that is precisely the kind of closeness the Lord wants with us. He is not interested in producing long-distance relationships. As the living bread, He wishes for people to receive Him—deeply, personally, until they are *"one spirit* with Him" (1 Cor. 6:17).

Since the beginning of time kids at dinner tables have been told, "Stop playing with your food!" Youngsters can be pretty inventive. They quickly discover that an apple can be thrown like a softball. Peas can be blown through a straw. A pancake can function as a Frisbee. But parents know that food is useless until it is received. That's why they frown on dinner being turned into toys. This was also why the Lord, in a very respectable way, told the crowd to stop treating Him like Santa Clause and start valuing Him as "the food which endures unto eternal life." When the "living bread" is adapted for other uses, like its physical counterpart, it loses the fullness of its meaning. However, if it is received, then Christ will immediately enter the deepest recess of a human being and satisfy the inward hunger of soul and spirit. That is exactly what God meant for us to do with Jesus in the first place.

How To Receive Christ

The Lord said, "*I* am the bread of life" (John 6:48)..."If anyone *eats* of this bread, he will live forever" (John 6:51)..."Whoever *eats My flesh and drinks My blood* has eternal life" (John 6:54). You've heard of following Christ and loving Christ, but *eating* Christ might sound very strange to your twenty-first-century ears. If so, then you should know that it had the same disquieting effect when it was heard by first-century ears.

Eat My flesh...drink My blood.

The disciples complained that "this is a hard saying, who can understand it?" (John 6:60). Maybe as they grappled with the meaning, they imagined some form of ceremonial cannibalism. The thought must have been too disturbing for them to take—"From that time many of His disciples went back and walked with Him no more" (John 6:66). But if they had really listened they would have heard the Lord also say, "the flesh profits nothing" (John 6:63)—a clarification that the phrase "eat My flesh" was not meant physically. Even if, through some bizarre ritual, a person had managed to consume the skin and tissue of Jesus, it wouldn't have profited the eater a bit because the Lord had also said, "It is the *Spirit* who gives life" (John 6:63).

Eating Christ is something spiritual. It has to do with deeply receiving His invisible, intangible person. We might think that for such a profound spiritual thing to take place, a complex technique is needed—maybe a pilgrimage or some religious methodology. Yet, the Bible shows us that the way to receive Christ is much simpler than we suppose. It says, "as many as *received* Him, to them He gave the right to become children of God, to those who *believe* in His name" (John 1:12). The words "receive" and "believe" are used synonymously in the same verse. They define each other. This informs us that receiving is not behaving or meditating or fasting. Receiving is *believing.*

If we want to receive a slice of bread, we do it through chewing. If we want to receive the *living* bread, we do it through believing. The day we believed in Christ, we didn't join a world religion. We *ate* something. It was our first bite of "true food" (John 6:55 NASB), and it brought the flesh of the Son of God into us.

CHRIST IN YOU –
HOW IS IT POSSIBLE?

In the minds of many people it is one thing to believe in the Jesus who walked the earth many centuries ago. It is another to believe that the very same Jesus can enter them. How could something like that be possible? Prior to His death and resurrection, Christ was physical and three-dimensional. He could not enter His disciples any more than you can enter a block of cement. With the exception of special miracles, as a man on earth the Lord obeyed the restraints of time and space. When He journeyed somewhere, He walked or rode. He didn't fly. Although we find Him walking on water, that was a miracle for the moment, exercised for the good of those in a storm-tossed boat. It had nothing to do with His personal convenience. Although His ministry was often miraculous, His personal living was subject to God-created physical limitations, like any normal man.

But after He rose from the dead, things changed. For one thing, the Lord appeared in a room even though the door had been shut (c.f. John 20:19). How did He get in there? Prior to His resurrection, He would have needed to open the door in order to walk through it. At this post-resurrection point, however, it seems that He simply walked straight through it. Later, we also find Him appearing (Luke 24:13-31; John 21:1; Acts 1:3), sometimes in recognizable form and sometimes not (John 20:14-16; 21:1-4, 7).

The only explanation for this is that "the Last Adam [Christ], became a life-giving *Spirit*" (1 Cor. 15:45). In that state, He was no longer under the limitations of time or space. Nothing physical could restrict Him. This is extremely meaningful for us, because if Christ can penetrate a closed door, then He will have no trouble entering a human body. It is as easy for Him to come into us as it is for us to step into a fog bank. In fact, on the day of your salvation He entered you so smoothly that you were probably not even aware that He did it at the time.

CHRIST BEING IN YOU IS BETTER FOR YOU

We all must come to terms with the fact that it is better to have Christ *in* us invisibly, than to have Christ *with* us visibly. I've met plenty of believers who wish their relationship with Christ could be a physical one. They think that Christ living in them is inferior to having a flesh-and-blood version of Him that they can see. An invisible, indwelling Christ is perceived as a consolation prize for those born too late to have walked with Him long ago. Now, as the concept goes, we are stuck with a "faith" Jesus who seems unreal at times, especially during personal emergencies.

While some of us think that the Christ we have today is a step down from the One who wore sandals and tunics, scripture says otherwise. When the Lord became the life giving Spirit He was not reduced to some lesser plane of existence as though He became only a semblance, a ghost of what He once was. The Bible shows us that somehow, mysteriously, the Lord continues to retain His humanity. In His newly resurrected state, He said to the disciples, "Behold My hands and My feet, that it is I myself. Handle Me and see, for a spirit does not have flesh and bones as you see I have" (Luke 24:39). The Lord is not a formless, immaterial phantom of some sort. Past the point of resurrection He could still be touched and He could even eat (Luke 24:42-43). He is substantial but spiritual, meaning that He can be inside, out of, or above physical matter at will. Thankfully for us, He entered *our* matter—epidermis, tissue, blood, bone, and cells—and got into our very spirit.

"Yes, but we can't see Him," some Christians argue. According to them, not being able to see Him with our eyes is a severe handicap. The Lord Jesus strongly disagreed with that thought. He told His disciples, "because you have seen Me, you have believed. *Blessed* are those who have *not* seen and yet have believed" (John 20:29). This is a startling concept, since we assume that sight always confirms faith, or at least stimulates it. But the Lord's word indicates that it is not the lack of sight but perhaps the abundance of it that creates a handicap.

We only need to open the gospels to witness this. There we have Jesus in the flesh, physically available to the disciples twenty-four hours a day for three and a half years. What did they see? One of them, Philip, told Jesus, "Lord, show us the Father, and it is sufficient for us. Jesus said to him, 'Have I been with you so long, and yet you have not known Me, Philip? He who has seen Me has seen the Father" (John 14:8-9). In other words, Philip missed it. By looking at Jesus' visible form, he saw a carpenter, a Jewish prophet, a holy man, a great teacher, perhaps even the Messiah, but not the biggest thing—God Himself. Philip's physical sight had become his limitation. While trusting in it, he failed to cultivate the deeper seeing of his heart (see Eph. 1:18).

The other disciples were no better off. While He was still on the earth with them, the Lord Jesus addressed them as "you of little faith" (Matt. 14:31). His visible presence evidently did not do much for them in the area of helping them believe. And we have an even more extreme example concerning the brothers of Jesus, His own family. They had grown up with Him in their home. Surely, they should have been the best candidates for a deep faith. But again, the eyes of the flesh were no help, "For even His brothers did not believe in Him" (John 7:5).

The limitations of sight actually bring more blessing than we realize: "Blessed are those who have *not* seen" because they have not been spoiled. A child can be spoiled very easily. Buy a toy for him whenever he wants it, or give her candy whenever she cries. It would also be very easy for the Lord to spoil Christians—to feed their lust to "see" things every time they are down, or shaken, or suffering. But after a few supernatural "visions" they will need them every time. This kind of Christianity, without exception, leads to very little knowledge or interest concerning Christ *in* you.

The Apostle Paul, who himself was no stranger to miraculous visions, said, "it pleased God... to reveal His Son *in* me" (Gal. 1:15-16). Though Paul had seen the Lord Jesus with his eyes, what controlled His Christian life was primarily inward. If the visible dimension of meeting Christ had become the foundation of His Christian life, even Paul might have been spoiled. He could very easily have required a Damascus road experience (Acts 9:3-6) on a regular basis to keep his faith afloat. Every time trying circumstances arose, Paul might have begged and pleaded with Christ to appear and reassure him. If it happened, a spoiled Paul would have been happy. If not, he would have gone into a depression, wondering why the Lord did not love him any more. Happily, we have a Paul who declared "we walk by faith, *not by sight*" (2 Cor 5:7). Whether he saw Him or not, Paul could say, "Christ lives *in* me; and the life which I now live in the flesh, I live by faith" (Gal. 2:20).

During the time Christ was on the earth, the disciples were with Him in the most tangible sense, but that experience lacked a certain completeness. At best, being *with* Him was like being *with* food. Anyone who has dieted knows the frustration of being *with* food. I once heard about a woman who hoped to lose some weight by going on a water fast. After three days had gone by, a coworker in her office went out for lunch and brought back a sack of cheeseburgers. The very smell of the food broke the woman's will to fast. She was so incensed over the whole thing that she sued the coworker! That extreme response illustrates the frustration of being with food— seeing it, and smelling it—without being able to receive it. It is only when you eat food, and it *vanishes from sight* into the depths of your being, that you can truly be satisfied.

My wife has made some incredible meals. I've never said, "Hmm, too bad the food is in my stomach now, and I can't see it anymore. I would rather be able to look at it here on my plate than have it disappear within me." If I ever start thinking like that, then it's time for some professional help.

We Christians have the Lord Jesus in us invisibly. He has gone into our depths where He now lives forever. If we go on to understand the blessedness of that fact, we will never desire a different kind of relationship with Him.

CHRIST IS NOT "STANDARD EQUIPMENT"

Many today who like to sound open-minded invoke the mantra "Christ is in *all* of us." Nobody wants to be the narrow guy who disagrees, since it might be taken as rude or judgmental.

The idea of Jesus being in everyone appeals to some politically correct sense of fairness, but it is a terribly misguided one. Let me paint a picture of the tragedy that can come from this kind of thinking. Imagine that you are part of a skydiving team about to parachute out of a plane. Everyone stands ready. They are all dressed and rigged for the jump. But then you notice that the parachute pack on one of your teammates appears to be deflated, as if nothing is inside of it. "Excuse me," you say, pointing to it, "Is everything okay with your pack?" Annoyed, the teammate replies, "What's that supposed to mean?"

"Nothing personal, but it looks—"

"Looks like what?"

The quick, curt reaction catches you off guard. "I uh, I was just wondering if you checked your chute." The others are watching now. "Hey, man, give him a break," one of them says. "Yeah," another adds, "Stop trying to scare him."

"But I'm not," you reply. "It looks like there's nothing in his pack."

This provokes even more outrage. "We're professional skydivers," one says. "Of course there's a chute in his bag. There are chutes in *all* of our bags."

The exchange continues until you are finally shouted into silence—the price of being a "trouble maker." But the price paid by the teammate in question will be much higher. He will literally die because no one wanted to humiliate him by making him check his pack.

Don't think that this parable is overly dramatic. The same situation is acted out on a daily basis, except it revolves around whether or not Christ is in a relative or a coworker or a dear friend. "Of course He is," they assure us, as though, along with our arms, legs, ears, and eyes, Christ is standard onboard equipment for every human being.

Quite to the contrary, the Bible limits the number of people who have Christ in them. John 1:12 makes clear, "*as many* as received Him [Christ], to them He gave the right to become children of God." The words "As many" are a dead giveaway that only a portion of the human race has received Christ and has Him living within them. Many may have received Him, but not all. The Bible also says, "*if* Christ is in you" (Rom. 8:10), a conditional statement which would be needless if everyone already had Christ within them. *"If Christ is in you"* means that He may be or He may not be. Even when scripture says, "Christ is...in all" (Col. 3:11), it does not mean "in all" the people of the whole world, but "in all" those who are part of the "new man" (Col. 3:10), the body of Christ.

The idea of Jesus living in everyone might sound like a noble way of viewing the world, but it is simply not true. As long as a person has never received Christ, then Christ is not in him. No one can skip the step of receiving. If he does, he will ultimately discover—perhaps too late—that there is no "parachute in his bag."

WHAT IT MEANS FOR CHRIST TO LIVE IN YOU

The Lord Jesus Himself was the One who introduced the concept of His living in us. He said, "In that day you will know that I am in My Father, and you in Me, and *I in you*" (John 14:20). But what does "Christ in you" really mean?

In order to answer this question, let's first clarify what it does *not* mean. For one thing, Christ does not merely dwell within His believers as a cherished memory. Sometimes people wear tee-shirts that say "Elvis Lives." Of course that means in terms of appreciation, he lives on in the hearts of his fans. By that definition anyone who has left behind some influence could live in another person. However, it would be strictly metaphorical. Many artists, politicians, scientists, entertainers, and founders of world religions lie in graves. The words, sounds, and ideas they left behind still reverberate in the hearts of their followers, but that is as far as it goes. Neither their souls nor their bodies are available to anyone now. When we say that Christ lives in His believers, however, it is not in reference to their fond reminiscences of Him. Yes, the Bible speaks of remembering Christ, but not as a long dead Person whom we are no longer able to contact.

Because of the persistent and clear way the Bible talks about Christ living in us, we know that it is not a figure of speech. The Lord's personal presence is within all true Christians. Even the Corinthian believers, as troubled as they were, knew this. They tested the Apostle Paul by seeking proof that Christ spoke in him (2 Cor. 13:3). Again, the prepositions used here are important. Speaking *in* someone means more than speaking *through* someone. Speaking *through* someone is to use a person like a relay or a channel. But speaking *in* someone is different. It involves a profound level of closeness in which a speaker inhabits a person while speaking. This is how Christ is oriented to His believers. He is not outside of us speaking to us and then expecting that we will relay His message. No, Christ speaks *in* us. An intense personal communication of this kind means that real believers are not merely switchboards or megaphones for the Lord's word. They themselves are the very place in which He speaks. This is not to advocate that we begin listening for voices in our heads. The speaking of Christ is spiritual and deep, usually in the form of impressions rather than words. The common sense point that I wish to make is that in order for Christ to speak in us, He must be...*in* us.

The idea of Christ being in us also lies at the heart of Paul's words in 2 Corinthians. There his desire was that "the life of Jesus...may be manifested *in* our mortal flesh" (2 Cor. 4:11). He hoped for the life of *Jesus* to be seen there and not merely our attempts to *act like* Jesus. Paul's thought of the Christian life went beyond only being "Christ-like." He saw it as Christ forging an internal organic bond with the believers. That was how Paul could refer to Christ as "our *life*" (Col. 3:4) and could also say, "to me to live *is* Christ" (Phil. 1:21). The Jesus of Paul's epistles was more than objective. He was the subjective, indwelling possession of all those who received Him.

CHRIST IN YOU OR CHRIST IN HEAVEN?

Once it is clear that the Lord Jesus does not indwell us only by sentiment or memory or poetic metaphor, we face the wonderful reality that He is actually in us. The Bible refers to it as "this *mystery*...which is Christ in you" (Col. 1:27).

Part of "this mystery" lies in the fact that Jesus occupies two places at once—heaven and the believers. The gospel of Mark ends by telling us that the Lord Jesus "was received up into heaven and sat down at the right hand of God" (16:19). Luke ends by saying, "He was parted from them and carried up into heaven" (24:51). From these two passages, we correctly gather that the Lord's final destination was heaven. But Luke and Mark are only two out of four gospels. The other two gospels, Matthew and John, conclude with Christ staying here. Neither records the Lord's ascension into heaven. Instead, one ends with the promise that "I am *with you* always, even to the end of the age" (Matt. 28:19), and the other concludes with a command, where Jesus tells Peter to "follow Me" (John 21:22). The accounts in Matthew and John do not contradict the accounts in Mark and Luke; they compliment them. The endings of the four gospels put together demonstrate that at the same time Christ is here on earth He is also in heaven.

We find this thought highly developed in the epistles, where Paul directs our attention to "Christ *in* you, the hope of glory" (Col. 1:27), but then tells us to "seek those things which are *above, where Christ is, sitting at the right hand of God*" (Col. 3:1). Both "Christ in you" and "Christ above" are simultaneously true. Figuring this out is a little bit like considering how electricity could be in both a generating plant and in your kitchen light bulb at the same time. Just where is the electricity? From your perspective, it is in the bulb, because the light comes on when you hit the light switch. But if we visited the generator, which is miles away and out of sight, we would realize that the same electricity is present there as well. How could it be in two places at once? That is like asking how Christ could be in you and in heaven at the same time. It is all part of a mysterious reality. Our spirit, where the Lord Jesus lives, is connected with heaven, where the Lord Jesus also lives.

THE BLESSINGS
OF CHRIST BEING IN YOU

When a person receives Christ within, it makes his world the best of all possible worlds. I often tell groups of Christians that with the Lord in them, they are doing better than they think. I sometimes get puzzled looks in return. I know why I get those responses. We frequently lose sight of our eternal wellness and focus instead on problems with kids, jobs, finances, homes, and health. In addition, there are spiritual failures—bad habits that we can't seem to break, good habits that we can't seem to cultivate, and occasional seasons of flatness. Those things have a way of making us see ourselves as crippled and barely making it. In order for us to accurately assess our condition, we need to stop and consider what it means for Christ to live in us. Only then will we get some impression of how supremely blessed we really are.

YOU ARE GREATLY BELOVED

John 3:16 tells us that "God so loved the world," but this primarily describes God's love for erring, unsaved creatures that have fallen into sin and death. It is a love full of concern and pity. The love He has for Christians, however, mostly involves delight and satisfaction. That is not because we always do the things that God likes. Behavior is not the issue here at all. Rather, God's love for a believer is *paternal* in nature. It irresistibly comes to us now because the *Son* of God is in us.

God said, "This is My beloved Son, in whom I am *well pleased*" (Matt. 3:17). No one delights the heart of God like the Lord Jesus does. Jesus acknowledged this when He said to the Father, "You *loved* Me before the foundation of the world" (John 17:24). Indeed, God's entire kingdom is the "kingdom of the *Son* of His *love*" (Col. 1:13).

Now this Person, so supremely favored by the Father, dwells in the believers. Because of this, no matter what happens, we will always in some way find favor with God.

His affections will be upon us because He sees His own Son in us.

Christ is not merely one item in a list of things that we receive. Make no mistake about it, He is *everything* in our salvation. The Bible speaks of "the salvation which is *in* Christ Jesus" (2 Tim. 2:10) and says that "there is salvation *in* no one else" (Acts 4:12 NASB). We might have thought that being saved was all about getting a collection of assorted works and blessings, but it is actually just a Person, and ultimately that very Person coming to live in us.

For those who have broken God's law, "Redemption...is *in* Christ Jesus" (Rom. 3:24). For the spiritually dead, there is "eternal life *in* Christ Jesus our Lord" (Rom. 6:23). Sinners have lost God, but they can get Him back in Christ, for "*in* Him dwells all the fullness of the Godhead bodily" (Col. 2:9). God does not give us anything outside of Christ. Instead, He "has blessed us with every spiritual blessing...*in* Christ" (Eph. 1:3). Apparently, from God's point of view, we do not need many things. We only need His Son.

Christ is truly the whole package of salvation. The Apostle Paul told the believers that "You are complete in *Him*" (Col. 2:10). It is no wonder that people who receive Christ often have some kind of inward registration, reaction, or change. It is a lot like what happens when we eat certain kinds of foods. For example, I once ate a spoonful of Vietnamese pepper paste and within two seconds felt like my mouth was melting. Some people have this strong, immediate experience when they meet the great salvation in Christ. They smash and trash sinful things while making radical changes in their lives. But there's also the "slow burn." That's like eating some so-called "mild" salsa and then bragging about how you can drink it like iced tea. Then it sl-o-o-o-owly catches up to you, making you wish you really did have some iced tea—a whole pitcher of it. This is the other way many people react to the salvation in Christ. You measure their response in months, not minutes. They might not have even noticed that the Lord affected them until much later, when a friend exclaimed, "Man, you're different!" In either case, whether immediate or gradual, reactions will come because the Christ who lives within us contains "so great a salvation" (Heb. 2:3).

While He was on the earth, the Lord Jesus performed a number of miraculous works for people. He described some of them: "the blind see, the lame walk, the lepers are cleansed, the deaf hear, the dead are raised..." (Luke 7:22). Then He mentioned the poor. What did the Lord do for them? He said, "the poor have the gospel announced to them" (Luke 7:22). Now to our understanding, the most obvious way to help the poor is to give them money. Why did Jesus preach the gospel to them instead? Why not create a pile of gold for them so they could fill their pockets and go home? The gospel was offered instead, because it gives the Lord Jesus to people, and when they receive Him, their previously impoverished condition changes to one of spiritual wealth. It is a wealth that "neither moth nor rust destroys and...thieves do not break in and steal" (Matt. 6:20). It is "the unsearchable *riches* of Christ" (Eph. 3:8).

"Riches" as it is used in Ephesians 3:8 does not refer to dollars and cents. It relates to all the aspects of Christ as portrayed in the Bible. When I was a young boy, my only concept of Christ was that He was some kind of superman. I imagined that He could lift a tractor-trailer rig with one finger. He could hear somebody whispering on the other side of the world. He could eat a thousand apple pies at one sitting. All these were feats of great importance to an eight-year-old boy. I might not have known Christ, but I figured that if somebody somewhere could do those things, he was okay in my book. When I finally read the Bible many years later I was surprised to find Jesus *Himself* so captivating, not just the powerful things He did. His miracles were impressive (I swapped my homemade ones for the

90

scriptural ones), but it was His very personality that hooked me. The gospels had managed to record a life that seemed to be everything that I could have wanted in another person. Being introduced to the Lord's humanity, was to me, an introduction to unsearchable riches.

I had never realized I was that hungry to know a real human being. I wasn't the odd case, either. Positive human virtues are in short supply today. People long for them so badly that they pay money to see them at the movies. The box office is kept afloat by a lot more than interesting special effects. John and Jane Doe want to see the courage of action heroes marching into a hail of bullets. They want to see exhibitions of self-sacrifice, kindness, and endurance.

Viewers glory in these virtues. Nothing, it seems, can entertain or encourage us more than seeing some aspect of humanity at its best, even if it is all just make-believe.

Unfortunately, the real-life human race is rarely in such form as its big screen counterpart. We hope that virtues like sympathy, gratitude, and honesty could be in ourselves and in those surrounding us. But this hope is often bitterly disappointed. An appalling lack of virtue results in damaged marriages, failed professional pursuits, and broken family relationships that might never be healed. The self-help industry tries to offset this by pumping out mountains of books and tapes. These attempt to correct bad character and guide the development of "strengths." But after trying so hard with so little positive outcome, it is clear that virtue requires an energy that most of us are not willing to spend. Even those who are willing often find their positive traits sabotaged by "holes" in other areas of their life. People lauded for their honesty are often without mercy. The merciful are often without righteousness. The righteous may not be affectionate. The affectionate may not be very honest. Ironically, being a whole human being is beyond human ability.

As portrayed in the gospels, the life of the Lord Jesus consisted of a perfect balance of virtues. For instance, He was courageous. On the way to Jerusalem to be crucified, Jesus led the way before the fearful disciples (Mark 10:32), yet He never became reckless or presumptuous. He said, "I can do nothing on My own initiative...I do not seek My own will, but the will of Him who sent Me" (John 5:30 NASB).

We find His honest judgment penetrating, as He rebuked his disciples: "Why are you fearful, O you of little faith?" (Matt. 8:26). But His strongest affections were for that very same group: "He loved them to the end" (John 13:1).

There was a highness to His Person, a dignity as He said, "You call Me Teacher and Lord, and you say well, for so I am" (John 13:13). Yet at the same time He was humble, saying of Himself, "the Son of Man did not come to be served, but to serve" (Mark 10:45).

As to His gentle feelings, Jesus "was moved with compassion" (Mark 1:41) to heal a leprous man. Yet He could also be firmly immovable: "Another of the disciples said to Him, 'Lord, let me first go and bury my father.' But Jesus said to him, 'Follow Me, and let the dead bury their own dead'" (Matt. 8:21-22).

His sweet simplicity appealed even to the smallest children as He took them into His arms and fervently blessed them (Mark 10:13, 16). But this same Person could be mysteriously deep, confounding the religious experts of the day as He spoke "things kept secret from the foundation of the world" (Matt. 13:35).

He could suddenly wield power, as when He stood in the middle of a storm and "rebuked the wind and said to the sea, 'Peace, be still!'" When He did this, "the wind ceased and there was a great calm" (Mark 4:39). But out of His love, this powerful Person would not lift a finger against His enemies as they beat Him in the face and mocked Him and killed Him.

The Lord Jesus did not have the extremes of character that come with damaged humanity. His love never degenerated into sappiness. Neither did His power and judgement warp into tyranny. His gentleness never became weakness. His firm resolve never made Him unmerciful. The gospels do not present us with a Savior whose personal traits are unbalanced and exaggerated. We find instead a genuine man whose character is a fine blend of all that we hope to find in others and all we hope to be. Now, this Person, with the extensive riches of His humanity, *lives* in us for our enrichment and for our daily need.

You Have Been Greatly Enriched—
By the Lord's Divinity

So far, we have touched upon the riches of Christ's *humanity* in you. However, we should remember that Christ is fully God as well as fully man. His *divine* nature, therefore, is also a storehouse of spiritual treasures.

In the book of Exodus, Moses asked God,

> "When I come to the children of Israel and say to them, 'The God of your fathers has sent me to you,' and they say to me, 'What is His name?' what shall I say to them? And God said to Moses, 'I AM WHO I AM.'...Thus you shall say to the children of Israel, 'I AM has sent me to you.'" (Ex. 3:13-14)

This strange, almost cryptic name might leave us asking, "I AM...*whom*? I AM...*what*?" God's name, I AM, is an open-ended sentence. It is up to us to fill in the rest. If we are struggling with a problem, God's name is "I AM *the answer*." Should there be a lack among His children, God's name is "I AM *whatever you need*." The riches that He has to bestow upon us are unlimited. The question is, how do we appropriate them?

Once again, the answer lies in receiving Christ. While He was on earth, the Lord Jesus repeatedly referred to Himself as "I AM." In essence, He was the heavenly "bank" coming down to enrich us all. To begin with, He said, "*I am* the bread of life" (John 6:48). That was a stunning declaration because He was describing Himself as the unique sustenance of mankind—the only spiritual food that a human being could ever need. There were no qualifications given. Jesus said, "he who comes to Me shall *never* hunger" (John 6:35). "He who comes" means anyone who comes—anyone at all, regardless of intellect, race, or social standing.

93

Sometimes people say, "Jesus might be good for you, but He's not good for me." That's wrong. The words "shall never hunger" is a guarantee that those who come to Christ will find fulfillment in Him regardless of who they are and what they've done. This is a miracle. Nothing else we know of can deliver the promise of satisfying any man, any time, anywhere. A potency of that magnitude is supernatural, yet we encounter it in the Lord Jesus. The ability to feed and fill all men is an element of His divine riches.

The Lord Jesus also said, "*I am* the light of the world" (John 8:12a). People commonly equate academic knowledge with enlightenment and a lack of education with darkness, but true light does not come from colleges, books, or ideas; it comes from Christ. He is "the *true light*, which coming into the world, enlightens every man" (John 1:9 NASB).

"Every man" in this verse, literally means *every* man. If it had been possible for Buddha, Confucius, or Mohammed to come to Christ, then Christ would have enlightened them all. They would not have enlightened Him. The Lord Jesus was described in an Old Testament prophecy as "the *Sun* of righteousness" (Mal. 4:2). He was the Sun and no more needed additional light than our sun, which illuminates everything but requires no illumination upon itself.

Still, a number of times in the gospels people tried to shed light on Christ by "straightening Him out." Martha, an outspoken Jewish woman, told Him, "If you had been here, my brother would not have died" (John 11:21). It was a thinly veiled complaint that the Lord just hadn't done enough. In another case, "the disciples of John came to Him, saying, 'Why do we and the Pharisees fast often, but your disciples do not fast?'" (Matt. 9:14). It was an accusation that the life Jesus was leading others into was short of godliness. On still another occasion, after Jesus spoke of His upcoming death and resurrection, Peter thought he was helping the Lord when he "took Him aside and began to rebuke Him, saying, 'Far be it from You, Lord; this shall not happen to You!'" (Matt. 16:22). In each of these cases and many others, people assumed that they had an understanding that the Lord didn't have, but His answers to them showed that they were the ones who were confused. They could not properly decipher His words and actions. As it is written, "the light shines in the darkness, and the *darkness did not comprehend it*" (John 1:5).

Divine light is not a natural commodity; we are not born with it. And as long as we live without it, we will be poor in our realization of the most basic spiritual things. It may be shocking to hear, for instance, that without Christ we will never realize who we are. Many conscientious people who work hard at being good are victims of such "low light" conditions. As they master one good behavioral trait after another, their pride grows and so does their darkness.

This attitude was exposed in the people around Jesus as He walked the earth. One of them, a rich young man, approached the Lord and confidently listed all the commandments he had kept from his childhood. "Jesus said to him, 'If you want to be *perfect*, go, sell what you have and give to the poor, and you will have treasure in heaven; and come, follow Me.' But when the young man heard that saying, he went away sorrowful, for he had great possessions" (Matt. 19:21-22). This proud fellow had met the "Light of the world," and only then had he discovered any real imperfection in his life. He was "righteous" in many things, yet he loved his "great possessions" to the point that they kept him from following the Lord. In his personal darkness he had unknowingly cultivated a life that continually broke the greatest commandment: "You shall love the LORD your God with all your heart, with all your soul, with all your mind, and with all your strength" (Mark 12:30). Without Christ we all could have easily remained on a path of blind self-appreciation just like the young man. But now that the Lord's light has enriched us, we can appreciate who we are and where we are in relation to Him.

In our natural human condition, we are blind to everything, even God. As the Bible says, "No one has ever seen God at any time" (John 1:18a). Thankfully Christ, the light of the world, can enable us to apprehend the God whom we cannot see— "The only begotten Son, who is in the bosom of the Father, *He has declared Him*" (John 1:18b).

Declaring God is to make Him known through all sorts of ways—words, deeds, attitudes, actions, reactions, likes, and dislikes. The Son was such an expression of the Father that there was nothing He said or did that would leave observers deficient in their knowledge of God. This is why Jesus said, "He who has *seen Me has seen the Father*" (John 14:9), and Paul said that we can find "the *light* of the knowledge of the glory of God *in the face of Jesus Christ*" (2 Cor. 4:6). Without Christ, God largely disappears from view, leaving men to think of Him as a faceless "force," a stone effigy, or any of a thousand bizarre religious concepts. The most fundamental spiritual item—God Himself—becomes impossible for us to see. However, now that Christ lives in us, the real God has started to come sharply into focus. His inward illumination has begun to cause a knowledge of God from the inside out.

Ultimately, all the riches of divine light are in Christ. John said that the face of Jesus "was like the sun shining in its strength" (Rev. 1:16). When the Lord entered into us, that same "sun" began to rise inside, somewhat like the gospel writer described: "The people who sat in darkness have seen a great light, and upon those who sat in the region and shadow of death light has dawned" (Matt. 4:16). Because His light is now in us, new realizations about things have begun—things we never would have understood while sitting in the region and shadow of death.

The divine riches in Christ progressively unfold as Jesus continued to say "I AM." He said, "*I am* the good shepherd" (John 10:14). Before a man receives Christ, he has no shepherd. He is left to his own devices. This is tragic, because the pace of life in human society has done nothing but speed up over the centuries. The forty-hour work week (at least for professionals) is now a thing of the past. With travel and lots of overtime, it is now seventy hours a week or more. With that kind of sustained pace, it's not uncommon for people to be too exhausted for their families and, of course, for the things of God. There has never been a time when the riches of "our Lord Jesus...the great *Shepherd* of the sheep" (Heb. 13:20) were more needed in society. Consider the phrase, "He makes me to *lie down* in green pastures; He leads me beside *still* waters" (Ps. 23:2). These experiences of the Lord's inward care—stillness and rest— are exactly what a person needs when he has gotten lost in the rat race.

David, the writer of Psalm 23, was no mere storybook character. He was a real person who faced tremendous challenges. His family had gone through crises rivaling the worst of what we see today. A superior (King Saul) stalked him and wanted him dead. There were conspiracies against him and betrayals. Then there were his own failures— murder, adultery, and terrible mistakes that cost the lives of thousands. If David had been alone, he would have collapsed into a heap of self-pity and overwhelming anxiety. Instead, when he surveyed his circumstances, including his stormy past and his unknown future, he wrote, "Yea, though I walk through the valley of the shadow of death, I will fear no evil; for *You are with me*; Your rod and Your staff, they comfort me" (Ps. 23:4). It is not exactly clear when David wrote those words, but they eventually became the hallmark of his life. With him as with all God's people, the most basic comfort lies in knowing that the Lord is present.

When the disciples were commanded to "go therefore and make disciples of all the nations" (Matt. 28:19), they had no idea what lay ahead of them. The world was a wild, dark place. Attempts to disciple all the nations could result in anything from abject humiliation to physical harm. So the Lord Jesus ended His command by saying, "I am with you always, even to the end of the age" (Matt. 28:20). He did not conclude with, "Behold, everything will go well for you" or some other shallow promise. By telling them "I am with you," He considered His own abiding presence as sufficient for all the disciples' future needs. There is no closer supervision that a shepherd could provide than by being personally installed within His sheep. From the immediacy of our own spirit the Lord Jesus renders the richness of His care to us—He "leads" (Ps. 23:2b), "restores" (Ps. 23:3), "comforts" (Ps. 23:4), and "anoints" (Ps. 23:5). Those who receive this inward shepherding can say in an even more profound way than David, "My cup runs over.

Surely goodness and mercy shall follow me all the days of my life" (Ps. 23:5-6).

The treasures related to "I AM" opened up even more when Christ said, "*I am* the resurrection..." (John 11:25). We are used to thinking of resurrection as an event that happened on the third day. But here it is personified. More than being a power or an occurrence, it is the Lord Himself. The word "resurrection" literally means " rising up." You can relate to this definition if you've ever tried to hold a beach ball under water. As soon as you let it go (assuming you can submerge it to begin with), the ball shoots to the surface like a rocket. It automatically rises. It only knows one direction—up. When Jesus said "I am the resurrection," He was saying "I am the rising up." Anytime He met a suppressing or depressing situation, He rose up and overcame it. Some of these situations in the gospels had to do with the heaviest affliction of all—death. In one case, a widow mourned the loss of her only son. Jesus said to her, "Do not weep. Then he came and touched the open coffin, and those who carried him [the dead man] stood still. And He said, 'Young man I say to you, *arise.*' So he who was dead sat up and began to speak. And He presented him to his mother" (Luke 7:13-15). Because Christ —"the rising up"— had come, the woman could no longer weep, the man could no longer be dead, and the crowd could not restrain itself from glorifying God.

Jesus is the resurrection itself, so wherever He is, rising up is sure to occur. That is why He spoke about Himself with such certainty: "The Son of Man is being betrayed into the hands of men, and they will kill Him. And after He is killed, He *will rise* the third day" (Mark 9:31). Of course, this is exactly what happened. The Lord proved too buoyant to be held down by death for very long. With this in view, what takes place when Christ enters the average person?

First, consider our condition before He comes along. Human beings find their mortal lives not as a beach ball rising up, but like an anvil, sinking down. We are often in the grip of despondent moods or brooding anger. With the many problems in which humanity is mired, it might seem that resurrection would meet its match in some people. Finding their situations too heavy, it would succumb and begin sinking rather than rising. But this is never the case. The Apostle Paul issued several impressive blanket statements to all who receive Christ. He told us that "you...were *raised* with Him through faith" (Co. 2:12) and that God "made us alive together with Christ...and *raised* us up together" (Eph. 2:5-6). The moment Christ came in, His rich resurrection became ours, and our spirit, no matter how burdened, rose up.

Today, even past the point of believing in Jesus, difficult situations continue. We pray that they would go away, yet God allows them to remain. Why? Because adversity is where we learn about the riches of resurrection that we have received in Christ. If we wish to know the power of a light, there is no better place to find out than in the deepest darkness. If we are to know resurrection, the best proving ground is the difficulties of human life. Paul knew this better than anyone. He wrote, "We do not want you to be ignorant, brethren, of our trouble which came to us in Asia: that we were burdened beyond measure, above strength, so that we despaired even of life" (2 Cor. 1:8). This was apparently a situation that the apostle found nearly unbearable. He was clear, however, about why God had allowed it to remain in his life: "that we should not trust in ourselves but in God who raises the dead" (2 Cor. 1:9). Paul had wished "that I may know Him [Christ] and the power of His resurrection" (Phil. 3:10). But it was only through a death-filled environment that such a thing could have been possible. For him, as for the rest of us, all that hardships can ultimately do is help us know "the rising up." The vast wealth of resurrection in Christ assures us of this.

Adding to His self-disclosure as the I AM, Jesus said, "*I am* the way, the truth, and the life, no one comes to the Father except through Me" (John 14:6). We rarely encounter such exclusive statements. Most destinations can be reached through multiple approaches; you could get there ten different ways. But God the Father is not in the same category as everything else. Sadly, many people think so, and choose whatever route they think might lead to Him. At the end of their journey what they find is something boring, disappointing, or even worse, devastating.

One student I knew named Shane, selected his own road to God. His self-chosen way, though, led him right into a cult. Shane had recognized signs of it—ultra-legalism, false teaching, leader worship, money mongering, and immorality—but he had excused them away. Out of a desire to stick with his new religion, he tried being obedient and self-disciplined, but this never seemed to lead him to God. Instead, the longer he remained on his road, the more it took him into delusional and life-sapping extremes. By the time I met him, Shane had given up on finding the truth. But the fact was he hadn't taken "the way" to it at all. If in the first place, he had taken Christ who is the way, he would certainly have arrived at the "truth and the life" because the way, the truth, and the life inseparably go together. Since Christ Himself is the way to the Father, the truth of the Father and the life of the Father, having Him within us guarantees that we will be led directly to the Father.

When something is "unsearchable" that means it cannot be exhausted or fully found out. Christ certainly fits that description. He told us, "*All* things that the Father has are mine" (John 16:15), "*All* things have been delivered to Me by My Father" (Matt. 11:27), and "The Father loves the Son and has given *all* things into His hand" (John 3:35). Christ has God's image (Heb. 1:3), God's glory (2 Cor. 4:6), and God's authority (Matt. 28:18). The Bible even tells us that Christ *is* God's power and God's wisdom (1 Cor. 1:24). It is no wonder that He is the One "in whom are hidden all the *treasures* of wisdom and knowledge" (Col. 2:3).

The man who is wealthy in material things, yet does not have the Son of God, is bankrupt in terms of true riches. At the grave, all his earthly wealth will suddenly be reduced to zero, proving that none of it was ever real—"When he dies, he shall carry nothing away; his glory shall not descend after him" (Ps. 49:17). But the poor man who has received the Lord Jesus is in a different situation. Underneath his material poverty lies great and eternal enrichment.

The limitless treasures of Christ are his—a full and wonderful humanity, food, light, shepherding, resurrection, the way, the truth, the life, and *all* things in God.

This is why the Lord Jesus presented Himself, rather than money, to the poor. He saw the poverty of the human spirit as something far more grievous than that of wearing hand-me-downs and driving old cars. So, He gave Himself to turn our empty condition into a surplus. Now His believers can say "we have this *treasure* in earthen vessels" (2 Cor. 4:7).

You Now Have Hope

When Paul wrote about our life before salvation, he said, "at that time you were without Christ...*having no hope*" (Eph. 2:12). Maybe some of us can't completely agree. When we recall our past, the gloomy label of "hopeless" seems a little extreme. Perhaps we were bettering our education or climbing a career ladder when we met Jesus. Even if we weren't doing any of that, "hopeless" is a radically negative description. However, to honestly think that there was hope before salvation only shows that our definition of the word needs an overhaul. Colossians 1:27 provides some help by speaking of "Christ in you, the *hope of glory.*" The biblical idea of hope is not related to the promise of worldly success. It has to do with anticipating the glory of God.

Now what is "the hope of glory?" We can demonstrate what the phrase means by using two pots of dirt. Both of them are identical, with the same soil and the same amount of light, water, and necessities. We will give one of them "the hope of glory," but we will allow the other to remain hopeless. How is this done? We only need to plant a rose seed into the soil of one of them. The action takes a mere second, but now, suddenly, that pot has the hope of glory. The seed planted inside of it contains the potential for blossoming into a brilliant crimson rose sometime in the future. The other pot, no matter what happens to it, has no such hope. We could spray paint it with liquid gold, drive it around in a limousine, or erect a shrine for it, but it would still not have the hope of glory. No matter what else was done for that pot of dirt, without a seed in it, it would never be anything more than a pot of dirt.

At the time we believed in Christ, He was planted in our little human "pot of dirt." Given time, this "seedling Christ" will grow and eventually be "glorified in his saints" (2 Thess. 1:10). That will be a marvelous blossoming in the future. On a particular date known only to God, the Christ that was hidden within us at the beginning of our faith will blaze forth in a show of divine splendor. As Paul said, "When Christ who is our life appears, then you also will appear with Him in *glory*" (Col. 3:4). This is true hope—that the silent spiritual reality currently inside of us will become visibly manifested on the outside. It will be a time of brilliant power as the Lord Jesus "will transform our lowly body that it may be conformed to His glorious body" (Phil 3:21). Since "the Lord of glory" (1 Cor. 2:8) lives in us, our hope of glory is not some expectation that will prove in the end to be the stuff of fairy tales. We are assured that "whoever believes on Him will not be put to shame" (Rom. 10:11).

There's nothing like a good mystery, especially one that has been carefully guarded for a very long time. The Bible mentions "the mystery which has been hidden from ages and from generations" (Col. 1:26a). Just from the standpoint of curiosity, a matter hidden for centuries ought to catch the interest of anyone reading this verse. But the mystery here is not something that the average person can casually discover. God must reveal it and, in fact, He has...to some. It has "now been revealed to His *saints*. *To them* God willed to make known what are the riches of the glory of this mystery" (Col. 1:26b). Of course, the reference to "saints" here simply means those who believe in Jesus. They, or more precisely, we, have received the revelation of "this mystery, which is *Christ in you*" (Co. 1:27). Now we can know firsthand what it means to be the beloved of God. We can experience the greatness of salvation. We can enjoy a treasury of spiritual riches. And, regardless of who we were, since the Son of God has been planted in us, we now have real hope.

5

WHAT IS SALVATION?

RECEIVING THE HOLY SPIRIT

WHO AND WHAT IS THE SPIRIT?

It's amazing how the human mind thinks in terms of pictures. Say the word "God" to a Christian and there's an immediate image in his head. It's rooted so deeply that he might not have even realized that it flashed through his brain. What's interesting is that the picture he sees may not be an accurate one.

For instance when hearing "God," the average Christian might visualize the celestial figure in MichaelAngelo's *The Creation*. This could be his frame of reference, although God is never described in the Bible as an elderly Caucasian man with a beard. If you mention the name "Jesus," for many people the image of a robed figure suddenly materializes—almost girlishly handsome with light brown hair and blue eyes. That is not a description derived from any biblical source. In fact it somewhat contradicts the Old Testament prophecies concerning Him where He is described as having "no form or comeliness" and "no beauty that we should desire Him" (Isa. 53:2-3). Regardless, inaccurate images lodge in people's minds. They are easy to pick up and they remain until more correct concepts come along to replace them.

Not all word-picture associations concerning God, though, materialize so effortlessly. Mention the Holy Spirit to a Christian and he might draw a blank—unless he has sat through years of Sunday services, looking at pictures of doves on stained glass windows. Even then he might wonder, What is *that?*

I remember wondering the same thing. Why did God need a bird? It seemed very strange. What confused me all the more was the way that some Christians said "Holy Ghost" instead of "Holy Spirit." Why did God need a ghost? Ghosts were supposed to haunt houses. The whole matter seemed incomprehensible to my young mind. However, I had some religious friends who were happy to explain. They told me that the purpose of the "Holy Ghost" was to enter people on God's behalf and make them do all kinds of peculiar things. As they described those things with enthusiastic zeal, worse confusion set in. Now the Spirit was not only related to a bird and a ghost, but strange behavior too.

Thankfully, the Bible brings clarity to the glut of strange ideas floating around about the Spirit. First of all, it dispels the thought that the Holy Spirit is an impersonal dumb force, like something out of a *Star Wars* movie. The scriptures speak of the Holy Spirit as a Person—

> "When *He*, the Spirit of truth, has come, *He* will guide you into all truth; for *He* will not speak on His own authority, but whatever *He* hears *He* will speak; and *He* will tell you things to come. *He* will glorify me, for *He* will take of what is Mine and declare it to you." (John 16:13-14)

Furthermore, the Spirit is described as possessing a personality. He wills to do things (1 Cor. 12:11), He has a mind (Rom. 8:27), He can grieve (Eph. 4:30), He teaches and instructs (John 14:26; Neh. 9:20), He intercedes for us in prayer (Rom. 8:26), He bears witness to our status as children of God (Rom. 8:16), and He calls people for spiritual work (Acts 13:2). If the Spirit were only an energy or power of some kind, none of those characteristics could possibly belong to Him. For example, electricity is a powerful energy. A bolt of lightening can split an oak tree in half, but it cannot instruct anyone, cannot grieve, and cannot will anything. Electricity is a power, not a Person. Since the Holy Spirit has all the qualities of personality, He must be a Person, and not merely a power.

If the Spirit is a Person, however, then *who* is He? This is an important question, because some of us might harbor a feeling that the Spirit is somehow inferior to God the Father and Christ the Son. Since He is mentioned last in the phrase "the Father, the Son, and the Holy Spirit," that could be understood to mean that He is the least in the divine Trinity. As the incorrect sentiment goes—"The Father and the Son sent the Spirit in their place, so at least I got *something* of God." No one, of course, would come right out and say that, but I have often heard new Christians unintentionally refer to the Spirit as some type of secondary agent. A concept of that kind suggests that the Spirit is a representative twice removed from someone important. It is as though a company president couldn't be somewhere in person, so he sent a delegate. Upon discovering he couldn't attend either, the delegate sent a stand-in of his own. Supposedly then, whoever shakes hands with the stand-in "kind of" shakes hands with the delegate who is friends with the president.

Is "the gift of the Holy Spirit" (Acts 2:38) someone several times removed from God? Is He such a blessing to us only because He knows someone who knows someone? The Bible gives an unqualified "no," because it speaks of the Holy Spirit as God Himself. In the book of Acts, we find the Spirit and God referred to interchangeably. The Apostle Peter asked a man named Ananias, "Why has Satan filled your heart to lie to the *Holy Spirit?*" (5:3). In the next verse he says, "You have not lied to men, but to *God*." According to Peter's estimation, lying to the Holy Spirit and lying to God were the same thing. Later on, the Apostle Paul writes something similar, also speaking interchangeably of the Holy Spirit and God. First Corinthians 6:19-20 says, "*the Holy Spirit* who is in you" while the following verse speaks of "*God* in your body." A related thought also occurs in 1 Corinthians 3:16, where the believers are called "the temple of *God*," yet in the very next phrase they were told that "the *Spirit* of God dwells in you." Apparently both apostles saw the Holy Spirit and God as identical.

These are not the only indications of the Spirit's Divine identity. We also find that characteristics belonging uniquely to God are possessed by the Spirit as well. These include omnipresence (being everywhere at once—Ps. 139:7-10), omnipotence (having all power—compare Micah 2:7 with Gen. 18:14), and omniscience (having all knowledge—1 Cor. 2:11; John 16:13). Besides these things, the Spirit is credited with the work of creation (Job 33:4) and is called *eternal* (Heb. 9:14). He is recognized as the writer of the Bible (2 Pet. 1:21), He has authority over the church, He distributes all gifts to the believers (1 Cor. 12:11; Acts 20:28), and He commissions and sends apostles into the work of God (Acts 13:2,4).

The Spirit is obviously not a lesser gift of some kind. He is God Himself. For this reason, when He enters into us, as the Bible promises when we believe the gospel, we immediately become aware of the presence of God. Like the Apostle John said, we know that God abides in us "by the *Spirit* whom He has given us" (1 John 3:24).

How Many Persons Do You Need to Receive?

Because of the emphasis in the last chapter on receiving Christ, we wonder where the Holy Spirit fits into the picture. Is He an additional Person who independently comes to live in us? Perhaps you've heard of the old college stunt of stuffing people in phonebooths. Maybe that's what salvation would look like if it were piecemeal—that is, if assorted persons crowded into us one-by-one after we believed.

The Bible has a better, "saner" way of looking at it. First there is the Lord, before His death and resurrection, telling the disciples, "The *Spirit* of truth...will be in you" (John 14:17), yet just three verses later saying, "you will know that *I* am...in you" (John 14:20). At that point, it looks as if there will be two parties living in the disciples—the Spirit and Christ. But at the finale of John's Gospel, the Lord commands them to "Receive the *Holy Spirit*" (John 20:22). He does not say, "Receive *Me*." Either that means Jesus forgot to tell them to receive Him too, or He knew that receiving the Spirit was the *same* as receiving Him. One receiving was required, not two.

This thought continues in the book of Acts. There, the bulk of Peter's gospel message to the great crowd in Jerusalem was all about Jesus and His work. Those hearing it and responding to it should have received Christ. But Peter's closing thought was not worded that way. He said that if anyone repented and was baptized, they would "receive the gift of *the Holy Spirit*" (Acts 2:38). Again, either Peter forgot to tell them to receive Christ, or he knew that receiving the Spirit was enough.

In order to be saved, we are said to either receive Christ or receive the Spirit. There are no conditions for salvation that hinge on receiving one in addition to the other. The Bible says to receive "Him," not to receive "them." Those who have "received Christ Jesus the Lord" (Col. 2:6) are identical to those who have received the Spirit (Gal. 3:2). When we respond to the gospel of Christ in faith, we become "partakers of the *Holy Spirit*" (Heb. 6:4). Yet, "having begun in the *Spirit*" (Gal. 3:2), we will realize that *"Christ* lives in Me"* (Gal. 2:20).

This is not to confuse the Persons of the Trinity by eliminating the distinctions between them. But where salvation is concerned, we simply cannot treat the divine Trinity as separate components that need to be received independently of one another. No one receives Christ without receiving the Holy Spirit. Conversely, no one has received the Holy Spirit without receiving Christ.

JESUS GOING AND THE SPIRIT COMING— A BETTER ARRANGEMENT FOR US

Jesus said to the disciples "I tell you the truth. It is to your advantage that I go away" (John 16:7a). If I had been there, I might have said, "Hold on just a minute! I already have enough trouble following You while You're here. How am I going to be better off if You leave?" The Lord explained, "If I do not go away, the Helper will not come to you; but if I depart I will send Him to you" (John 16:7b). This "Helper" is the "Spirit of truth" (John 16:13). The Lord Jesus went away so that the Spirit would come and, from the Lord's point of view, this was a much better arrangement for us.

Jesus had said, "I will pray the Father, and He will give you another Helper, that He may abide with you forever— the Spirit of truth...you know Him, for He dwells with you and shall be in you" (John 14:16-17). At first this sounds like an entirely different Helper than the Lord Jesus. It could have been disappointing to the disciples. Surely, no one can replace Christ. But when we are dealing with the Spirit, remember that we are not talking about a secondary agent performing secondary tasks. As the Lord had told them, "the Spirit of Truth...will be in you" (John 14:17), but in verse 18, He said, "*I* will come to you" (John 14:18) and "you will know that *I* am...in you" (John 14:20). All of these verses tend to indicate that the "truth" the Spirit is "of" has to do with the truth, or, reality of Jesus Himself. The Spirit brings the reality of Christ's presence, the reality of His accomplishments, the reality of His life, and the reality of His words into our experience. Without this vital function of "the Spirit of truth," nothing of Christ would seem very true in our experience.

GOD'S PRACTICAL HELP FOR US

For most of us, the term "Spirit," is associated with something mysterious. But actually, the Spirit is the most practical help that God could give a believer. The Lord Jesus spoke of Him as "the *comforter*" (John 14:16, 26; 15:26; 16:7), which is adapted from the Greek word *parakletos*. The term refers to one who draws alongside another for the giving of help.

If you are a Christian, the Spirit has been given to you "that He may be with you forever" (John 14:16). This promise indicates that you will always need emergency "roadside assistance" in the Christian life. The Spirit is the best aid that God could give us since the Spirit brings the true presence of the Lord Jesus to us in all places at all times in all situations.

Many believers fancy that they need something more than the Holy Spirit, but that is only because they do not know what they have. R.A. Torrey, noted Christian teacher, told the story of an old lady who was a country peasant. She was poor and hungry, but too ashamed to ask anyone for help.

"My son has gone away to work in England," she said to a friend.

"Does he send you money?"

"No, but he sends me pretty pictures."

"Could I see them?" the friend asked.

To this the old lady produced a fistful of colored paper.

"Ma'am," the friend said, shocked, "This is English *money!*"

Many Christians are in those shoes. They have received the Holy Spirit, but are hardly aware of His worth or what He can do. Because of this ignorance, they live in spiritual poverty. The Lord has graciously granted them help, but they haven't recognized it yet.

This is like Hagar, an Old Testament woman who nearly

died of thirst in the wilderness. While she was dehydrated and despondent, God opened her eyes and immediately she saw a well of water (Gen. 21:19). Apparently, it had been there all along; she simply hadn't been able to see it. In another instance, the Prophet Elisha and his assistant found themselves in the middle of a war and severely outnumbered. When the assistant became afraid, Elisha said, "'Do not fear, for those who are with us are more than those who are with them.' And Elisha prayed, and said, 'Lord...open his eyes that he may see'" (2 Kings 6:16-17). Suddenly all around them, an army of flaming chariots became visible to the shaken young man. It was another case of the heavenly resources having been there, albeit undetected. Like some of these short sighted-people from the Old Testament, we Christians must also have our eyes opened to see the great provision that God has provided for us—the Holy Spirit.

WHAT THE SPIRIT DOES—
HE ENABLES US TO PARTICIPATE IN CHRIST

It is very likely that only one out of thirty people can name a single thing that the Holy Spirit does. His work is something that tends to be a part of the great unknown. Yet this need not be the case. We have the Bible, the sourcebook of all the truth related to the Spirit's mysterious operations.

Second Corinthians 13:14 contains the phrase "The *fellowship* of the Holy Spirit" (NASB). The term "fellowship" comes from the original Greek word *koinonia*. It means "mutual participation." "The fellowship of the Holy Spirit," then, indicates that a substantial part of the Spirit's work is to cause us to participate in our salvation.

When we were saved, we were elevated from spiritual bankruptcy into the "riches of Christ." But what good is something like that if you can't participate in it? Since some gifts are non-participatory, even if they are valuable, they are not enjoyable. For instance, a five thousand-dollar savings bond is valuable, but untouchable for a long time. If Mom and Dad were to give Junior one of them for his birthday, upon opening it, he would sigh, say a dutiful thank-you, and hunt for something he could currently enjoy, like a bee-bee gun or a model airplane.

There is a common thought among Christians that the gift of salvation can only be enjoyed after death, and in the meantime, it is largely non-participatory. In other words, the Christian faith only becomes truly experiential in the funeral parlor. But the Spirit has brought fellowship into us. He enables us to *currently* participate in our salvation—that is, in everything from the relief of forgiven sin, to the enjoyment of the riches of Christ, to the experience of eternal life. Because of the Spirit, our salvation is not padlocked. We believers can enter and thoroughly participate in it, since now "we...have *access in one Spirit* unto the Father" (Eph. 2:18).

The Lord Jesus said concerning the Spirit, "He takes of Mine and will disclose it to you" (John 16:15 NASB). Thus the Spirit brings into us such things as the joy of Christ—"*My joy may be in you*" (John 15:11) and the peace of Christ—"*My peace I give to you*" (John 14:27). When this happens, we are ushered into an immediate, firsthand contact with the Lord. Over time, the quality of our Christian lives will largely depend upon that kind of participation.

The happiest men on earth are the ones who are in the fellowship of the Holy Spirit. The reason for this is simple: joy and the Spirit are inseparably connected. The early disciples found this out as they were "filled with joy and the Holy Spirit" (Acts 13:52).

The disciples of today are finding it out, too. As we drove away from a Christian gathering, Sheila, a new believer told us, "This was the best night of my life." For a moment I wondered if that wasn't a bit of an overstatement. The meeting itself had not been explosive—there had been no loud singing or powerful preaching, just an informal Bible study with ten people. It had not been held in a giant sanctuary with vaulted ceilings and marble pillars. The setting had been the front room of a house that smelled of old furniture. Yet in that unimpressive environment, this woman, who was nearly fifty years old with an accomplished life, could tell us that it had been the best night of her life. She could only say something like that because she had touched the Spirit. The result, or "fruit of the Spirit is...joy" (Gal. 5:22), and in Sheila's case it was a joy profound enough to eclipse everything else in her life up until then.

The durability of joy in the Holy Spirit is also incredible. It manages to coexist alongside all kinds of contrary feelings and situations. Often a follower of Christ gets hit with a sudden load of emergencies or irritations. Everything on the fringes of his life becomes chaotic. Yet even in the midst of the most serious tribulations, as our bodies are hurting and our souls are wracked by emotions of every kind, the deep-seated joy of the Spirit is still present. Christians in the ancient city of Thessalonica were examples of this. They received the worst kind of treatment from hostile, anti-Christian neighbors. The preacher they highly esteemed, the Apostle Paul, was hated, and the gospel message they believed in was mocked. Still, they had "much *affliction*, with *joy* of the Holy Spirit" (1 Thess. 1:6).

The Spirit has an amazing power to satisfy man. Jesus said, "Whoever drinks of the water that I shall give him [the Spirit] will *never* thirst" (John 4:14, see also John 7:38-39). This was a promise that our cravings for the trivial, the sinful, and the worldly would be eliminated. Whoever takes in the Spirit will find Himself released from those things. Not only so, but if a man receives one gulp of this "water," it will "become in him a *well* of water, springing up to eternal life" (John 4:14b). As soon as the Spirit gains entrance into a heart, He becomes a well *installed* within to bring a constant source of fellowship and thirst-quenching joy.

When some people become Christians, they think of it as entering a religious boot camp. It is an excellent arrangement for them. Their personality types appreciate duty and gravitate to self-discipline and rules. I wasn't one of those people. I had abolutely no interest in being religious or whipping myself into shape. The thought of a more disciplined me, a more wonderful version of myself, just wasn't enough to drive my Christian life. What propelled me was the simple joy of the Spirit. I had plenty of friends who couldn't believe this. They thought I had been brainwashed, or that perhaps I was just some kid who was trying to change himself while secretly hating it. They couldn't believe it was real. But it was and it is. The enjoyment of the Spirit can empower anyone to have an authentic Christian life. This includes living above the addictive thirsts of the material world.

A woman once approached D.L. Moody, the great gospel preacher, and said, "Mr. Moody, I do not like you."

He asked, "Why not?"

She said, "Because you are too narrow."

"Narrow! I did not know that I was narrow."

"Yes, you are too narrow. You don't believe in the theatre; you don't believe in cards; you don't believe in dancing."

"How do you know I don't believe in the theatre?" he asked.

"Oh," she said, "I know you don't."

Mr. Moody replied, "I go to the theatre whenever I want to."

"What," cried the woman, "you go the theatre whenever you want to?"

"Yes, I go to the theatre whenever I want to."

"Oh," she said, "Mr. Moody, you are a much broader man than I thought you were. I am so glad to hear you say it, that you go the theatre whenever you want to."

"Yes, I go to the theatre whenever I want to. I don't want to." (Torrey 123).

The world does not understand that the root of all our true change is not the power of duty—"should's," "ought-to's," or "have-to's." It is a well of living water. The concept is elementary. If you have just finished drinking that pure water, you won't feel the urge to drink from the ditch in your front yard.

After enjoying the fellowship of the Spirit for a period of time, many of us found that we no longer wished to waste our lives on trivial pursuits. It was not only that those things were wrong, they were just not *needed* anymore. The Spirit brought in joy and though we hardly noticed, washed out lots of junk. This happens when a flow of water as clean as heaven visits our inward parts—*"rivers* of living water" (John 7:38-39).

The book of Ezekiel speaks of that river's invisible current. When we first believe, we step into it where it is "water reaching the ankles" (47:3 NASB). At that point, the flow of the Spirit is somewhat shallow. We have a habit of splashing around in spiritual things for a short time, but getting out whenever we want. Our flow of fellowship, that is, our participation in Christ, is not yet that deep. But Ezekiel then proceeds to show us that the flow will deepen. It rises to the knees and to the loins (47:4). Later, the prophet described it as becoming so deep that it was "a river that I could not cross; for the water was too deep, water in which one must swim" (47:5). This is exactly the way that the Spirit gradually floods our inner being with His fellowship.

The result is that "everything shall *live* where the river flows" (Eze. 47:9). Moving water characteristically heads toward the deepest, emptiest place. When the Spirit, who is the "living water" (John 4:10) streams into us, the first place He brings His living fellowship is into the deep hollow void at the center of our being. Immediately, that dead spot, our human spirit, springs to life. This is because the life that the Spirit brings into us identical to the life that is in Christ. Indeed, the Holy Spirit Himself is called "the Spirit of life" (Rom. 8:2). He is "a pure river of water of *life"* (Rev. 22:1), flowing into us whatever is in the Son. That is how He causes us to participate, to fellowship, in the Lord Jesus.

THE SPIRIT SHOWS JESUS AS HE IS

Although experience in the Christian life is good, without understanding, it still falls short of the ideal meant for each of us. God does not want us to simply have many happy feelings and not know what they are related to and why we are having them. That would be a "blind" enjoyment, like eating ice cream in the dark. Therefore, the Spirit shows us Jesus as He really is. The Lord said, "He will *glorify* Me"

(John 16:14), an activity which means the Spirit would demonstrate, exalt, and show forth the true worth of Christ. Any man with the Holy Spirit inside of him has encountered this work. Perhaps as he was reading the Bible, or singing a hymn, or attending a Christian meeting, the Lord Jesus suddenly seemed very attractive. Some aspect of Him blazed with a beauty that made the believer appreciate Him more than ever. That is part of the Spirit's work to glorify the Son. Back when I was in the Army, I had a barracks roommate who was not saved. He couldn't fathom why I was so interested in Christ and why Sunday morning church service wasn't enough to satisfy my "religious drive." Well, at the time, I was a little puzzled by it, too. I didn't have enough knowledge to explain that the Holy Spirit within me was glorifying the Son. However, now I know that my passion for Christ was a product of seeing with the eyes of my heart the greatest sight of all—Jesus Himself.

The Spirit glorifies Christ by illuminating who He is. He never dresses up the Son of God to make Him more attractive. No improvement is necessary because Christ is already incomparable. Glorifying the Son only requires that the Spirit show Him according to His true magnificence.

Through mortal eyes, Jesus is nothing special. If you read the most touching, powerful verses in the Bible to a man who does not have the Holy Spirit, it might be the same to him as reading the back of a milk carton. But read the same verses to a person under the glorification work of the Holy Spirit, and his heart will burn for Christ. The same Jesus discarded by one person becomes "Chief among ten thousand" (Song 5:10) to another.

The Spirit always brings Christ sharply into view and sets Him on center stage. In Acts chapter 2, Peter was filled with the Holy Spirit. His words and emphasis and power were all of the Spirit. The result, however, was not with the Spirit being uplifted as an object of faith before the crowd. No, Jesus Christ was exalted in front of them. When the crowd positively responded, it was to the Spirit's work of glorifying Him.

THE SPIRIT SOLVES THE PROBLEM OF "THE ANTIQUE" JESUS

Before I was saved, I often felt an impassable gulf, two thousand years wide, separating me from Christ. The year 1976 seemed to be an incredibly modern time. It was all about Camaros, silk shirts, Converse sneakers and everything else that went along with the freshman year of high school. There was a pervasive modern attitude. Kids were experimenting with sex and alcohol at a much earlier age than ten years before. Others were getting into things like smoking pot and shoplifting. My impression was that an ancient Jesus couldn't fit anywhere in that landscape. It seemed that He belonged "back then" with things like camel trains and pyramids.

The Lord, however, worked long ago in a way that circumvented the "antique Jesus" problem. Now, no matter what age or generation, Christ is never outdated. It is not possible for Him to become irrelevant. When Jesus died on the cross, He offered Himself up "through the eternal Spirit" (Heb. 9:14). "Eternal" means timeless, unbounded, unlimited. It means that yesterday is the same as today and tomorrow and the day after. Eternity is where time is no longer a factor. Since the Lord is "through the eternal Spirit," He is the same loving, compassionate Savior as He was long ago. The steady march of centuries cannot dim His personal vitality, as it is written, "You are the *same*, and your years cannot fail" (Heb. 1:12).

Eventually, the "progressive" seventies passed away, becoming just another source of amusing nostalgia. The styles of that era are now downright funny to someone like my daughter, who is a child of this new century and millenium. However, the Jesus I had suspected was obsolete at that time has continued to remain fresh and untouched by age. He is through the eternal Spirit. The seventies were not.

The Spirit is the realm in which Christ, His death, and His resurrection are current realities, not yesterday's news. When He enters us, the things of God become a present reality. Although the work of redemption was accomplished on the cross two thousand years ago. Whenever a person receives the Spirit, he can say, "*Now* is the day of salvation" (2 Cor. 6:2). With the Spirit there is only now. He never brings the things of yesterday. Nothing He has to offer is stale. The Christ He conveys is current, fresh, and not even one minute old.

THE SPIRIT IS GOD'S MARK OF OWNERSHIP

Items that are privately owned often bear marks of ownership. This protects them from being stolen or confused with things that belong to others. The practice of branding personal possessions is also found in the spiritual world. For example, in the book of Revelation, human beings that belong to the Antichrist have the number 666 on their hands or foreheads (Rev. 13:11, 16-18; 14:9-11). It is debatable whether the mark is literal or not. Regardless, the person bearing that number is satanic property.

When we heard and believed the gospel, we were "*sealed with the Holy Spirit of the promise*" (Eph. 1:13; 4:30). A seal is a personal stamp that functions as a mark of ownership. This does not mean golden letters will appear inside of you that spell G-O-D. The Holy Spirit Himself is God's stamp, God's mark of ownership. His very presence within us shows all the inhabitants of the spiritual world that we are God's possession.

In my early days of ministry, I knew a young Christian named Jared. He must have held the world's record for "disconnects." That is, he would follow Christ with all his heart for one week and then suddenly drop completely out of the picture for four months. Then, just when you figured he was gone for good, Jared would surface again, sorry for where he had been. His return would always last for a couple of weeks before disappearing once more. But even so, you could always count on him coming back. Jared's "rollercoaster" Christian life has been going on for over twenty years. The reason he can't seem to vanish for good is very simple: every time he tries to wholeheartedly resign himself to being the property of the devil, something disagrees. The holy seal inside of him insists that, "You belong to *God,* not Satan."

This experience is by no means peculiar to Jared. All who have the Holy Spirit have God's mark of ownership, and will feel a certain awkwardness when they try to give themselves to something else. The living seal within them will disagree and only give them peace when they present themselves to the One who bought them with His own blood.

THE SPIRIT GUARANTEES THE FULLNESS OF SALVATION

When a person rents an apartment, he makes a deposit guaranteeing that he will leave it the way he found it. God does something better. He pledges *not* to leave His dwelling the way He found it. Once you "come to Jesus just as you are" God guarantees that you will not remain "just as you are." In fact, His salvation will fully change you to become just "as *He* is" (1 John 3:2).

This promise is otherwise known as the inheritance of full salvation—the guarantee that we will go on to inherit all that the Lord has for us. There is "an inheritance incorruptible and undefiled and that does not fade away, reserved in heaven for you" (1 Pet. 1:4). It is "salvation ready to be revealed in the last time" (1 Pet. 1:5), that is, salvation in its final glorious stages. We have entered the initial stages of salvation already—being forgiven of sins, being delivered from the lake of fire, receiving Christ, receiving the Holy Spirit, receiving eternal life, and becoming children of God. But one day the full effect of those things will be realized in every part of our being (see 1 Thess. 5:23).

It all sounds wonderful at first, until we start noticing serious shortages in our personal lives—problem areas that make it hard for us to even imagine ourselves in glory. "How could God break through that habit?" we wonder. "It's *impossible!*" Once we allow habitual sins, backsliding events, personality quirks, and character weaknesses to define our future, of course the picture becomes very dismal. Looking at our mortal flesh in a full-length mirror, so to speak, we wonder if there is any reasonable hope that we will be "just as He is" (1 John 3:2).

All of this doubt necessitates a pledge of some kind, so God has made "the Holy Spirit...the *guarantee* of our inheritance" (Eph. 1:17-18). God is like a farmer who promises to one day give an apple orchard to his sons. Since the sons are immature and cannot appreciate the promised gift, for the time being the farmer gives them a slice of apple pie instead. Naturally, the pie is only a very small representative of the orchard. Even if it were the most delicious dish the boy ever had, it is still merely a taste of the one thousand-acre orchard that it came from.

Similarly, since we cannot fathom what lies ahead of us— "It has not yet been revealed what we shall be" (1 John 3:2)— God has provided us a foretaste. Every time we enjoy the Spirit, we taste His pledge to us that there is more salvation to come. Even our highest spiritual experience to date is just a sample of what lies ahead in our future.

THE SPIRIT HELPS US KNOW HOW TO PRAY

If you've uttered hundreds of mealtime and bedtime prayers throughout your life, you might think that you don't have a problem with prayer. It's easy. Just fold your hands, bow your head, and say something. We all feel quite secure in that kind of prayer life until we find ourselves troubled, pressured, sad, afraid, or disappointed. It is then that we discover "we do not know how to pray as we should" (Rom. 8:26b NASB).

During emergency times, no wooden prayers suffice. It seems that nothing is more important to us during days of crisis than authentic prayer that makes a connection to God. Yet those prayers are precisely the ones we do not know how to pray, so we often end up praying wildly, even evilly (James 4:3). For instance, we might ask the Lord to hurt someone or to help us get something that is not part of His plan for our lives. If we descend into true need for a moment, the theme of prayer is no longer "*your* will be done" (Matt. 6:10), but *my* will be done.

Amidst emotional flurry, we pray words and vent

frustrations that are not accurate. Yet, "the Spirit joins in to help us in our weakness" (Rom. 8:26). Deep within our murkiness and confusion "the Spirit Himself intercedes for us with groanings too deep for words" (Rom. 8:26 NASB). These spiritual sentiments—groanings—are things you'd probably never say in your prayer. For instance, because of an ugly, pressuring situation at work, you might pray, "Lord, please punish those at the office who are gossiping about me." Such vengeful sentiments might actually be coming out of your weakness. That is when the Spirit joins in to help you by deeply imbedding His own cry into your words. Together with you, He might pray concerning the unfair treatment, but instead of your escape from it, He "groans" for you to develop endurance. Concerning the gossip, He might not intercede for you to be vindicated. Instead, the Spirit might plead with God that in your discomfort, *you* would learn to hate gossip. Perhaps you gossip in other circles. You just don't do it in the office. So, as you vent many heavy feelings to God over being the target of ugly talk, the Spirit may at the same time be groaning over your own gossip habit. His burden is that you would never engage in loose, destructive talk again. And how about those troublesome coworkers? Like you, the Spirit may indeed have deep troubled feelings concerning them, but that does not mean He agrees with your desire for revenge. Instead, He may add to your prayer a profound yearning for them to see the error of their ways and come to salvation.

The Spirit helps us to pray in such a fashion, but that does not mean our only real prayers will be the ones we didn't know we were praying. Paul said, "I will pray also with the mind" (1 Cor. 14:15), indicating that understanding and prayer ought to accompany one another. You should "be renewed in the spirit of your mind" (Eph. 4:23) through Bible study and growth in the Christian life, so that you can pray accurately and with proper comprehension.

The Spirit gets involved with our prayer life because at times even the mature among us have trouble praying in harmony with God's will. So, "He makes intercession for the saints [the believers] according to the will of God" (Rom. 8:27).

THE SPIRIT SHOWS US HOW TO CONTINUE FOLLOWING CHRIST

Now that we have believed in Jesus, what do we do? It stands to reason that if we don't know how to pray, then we probably won't know how to act, either. Following Christ could degenerate into something that we merely make up as we go along. So, once again, there is the need for thorough, detailed help.

The Lord said, "When He [the Holy Spirit] comes, He will convict the world concerning sin and concerning righteousness and concerning judgment" (John 16:8). To convict someone is to convince them that they are unrighteous and going the wrong way. This is what the Spirit does among unsaved people. He operates upon them in such a fashion that they become worried about their sins and lose their peacefulness. In principle, however, the Spirit doesn't stop His convicting work when someone gets saved. On this side *or* on that side of salvation, He still dislikes sin. This explains why, as a Christian, you will feel troubled by even the possibility of involvement in sin. That is the Spirit's inward work to guide you away from unrighteousness. Because we tend not to be very sensitive about such matters, He must help us know what to do.

A Christian friend described to me how that he bought a gift for someone at a department store. The cashier gave him the sale price, but it was a mistake. The sale was supposed to have expired a few days before. The oversight saved him eight or ten dollars. Leaving the store, he began to feel a little uncomfortable. "I didn't do anything wrong," he told himself. "It was the cashier's mistake. Besides, it was *almost* still on sale." As he circled the mall, quietly arguing within himself that everything was okay, that no harm was done, and that he had even saved a few dollars, his peace with God faded. At length, he realized he was locked in a contest of wills with the Holy Spirit. When that became clear to him, he returned to the store to tell them about the mistake. Immediately, his inward peace came back.

And, as it turned out, my friend was given the discount anyway.

Now, before this man had been saved, he might only have had an uneasy feeling if, perhaps, he had stolen the item and was in danger of getting caught. However, in his case, he had technically been within the letter of the law. He had paid for the gift, and had paid what they charged him. No court in the land would indict him for that. The Spirit's feeling about sin, however, is more sensitive than human law. He keeps us walking according to God and not to some lower human standard.

"The anointing [the Spirit] which you have received... teaches you concerning all things" (1 John 2:27). That is, "all things" as they pertain to your relationship with Christ. The question is, if the scriptures already provide instructions on living the Christian life, then why is the Spirit's teaching needed at all? It is because we do not know how to *apply* the Bible. The Bible has definite limitations on what it will directly tell us. For instance, 1 Corinthians 11:14 says, "if a man has long hair, it is a dishonor to him." The question is, how long is too long? What is acceptable? The scriptures do not give us an answer in inches. Only the Spirit can do that.

Over the centuries, millions of Christian men have read 1 Corinthians 11:14. Their obedience to it as taught by the Spirit, led to bald heads, buzz cuts, hair to the collar, hair off of the collar, hair to the shoulder, hair not touching the ear, and as many other variations of length as can be imagined. The teacher in so many of those cases was none other than the Holy Spirit. In each individual case, He helped the believer to know what "short" meant.

Many areas require the Spirit's teaching, including how we dress. The Bible tells us that women should not adorn themselves in a flamboyant way (1 Pet. 3:1, 3). But anything beyond the blandest fashions might be seen as too fancy. Where is the line? The Spirit teaches each one of us.

Again, the Bible says, "Do not lay up for yourselves treasures on the earth" (Matt. 6:19). Does this mean we shouldn't have savings accounts? How much are we allowed to save before it becomes "treasures"? We must have the Spirit's instruction, for the Bible does not give us that information in terms of dollars and cents.

Often new believers ask these questions of someone they consider more mature and knowledgeable than they are. Yet, since we have the Spirit, we must remember that, "you do not need that anyone teach you" (1 John 2:27). This does not disallow human teachers, for God Himself has given them for our benefit (see Eph. 4:11). The counsel of godly Christians can be very valuable. These more learned believers can confirm what the Spirit *has* taught you or can draw your attention to what the Spirit is *currently* trying to teach you, or open the way for what the Spirit *will* teach you. Never fall into the trap of independence, so that you begin thinking you are supremely spiritual and do not need anyone else. God has placed us in the body of Christ, to a very large degree, because we need others. Nevertheless, you should not come to the point that you neglect the Spirit, always looking instead for someone to tell you what to do. That produces a Christian life prone to frustration. Such a believer will find himself pulled in many different directions as he tries to follow advice from one corner and contrary advice from another.

Christians can make very poor decisions. They often act on whims, moods, and other things that distract them from following Christ. That is why we must be "*led* by the Spirit of God" (Rom. 8:14). Apart from Him the guidance of the Lord Jesus would remain unknown to us and we would be sheep without a shepherd. But through the Spirit, "the sheep hear His voice" (John 10:3) and "know His voice" (John 10:4).

This "still, small voice" (1 Kings 19:12-13) does not come in audible words. Since the Spirit lives in us, He speaks directly to our hearts through spiritual impressions. For instance, in discouraging us from certain foolish intentions, He might give us troubled or uneasy feelings. If we decide to ignore the uneasiness, it turns into grief. That is not a happy state of being, which is why the Bible says, "do not *grieve* the Holy Spirit of God" (Eph. 4:30). Positively speaking, however, when our direction is properly aligned with the Spirit, our inner situation will be one of "life and peace" (Rom. 8:6). These kinds of sensations are the language of the Spirit, showing us how to specifically follow Christ in all circumstances.

HOW DOES A PERSON GET THE HOLY SPIRIT?

We *"receive* the Spirit...by the hearing of *faith"* (Gal. 3:2), meaning we received Him the second we believed in the Lord Jesus. As soon as He enters, the Christian life begins, which is why Paul told us we have *"begun* in the Spirit" (Gal. 3:3). Everything comes down to whether a person has the Spirit, because "if anyone does not have the Spirit of Christ, he is not His" (Rom. 8:9). Without the Spirit, a man cannot say he has begun to be a Christian, or that he belongs to God at all.

Believers sometimes become a bit nervous at this word. They wonder if they have actually received the Spirit because there were no immediate evidences of it. But in the beginning there may not be any outwardly compelling proof of His presence. The Greek word for Spirit, "pneuma," means air, or breath. In John 20:22, the Lord Jesus *"breathed* on them and said to them, 'Receive the Holy Spirit [*breath*].'"

Air is invisible, so what kind of proof should we look for to know that it has entered our lungs? Maybe we could hope for a tornado to burst out of our nose. That would certainly suggest the presence of air within us. But a more reliable test is to just ask whether we're alive or not. Without air in a person's lungs, he'll turn blue and die. Just the same, without the Holy "breath," there will not be any indications of life in you—no joy, peace, or appreciation within toward the Lord Jesus—just a flat line. If you are void of the Holy Spirit, you will not be able to identify even a single "spike" in your spiritual past. However, if the Spirit has come into you, sooner or later, certain life registrations will become evident like "love, joy, peace" (Gal. 5:22). These are called "the *fruit* of the Spirit" (Gal. 5:22a).

Many efforts have been made to exactly determine what

counts as evidence of the Spirit's presence. At the top of the list are things like special gifts and miraculous experiences. No doubt such things happen with some people, but certainly not all. Much more stable than any question of experience, though, is one of fact. If you really want to know if you've received the Holy Spirit, ask yourself, "Have I believed in the Lord Jesus and received Him?" If so, you have received the Holy Spirit. That is the Bible's logic and the last word on the subject, even if we have not felt a rush of special sensations.

THE GLORIOUS OUTCOME OF THE SPIRIT IN US

Now that "the Spirit of God *dwells* in you" (Rom. 8:9), your dignity, worth, and standing in this universe have been elevated to the highest level. This is due to one very important reason—the Spirit living in you now is the *Holy* Spirit. "Holy" refers to God's own nature, something set apart, special, totally different than everything else. So, the *Holy* Spirit refers to that Spirit who is distinct from everything else in the universe and above all. Before He came in, we weren't just evil, we were *common,* meaning not special and not set apart. As common people, we were potentially available to anyone or anything for any purpose. Our minds and bodies were high-traffic areas.

I once knew of an old house that fit that description. First, it had an ant infestation. Later mice came along. Then, after a while, squirrels began infiltrating the upstairs area. Finally, a family of possums moved in to the attic! It seemed that *everything* was living in that place. Perhaps that is a commentary on all of us before we were saved—*everything* was living in us. Sinners make themselves lodgings for everything from the filthy to the trivial—pornography, blasphemies, evil words and meditations, a multitude of worldly concepts, and anything else "interesting" that can fit inside. All of it lowers the human sense of worth. Some sinners willingly make the abasement complete by idly going on to damage their physical bodies. It is as though they are vandalizing or spraying graffiti all over a slum tenement.

When the Holy Spirit came in, though, everything changed. We ceased being a home for whatever could crawl into us and became instead "the *temple* of the Holy Spirit" (1 Cor. 6:19). This was a major upgrade of our status as human beings. Now, twenty-four hours a day the Holy Spirit resides in us. The significance of this cannot be appreciated without a picture of some kind for reference. If we turn to the Old Testament, we will find in 1 Kings 6-8 a physical description of God's temple. It was a marvel of the ancient architectural world, constructed with tons of precious stones, intricately carved wood, gold, silver, and bronze. In the deepest part of that magnificent structure was a chamber called "the Most Holy Place" (1 Kings 6:16; 8:6). It was the most sacred spot of all—the ultimate place set apart, because God Himself dwelt inside of it. There was simply nothing like that awesome house anywhere on earth. Today, whoever receives the Holy Spirit becomes the reality of that temple. God will enter and instantly cause the deepest part of the believer to become "the Most Holy Place." Thus the Christian is a walking temple, a wonder of the world. For he carries within him the massive spiritual riches symbolized by the fine wood, gold, silver, and bronze of the Old Testament temple picture. The Holy Spirit is in him and he is now "the *temple* of the Holy Spirit" elevated far above all that is common and separated from everything evil.

THE BEST THAT THE FATHER AND THE SON CAN GIVE US

The Lord Jesus said, "I will ask the Father, and He will give you another comforter" (John 14:16). This shows the first and second Persons of the Trinity working together to give us the third. It is a grand undertaking. The Spirit is *"the* gift" (Acts 2:38), simply the best gift that the Father and the Son can give us. In fact, if all the promises of God in the entire Bible were boiled down to one central item, it would be, as Paul called it, *"the* promise of the Spirit" (Gal. 3:14).

The Holy Spirit is where everything happens for a believer. The marrow of the Christian life is there. It is only in the Spirit that we can freshly enjoy Christ, see Him as He is, and receive guidance concerning how to follow Him on a daily basis. None of us are left having to "make it up as we go along." By the Spirit's indwelling, the "teacher" (John 13:13) and "the Good Shepherd" (John 10:11) Himself is with us leading us to "abide in Him in all things" (1 John 2:27). "I will not leave you as orphans" (John 14:18) was the promise the Lord made to the disciples. The coming of the Spirit was the keeping of that promise. Because of Him, no disconnect now exists between Christ and the believers. The Spirit has anchored salvation within them, effectively tying heaven to earth.

Reference Notes

Torrey, R.A. *The Person & Work of the Holy Spirit.* New Kensington: Whitaker, 1996.

6

WHAT IS SALVATION?

RECEIVING ETERNAL LIFE

THE LIVING DEAD

Our little cat died. My parents found him stiff and goggle eyed as they were stepping out the door to take us somewhere. It was an emergency moment. They tried to hide the corpse from us, by quickly stuffing it in the trash can—anything to spare me and my younger brother, Jason, from the trauma of seeing it. Alas, the trashcan had no lid and Jason saw it anyway. "Hey," he said, "Our cat's in the garbage." My mother steered him away from the sight. "I'm sorry, son, he's...well, he's dead."

"No, he's not."

"Yes, he is."

"Nuh-*uh*," Jason persisted.

"Sweetheart, he *is*."

"But," Jason said, mustering all sincerity, "His eyes are still open."

In a nutshell, that is what death means to a five-year-old—your eyes close.

The adult version is not much more advanced. Death means no pulse and no more brain wave activity. It's all about the funeral parlor and the cemetery.

Yet the Bible speaks of death in a way that goes beyond the biological sense of the word. It speaks of *spiritual* death. In the very beginning, God warned Adam about eating from the wrong tree, saying, "in the day that you eat of it, you shall surely *die*" (Gen. 2:17). However, the day Adam ate of it, he did *not* die—at least not the way we think. He didn't drop dead in the garden. His heart didn't stop. So, did God make an idle threat to Adam? No. Death did occur; it just wasn't physical. Adam's *spirit* died. Over time that spiritual death spread throughout his entire being like a slow cancer and finally even killed his body—but not before he passed that same death on to all of us. That's why the Bible says, "*death* spread to all men" (Rom. 5:12). Now the entire human race is in a condition of spiritual death. We are not only born sinners, but we are also born dead.

In the eyes of God, people who are biologically alive and perfectly healthy are as dead as those who are in the grave. A man said to the Lord Jesus, "Let me first go and bury my father." But Jesus said to him, "Follow Me and let the dead bury their own dead" (Matt. 8:21). The idea of dead people burying dead people might sound strange to our ears, but it clearly demonstrates God's view of humanity: some of the dead have a pulse and some do not.

The dead can also be the busiest people in the world. They often invest huge amounts of energy into humanitarian and religious efforts. However, the Bible describes their activities as "*dead* works" (Heb. 9:14). Those who are dead in spirit can only do dead things, regardless of whether those things are good or bad.

And before anyone accuses them of being dull, the dead

can really have fun. In fact, they often advise others to "get a life" which means to get a social calendar and fill it with entertainment. The prodigal son did that. He threw himself into wild parties and liaisons with the opposite sex, but the Lord Jesus described him as "dead" (Luke 15:24). In a similar way, the Apostle Paul said, "she who lives in pleasure is dead while she lives" (1 Tim. 5:6). It all proves that at times the most socially stimulated people can be the living dead.

SPIRITUAL DEATH
AND WHERE IT TAKES YOU

When the Bible says, you "were *dead* in your offenses and sins," (Eph. 2:1), it obviously does not mean something biological or social. It means death toward God. A person in that condition has no sense of the presence of God. He has no sense of God's worth or any real fear of God's holiness and strength. Simply put, spiritual death is an inward numbness toward the Lord, a lack of consciousness of the divine. The Bible calls it "being alienated from the life of God" (Eph. 4:18), and as a result, "being past *feeling*" (Eph. 4:19).

A man with no spiritual sensitivity is like a truck without brakes. He can manage to do many evil things, since he has no real awareness of God's presence. He is neither charmed by God's beauty nor is he deterred by the possibility of judgment. Such deadened persons "have given themselves over to lewdness to work all uncleanness with greediness" (Eph. 4:19).

I'm reminded of Cal, a hulk of a man that I knew while I was in the Army. He was strong, mean, and always in some kind of trouble with the authorities. You could often find him on Monday morning bragging about his weekend exploits—acts that were either illegal or immoral. One time he described how he had picked up a hitchhiker who was carrying a six-pack of beer. When the man was reluctant to share it, Cal pulled the car over and beat him up. It was terribly funny to Cal, who couldn't tell the story without laughing. Since his numb spiritual condition acted as insulation between Himself and God, he felt no conviction over the incident. The deadness within him had subdued normal virtues like mercy and compassion.

Spiritual death has a habit of warping human decency. That is why the dead often view sin as an achievement. They are those "whose glory is in their shame" (Phil. 3:19). My wife and I knew someone who got a job as a secretary. In the course of time, she went on to break up her boss's marriage. Later, the young woman proudly described her adultery as though it were an accomplishment. According to her twisted logic, it was a career ladder that had begun with making coffee and then ended with the conquest of another woman's husband.

This is typical of spiritual death. It prevents a person from feeling the weight of sin. "I don't get it," the unsaved often say. "What's wrong with getting drunk and having a good time? Where's the harm in enjoying the opposite sex without a bunch of marriage talk? I don't feel that there's anything wrong with any of it. I'm not the one with hang-ups." Of course arguments like those prove nothing. If you place a five hundred-pound anvil on a corpse, it will not feel anything either. The weight is very real, but since it sits on something dead, *apparently* there is no problem.

When a man's spirit is dead, the only "life" he has is in the outer shell of his body and mind. That is a serious problem, for, as Paul said, "our outer man is *perishing*" (2 Cor. 4:16). It is like an apple with a large bruise. Given time, the bad spot will spread until the whole apple becomes a lump of acidic mush. As long as a human being ignores the death within him, that will also be his final state. The spreading death within him will render his entire being like that apple. Thus, he will one day stand before the pure, holy God as something rotten.

We have already seen that at the end of the age, when God judges the world, it will be according to the sinful works that have been "written in the books" (Rev. 20:12). Yet there is another book opened in the final judgment, "the Book of *life*" (Rev. 20:12). Ultimately, everything revolves around the issue of life and whether a person has it or not—"Anyone not found written in the Book of *life*, he was cast into the lake of fire" (Rev. 20:15). The man who does not have life, from God's viewpoint, is dead and therefore not worth keeping in eternity. Death, it seems, disqualifies everything.

For the better part of my growing up years, my family had a cocker spaniel named Angel. We all loved her. Although she had been a steady presence in our home for so many years, the day she died she was no longer welcome there. Death only made her suitable for a hole in the backyard. Tragically, many will experience this at the end of the age. Because they never received eternal life, nor even cared about it, they will end up standing before God without it. Their names will not appear in the Book of Life and God will count them as dead men. Hell will be the only suitable place for them, because in eternity, death and everything associated with it will be thrown there. As we are told, *"Death* and Hades were cast into the lake of fire" (Rev. 20:14).

WHAT IS ETERNAL LIFE? —
SOMETHING MORE THAN YOUR LIFE LASTING FOREVER

The solution to the problem of death is found in John 3:16—whoever believes into the Son of God, "shall not perish, but have eternal life." It is easy to think that eternal life merely means to live forever. Some people, though, do not find that thought particularly rewarding. No one wants to die, but is the idea of living forever that attractive? Is that the best God can do for us—to extend our natural lives into infinity? After all, people in hell will continue their existence forever too. We will all continue in some way or another.

We must think of eternal life not only in the sense of longevity, but of *quality*. A person in hell has a miserable existence for obvious reasons. But what makes the quality of eternal life so great? Perhaps it is found in the things we will be doing. Maybe we can expect to play harps, sit on clouds, and sing. Those not attracted to such things try to imagine something better. They fancy eternal life with movie theaters and bass fishing and golf courses. The Bible, however, does not describe the blessing of life as an endless future full of hobbies and other pursuits. Its emphasis lies more on the fact that we will simply have eternal life than upon anything we will be doing besides.

In order to understand why this life could be so sufficient by itself, we need to define it. According to the original Greek language in which the New Testament was written, there are different ways in which the word "life" is used. One way is purely physical—"bios." That is where we derive our English word "biology." Every physical living thing has bios. It is created life with a birth date and a limited life span. Bios is mortal and fragile. Practically anything can end it, from harmful microorganisms to old age.

The next way the Bible expresses life is as "psyche," which is where we derive the word "psychology." This has to do with the mind, emotion, and will—the personality, or according to biblical terminology, the soul. The soul of a man is the very man himself. In Exodus 12:16 the phrase "everyone must eat" is, in the original Hebrew language, "every *soul* must eat." When Peter referred to the eight people in the ark, he said, "eight *souls* were saved through water" (1 Pet. 3:20). When a count of Joseph's family members was given, it was "seventy-five *souls*" (Acts 7:14). The number of men that were onboard Paul's transport ship in the book of Acts was "two hundred and seventy-six *souls*" (Acts 27:37). Adam himself was called "a living *soul*" (1 Cor. 15:45 NASB). Psyche life, therefore, describes the mortal man with his thoughts, feelings, and decisions.

The most profound way in which the Bible speaks of life is "zoe," the word commonly used to describe the eternal life of God. This is completely different from "bios" and "psyche." Eternal life is no mere extension of mortal life. It is not our life minus the expiration date. It is *another* life, distinct from our own.

When Jesus visited this earth and found us conducting business, being educated, raising families and even worshiping God, He saw us all as being dead. We had bios and psyche, but not zoe. That is why He said, "I have come that they may have life [zoe]" (John 10:10). In the Bible's estimation, only the life of God is "that which is life indeed" (1 Tim. 6:19). Everything else is a shadow.

A LIFE WITH NO BEGINNING OR ENDING

"The life of God" (Eph 4:18), as Paul called it, is remarkable in many ways. First, it is eternal, meaning it is not confined by time. The Psalmist said to the Lord, "From everlasting to everlasting, You are God" (Ps. 90:2). This, in itself, sets God's life apart from any other life in the universe. Only He is uncreated. While everything else had a beginning, He did not. God has created lower life than His own life—angelic life, human life, animal life, plant life, all the microscopic life—but because they are created, none are eternal. Even Satan must acknowledge that there was a time when he did not exist (or, maybe he doesn't admit it, but that still doesn't alter the fact). God's life knows neither beginning nor ending. It alone is eternal.

A LIFE THAT CANNOT SPOIL

Secondly, the life of God is incorruptible. Since it is not subject to time, it does not change with the endless passage of the ages. In contrast, this world, so full of shiny toys, fads, and fashions, "is passing away" (1 John 2:17). Physical things become feeble and weak. They eventually decay, because all creation is under "the bondage of corruption" (Rom. 8:21). Only God continues existing in an endless untarnished state:

> "You, LORD, in the beginning laid the foundation of the earth, and the heavens are the work of your hands; they will perish, *but You remain;* and they all will grow old like a garment; like a cloak You will fold them up; and they will be changed. *But you are the same, and your years will not fail."* (Heb. 1:10-12)

It is true that some life created by God has not been subjected to time, and therefore does not age, like the angelic life. Angels do not become "old folks." In that sense, they are incorruptible. However, in an even more serious sense they are vulnerable to *moral* corruption. The brightest, mightiest archangel, Lucifer, fell into this kind of corruption when he sinned. He also persuaded a number of God's angels to become "*his* angels" (Matt. 25:41), and join him in rebellion against God. Thus the purity of angelic life can be lost. God is, on the other hand, "the *incorruptible* God" (Rom. 1:23). Phrases such as "in Him is no darkness at all" (1 John 1:5) and "it was impossible for God to lie" (Heb. 6:18) are reminders that no kind of corruption can penetrate His life.

A LIFE THAT IS INDESTRUCTIBLE

The life of God is also indestructible (Heb. 7:16 NASB). This, of course, is much different than physical life, which can end in a moment and for any reason. Extreme care must be taken with our life, or it will not last long. Even so, non-drinkers, non-smokers, and non-risk takers still die of things like cancer and heart defects. James said, "What is your life? It is even a vapor that appears for a little time and then vanishes away" (4:14). This is not so with eternal life. No force or person can nullify it. No one can kill it. When death crashes into the life of God, it is like a child with a tack hammer assaulting Mount Everest. God's life cannot be vanquished with any instrument or by any means. That is why the Lord Jesus was so bold to say that those who receive eternal life "would not perish" (John 3:16). It was not because the believer would be granted an indefinite life span, but because he would receive a life that cannot be killed.

When Jesus came, the Bible says, "In Him was life" (John 1:4), that is, eternal life. But eventually, death confronted Him. Under the instigation of Satan, the whole world, represented by Jews and Gentiles conspired to destroy Him. He was taken and crucified. This was a tremendous test to the life within Him. We cannot deny that He died, was buried, and then rested "in the heart of the earth" (Matt. 12:40). However, it was only "for three days and three nights" (Matt. 12:40). Because eternal life was in Him, death could only be a temporary experience that He passed through. Death was powerless to contain Him, indeed, "It was not *possible* that He should be held by it" (Acts 2:24). Although the devil's entire arsenal had been exhausted against Him, the life in Jesus emerged from that dark tunnel of death as the *resurrection* life. It enabled Him to say, "I am He who lives, and was dead, and behold, I am alive forevermore" (Rev. 1:18).

LIFE IS A PERSON

Up until now I have used the phrase "the life of God" (Eph. 4:18). Yet, God's life should not be thought of as separate from Himself. Christ equated Himself with life, saying, "I am the way, the truth, and the *life*" (John 14:6), and "I am the resurrection and the *life*" (John 11:25). It is also written that, "He who has the Son has *life*. He who does not have the Son of God does not have *life*" (1 John 5:12). Having Jesus Christ is the same as having eternal life. The Lord not only bestows it; He *is* it.

In the same way, the Holy Spirit is equated to the life of God. When Jesus spoke about "rivers of *living* water" (John 7:38), He spoke "concerning the Spirit" (John 7:39). The Spirit is "the Spirit of *life*" (Rom. 8:2), which explains why the experience of a man filled with the Spirit is that of "springing up into everlasting *life*" (John 4:14).

In the final analysis, God Himself—the Father, the Son, and the Holy Spirit—is eternal life. Wherever He is, life is. So, when a person hears the gospel and receives Christ and the Holy Spirit, what happens is truly a miracle. The greatest life in the universe comes into that person, a life that cannot die or be corrupted, and one that has no beginning or ending. Not even the mightiest of God's angels like Michael or Gabriel, possesses such a thing. Neither does the worst of God's enemies, such as Satan or his angels. The believer is truly a phenomenon in this universe, for hidden within his mortal shell is the life that is really life.

A BLUEPRINT FOR GIVING LIFE

For a very long time the life of God was confined to Himself alone. No one shared it with Him. Mankind only had a mortal life that would begin aging and then dying shortly after it was born. God could have remedied the problem by simply giving His life to us. With a wave of His hand, He could have conferred it upon us from heaven.

But He refused to do it in such a superficial way. God had a plan. From the very beginning of the Bible, we find Him establishing principles that would govern how He would one day share His wonderful life with us.

For instance, in the book of Genesis the principle is established that life comes through something that dies and is broken open. When God desired to bring forth Eve, He did not will her into existence. Instead, "the Lord God caused a deep sleep to fall on Adam, and he slept; and He took one of his ribs, and closed up the flesh in its place. Then the rib which the Lord God had taken from man, He made into a woman" (Gen. 2:21-22). Adam's "deep sleep" was a kind of death experience, while the opening of his side to remove the rib illustrated a breaking experience. The issue of this dying and breaking process was Eve, who was entirely constructed with the life taken out of her husband. This established a great precedent for the future. When God would eventually be ready to share His divine life, it would be through a "container" that would die and be broken open.

There is a second great principle in Genesis governing the sharing of God's life. We find that God will never place His life where sin has not been properly dealt with. Directly following Adam's sin in the garden, the Tree of Life was suddenly closed to him. God "drove out the man; and He placed Cherubim [a special kind of angel] at the east of the Garden of Eden, and a flaming sword which turned every way, *to guard the way of the tree of life*" (Gen. 3:24). God would not tolerate the sinful Adam eating from that tree.

Its fruit represented the holy, uncreated, indestructible life of God. And if it got into Adam, that life would unavoidably mingle with man's sin nature. So, the Tree of Life was closed and would not be open again until sin was satisfactorily dealt with.

The principles that were established in Genesis were literally fulfilled in the New Testament. There we find Jesus giving His life to us in perfect accordance with them. First of all, the Bible says, "In Him was life" (John 1:4). This means that while He was on the earth, the Lord was a human container of divine life. In the entire world He was unique, because from God's viewpoint the rest of the world was dead. The prophet Isaiah said, "He [Christ] shall grow up before Him [God the Father] as a tender plant and as a root out of dry ground" (Isa. 53:2). A "tender plant" and a "root" are things of life describing Christ. But the "dry ground" is something dead, describing the entire human race surrounding Jesus. On this lifeless landscape of a world, only He was alive to God.

That fact alone made this "container" extraordinary. Men had never encountered a person who embodied the very life of God. The impact of such a Person living among us was tremendous. Consider the following passage by an anonymous author:

> "He is a man who was born in an obscure village, the child of a peasant woman. He grew up in another village. He worked in a carpenter shop until He was thirty, and then for three years He was an itinerate preacher. He never owned a home. He never wrote a book. He never held an office. He never had a family. He never went to college. He never put his foot inside a big city. He never traveled two hundred miles from the place where He was born. He never did one of the things that usually accompany greatness. He had no credentials but Himself. . .While still a young man, the tide of popular opinion turned against Him. His friends ran away. One of them denied Him. He was turned over to His enemies. He went through the

mockery of a trial. He was nailed upon a cross between two thieves. While He was dying His executioners gambled for the only piece of property He had on earth—His coat. When He was dead, He was taken down and laid in a borrowed grave through the pity of a friend.

"Nineteen long centuries have come and gone, and today He is the centerpiece of the human race and the leader of the column of progress. I am far within the mark when I say that all the armies that ever marched, all the navies that ever were built; all the parliaments that ever sat and all the kings that ever reigned, put together, have not affected the life of man upon this earth as powerfully as has that one solitary life."

This was the divine life making itself known to men on their own turf. As John said, "the life was *manifested*" (1 John 1:2). Yet that life was still only in Christ and in no one else. He was a container, but to the detriment of the world, He was a sealed one.

That was why it was a great thing when Jesus said, "I came that *they* may have life and that they may have it more abundantly" (John 10:10). In saying this, the "sealed container" was declaring that what was in Him was supposed to get out and get into others. How was this to happen?

Let's ask the same question about one of those big ceramic piggy banks, the kind completely enclosed, without the little door in the bottom. The bank might be full of money, but your pockets are empty. How will the treasure in the piggy bank get into your pocket? There is only one way: it must be broken open. Unless the bank is smashed, you will continue being poor.

Just as in the pattern established with Adam, the Lord Jesus went into the "deep sleep" of death and He was "opened": "One of the soldiers *pierced His side* with a spear, and immediately blood and water came out" (John 19:34). This was a breaking of the container to release something. In this case it was not to obtain a physical rib, but "blood and water."

When water came out of the Lord's side, it signified that His divine life had been released. He was no longer a sealed container, but one broken for the life of the world. Human eyes saw a small stream coming out of His side, but the reality was that a spiritual "Hoover Dam" had broken. It would begin to fulfill the Lord's mission "that they may have life and that they may have it more *abundantly*." Enough divine life had been released to supply the entire population of the world, then, now, and forever. If this wonderful container had not been willing to be broken on the cross, the life of God would have forever been confined within Christ. He would have remained "a tender plant" but the *only* one on a whole world of "dry ground." As He Himself said, "Unless a grain of wheat falls into the ground and dies, it remains *alone*; but if it dies it produces much grain" (John 12:24).

Blood also came out of the Lord's side, fulfilling the second principle that sin must be dealt with before life can be given. Since Christ died for our sins, God reopened the way for us to the tree of life. Like a bulldozer, the Lord's blood cleared away all the obstacles that once blocked our approach. Now in Christ, men can come and eat freely from that tree.

HOW TO RECEIVE ETERNAL LIFE

Most people are pragmatic when it comes to spiritual things. They want to know how deep truths are supposed to work out in their own experience. Eating from the Tree of Life would be one of those things they'd want to know about. If that tree is not a literal one and can't be located anywhere on earth, then how does a person go about getting eternal life? The simple answer lies in John 3:16. This verse, which is the most famous in the Bible, is also the least understood. Many Christians read it, "God so loved the world, that He gave His only begotten Son, that whoever believes in Him should not perish, but *go to heaven*." This, of course, is not what it actually says. The promise is that we "would have eternal life." John does not tell us how to go somewhere after we die, but how to receive eternal life, right here and now. The operative word in the verse is "believe." If we "believe in Him," then the life of God becomes ours immediately. John's entire gospel was constructed so "that you may *believe* that Jesus is the Christ, the Son of God, and that *believing*, you may have *life* in His name" (John 20:31).

By believing, eternal life becomes a current possession and reality to you. It is not something only for the future, after you die. John said, "These things I have written to you who believe in the name of the Son of God, in order that you may *know* that you *have* eternal life" (1 John 5:13). According to him, there is no need to wait and find out whether you will get it. If a man wants to know whether he has received eternal life, he only needs to ask himself whether he has believed in Jesus.

A New Life for a New Birth

It would be a very incomplete discussion to talk about eternal life and even how to receive it, yet not mention what that life does to us. The fact is, nothing will ever bring about a greater change in you. The coming in of life triggers a new beginning so radical that the Lord Jesus calls it being born again.

Many years ago, you were born "of the flesh" (John 3:6). Two human parents came together according to "the will of the flesh" (John 1:13) and conceived you. As a result, you were given skin, bone, tissues, and five senses, everything needed for life in this world. Perhaps just recently, you received Jesus Christ. When that happened, you received eternal life, causing you to be born all over again.

This second birth is "of God" (John 1:13) and "of the Spirit" (John 3:8), making it a miraculous work unparalleled in scripture. The God that has created the universe, parted the Red Sea, fought for His people, and thundered from heaven has topped His list of wonders by desiring to produce children. We find this incredible fact firmly imbedded in the ministry of the Lord Jesus. He repeatedly referred to God as "the Father," a title related to the giving of life and the begetting of children. Additionally, the new birth was an undeniable feature of the Lord's teaching:

> "Most assuredly I say to you, unless one is *born* again, he cannot see the kingdom of God." (John 3:3)

> "Most assuredly, I say to you, unless one is *born* of water and the Spirit, he cannot enter the kingdom of God." (John 3:5)

> "That which is born of the flesh is flesh and that which is *born* of the Spirit is spirit." (John 3:6)

> "You must be *born* again." (John 3:7)

The Lord's repetitive references to birth in those passages tell us of God's desire to produce children through His own life.

THE NATURE OF THE SECOND BIRTH

Maybe in the past you thought being born again was simply another metaphor for a new beginning, like "turning over a new leaf." Some think if a person dramatically changes for any reason he might be considered "born again." Perhaps a woman who once appeared in ads for cigarettes suddenly quit smoking, joined an anti-tobacco lobby and gave lectures in high schools about the hazards of nicotine. Was she born again? No. Mere change in itself is not what the Bible means when it speaks of being "born again."

In fact, just mention the phrase "born again" to someone and misunderstanding abounds, not only today, but in Bible times as well. Nicodemus was a man who thought being born again involved a physical rebirth. He questioned Jesus,

"How can a man be born when he is old? Can he enter a second time into his mother's womb and be born?" (John 3:4). To him the second birth meant a repeat of the first one, complete with a pregnant woman, contractions, and a delivery.

The Lord responded to Nicodemus, saying, "That which is born of the flesh is flesh and that which is born of the Spirit is spirit" (John 3:6). By stating this He established that the first birth is physical; the second is *spiritual*. Some people say, "Oh, so it's only spiritual." By that remark they mean to imply that spiritual things are not as real as physical ones. But the fact that the second birth is spiritual does not make it any less true. The Bible talks about spiritual things as being the things that are the *most* real. Paul said, "We do not look at the things which are seen, but at the things which are not seen. For the things which are seen are temporary, but the things which are not seen are eternal" (2 Cor. 4:18).

The second birth is not only more real and enduring than the first, but a lot more mysterious. Observers can track the process of human conception. They can observe the developing stages of an embryo. Through ultrasound technology they can even look at the baby while it is still in the womb. None of this can happen with the second birth. It is beyond human scrutiny. The Lord described it this way: "The wind blows where it wishes, and you hear the sound of it, but cannot tell where it comes from and where it goes. So is everyone who is born of the Spirit" (John 3:8). As the Lord indicated, studying the second birth is like trying to observe the origin and destination of a breeze. The human eye is not capable of perceiving it.

The entire process transpires in a place deeply buried within "the spirit of the man" (1 Cor. 2:11). We are beings of three parts—"spirit, soul, and body" (1 Thess. 5:23). Your spirit is your spiritual "womb," the spot reserved within you to receive the life of God. It is where the new birth occurs, as the Lord said, "That which is born of the Spirit [the Holy Spirit], is spirit [our human spirit]" (John 3:6). This is the beginning of our Christian lives and is the most indispensable experience we could ever have.

"BORN AGAIN" IS NOT ANOTHER BRAND OF CHRISTIANITY

Occasionally, I've run into people who said, "Don't tell me you're one those *born-again* Christians?!" The question comes from thinking that there are different kinds of Christians—some of the first birth and some of the second. It makes the second birth sound like just another religious tradition that one can choose. But did the Lord Jesus mean to tell us that being born again was optional? Is it simply one among many ways that we can be saved?

Let's look at the facts: He said, "You *must* be born again" (John 3:7). He also said why: "Unless one is born again, he *cannot see* the kingdom of God" (John 3:3), and without the second birth, "he *cannot enter* into the kingdom of God" (John 3:5). Those are strong words, telling us that the worship style we happen to prefer or what we like to call ourselves is immaterial. Unless eternal life gains an entrance into our being and triggers the new birth, we have nothing to do with God's kingdom.

The Savior only saves through one means. There are no other options. Either it is new birth, or nothing. From the physical perspective we were not given any options concerning how to begin our human lives. No one selected the way in which he or she would become a part of the human race. The entryway into this world is the same for all—birth. By the same token, we were given no choices concerning how to begin the Christian life. We must also begin through birth.

WHY BEING BORN AGAIN IS SO NECESSARY

The new birth enables a person to see and enter the kingdom of God (John 3:3, 5). The reason for this is simple: Every birth is related to a kingdom. When we were born as human beings, we automatically became members of the human kingdom. There were no applications or lessons required. Human life automatically enabled us to enter the realm of mankind, a domain that life in other kingdoms could never understand.

For instance, suppose a man goes outside with his dog to throw a stick. He needs a little diversion after a long work-week. Who among us couldn't understand this? For one, Fido doesn't. He might like to run and fetch the stick, but he has no idea what has motivated the whole activity. He cannot see or enter his master's mysterious reasoning because he is a member of another kingdom—the dog kingdom. That kingdom has a different life with a different birth, one that has no ability to comprehend difficult bosses and the next quarter's sales projections.

Our example works the other way around, too. As Fido goes after the stick, he stops and suddenly sniffs a fire hydrant. What invisible messages are there? Why are faint traces of urine so interesting to him? All that his owner can do is theorize. He is a member of the human kingdom, one that does not receive messages by sniffing fire hydrants. The man cannot "see" (understand) or "enter" (experience) the dog kingdom because he was not born a dog. He can be an expert in canine behavior, but at best, that is only a member of one kingdom studying the members of another.

Now it should be easier to understand why we need another birth in order to see and enter the kingdom of God. Without it we cannot begin to comprehend truly spiritual things. Unfortunately, good religious behavior is often prioritized more highly than being born again. A polished first birth is valued more than a genuine second birth. This might result in a good imitation, but that is all. Years ago, there was a children's program whose complete cast was chimpanzees. There were no human actors. All the chimps were dressed like people and they even had "lines," that is, when they moved their lips, sound technicians dubbed in human talk. "OOO OOO, AH, AH," turned into "Mrs. Jones, take a letter, please." The chimps wore three-piece suits, drove cars, and played golf. But no matter how convincing their performance was, as soon as the cameras stopped rolling, they would go back to picking fleas off of one another and climbing on studio equipment. They could mimic life in the human kingdom, but it was all an act. It would have taken a miracle to bring those chimps into true human behavioral patterns. In order to enter our kingdom, they would have needed a rebirth with human life.

Men who try to act like they are in the kingdom of God, without the new birth, are actually providing reruns of the chimp show. It is once again a life in one kingdom acting like the life in another. Yes, there are verses that tell us to emulate the example of the Lord Jesus and the apostles, *but never without the new birth*. It may be reasonable to tell a young boy to act like a man, but it's unrealistic to expect a monkey to act like a man, because the birth is wrong. The bottom line of membership in the kingdom of God is birth, not behavior.

Nicodemus was an accomplished religious person, "a man of the Pharisees," (a strict, pious sect of the ancient Jewish religion). He was also "a ruler of the Jews" (John 3:1). But when he came to see Jesus, the Lord didn't say, "Thank you for joining my cause. Because you're such a good man, you'll make a fine disciple and will be a credit to my movement." Instead, from the moment Jesus laid eyes on Nicodemus, He said to him, "Truly, truly, I say to you, Unless one is born again, he cannot see the kingdom of God" (John 3:3). Even the excellent religious behavior of a sincere man was not enough to enter the kingdom. Nicodemus could not behave himself into it. The Lord confirmed that he had to be born into it.

He went on to add, "Do not marvel that I said to you, You must be born again" (John 3:7). In other words, don't think the requirement is incredible or unreasonable. Our first birth produced flesh and blood, but "flesh and blood cannot inherit the kingdom of God" (1 Cor. 15:50). It simply is not sufficient for seeing, entering, and possessing a kingdom of spiritual reality. A second birth is entirely necessary.

WHAT THE SECOND BIRTH DOES TO YOU —
IT RENEWS AND ENLIVENS YOUR HUMAN SPIRIT

An immediate consequence of being born again is that

we see and enter the kingdom of God. That means seeing and entering a whole new world with all its varied experiences. This requires a different inward situation than what we had before in the old human kingdom. At that time we got along just fine with a deadened human spirit. There was simply no need for spiritual sensitivity because our whole life was lived in a non-spiritual world. But when the new birth occurs, God promises to "put a new spirit within you" (Eze. 36:26). Your old human spirit was numb and mostly without function. It underwent a serious change, however, when the life of God entered you. Although it is the same human spirit that you always had, when it became alive and functional, for all practical purposes it became new.

This is like having a nice watch that only runs on a rare brand of battery. Suppose you never located that kind of battery, so you never used the watch. You allowed it to just sit in a jewelry box for ten years under cufflinks and tie clips. It laid there for so long that it almost became indistinguishable from the junk around it. Then one day you find the rare battery that fits the watch. You insert the battery, it immediately begins working, and you begin wearing it. Then your friends notice. They say, "Got a new watch, didn't you?" Though you might explain that you've actually had it for years, in a sense you have to admit that it's new. This is just like your human spirit. For so many years it laid idle within you, but having been enlivened with the life of God, it is now "running fine." For the first time, you will begin enjoying the spiritual things of Christ, all because of your "new" spirit.

This fresh sensitivity toward God is in itself a wonder. Try to imagine a telephone pole suddenly springing to conscious life, feeling the sun, hearing the rush of cars along the road, and being tickled by the roosting of birds upon its lines. That would truly be an extraordinary event. An old dead chunk of wood, alive with a consciousness that it never possessed before, would really be a new thing on this earth. Men who are born again are no less of a wonder. Indeed, Paul says of the man who has been born of God, that "He is a *new* creation; old things have passed away; behold, all things have become *new*" (2 Cor. 5:17).

Resurrecting someone means bringing him back to life or raising him from the dead. People who have been born again have been resurrected because their dead human spirit was made alive. At the believer's core, death has been vanquished. I made a point earlier that a dead human spirit would spread death through a man's being like a bruise spreads over an apple. The same thing is true in reverse for a spirit that is alive. Once resurrection has occurred there, it will spread as well. It will reach all the parts of our being, enlivening them as time passes. First of all, "the spirit is life" (Rom. 8:10 NASB). Then, "the mind set on the Spirit is life" (Rom. 8:6 NASB). Ultimately, "He who raised Christ from the dead *will also give life to your mortal bodies* through His Spirit who indwells you" (Rom. 8:11). The believer will eventually be able to say, "Death is swallowed up in victory. O death, where is your victory? O death, where is your sting?" (1 Cor. 15:54b-55).

The resurrection life in a believer is "death-proof." That is why the Lord Jesus could say, "He who believes into Me, though he may die, he shall live" (John 11:25). The death of a Christian and a non-Christian might outwardly look very much the same. Either one of them may die of cancer or in a car crash, or violently, as in a murder. From the newspaper's point of view, it all looks the same. But there could not be a greater difference between the two. Those who die without resurrection life "have no hope" (1 Thess. 4:13). In a sense, they also will one day be resurrected, but negatively, as Daniel portrayed it: "Many of those who sleep in the dust of the earth shall awake...*some to shame and everlasting contempt*" (Dan. 12:2). For them, resurrection will not be a blessing.

Death is a terrifying thing to the world because it is the end of the "party" and the beginning of the dark unknown. But for those who have eternal life, it is a portal into blessing, for we will "depart and be with Christ" (Phil. 1:23).

The promise of a glorious resurrection works to "deliver those who through fear of death were subject to slavery all their lives" (Heb. 2:15 NASB). A believer is thus equipped to meet death with a very different attitude than his unsaved neighbors.

This does not mean that since they are certain to be resurrected, Christians are all emotionally neutral about death. There will certainly be some level of nervousness about it. Think about death as though it were bungee jumping. In a bungee jump the participant stands on the rail of a bridge, preparing to leap. His stomach is full of butterflies. He wouldn't do this at all if it were not for an elastic cord tied to his ankle. He knows he will only fall so far because the cord will stop his descent and jerk him back up in the opposite direction. If the jumper had no cord, then he would kick, scream, and do anything to keep from going over the side. He knows better than to leap without a strong connection. Like the bungee jumper, as the believer stands at the brink of death, he also might feel apprehensive. But he has an unbreakable cord—the resurrection life of Jesus Christ. He is not enslaved by fear because he has a secure connection. When he falls, the life within him will stop his downward plunge and eventually get him moving in the opposite direction. The unsaved should consider it a serious matter to face death without resurrection life. It is very much like leaping off a bridge without a cord!

I used bungee jumping as an example of death, but I do not want to give the impression that death is a game. Being freed from the fear of death does not mean that Christians should be reckless with their lives. Death brings grief to our loved ones, ends the work of the Lord in our lives, and terminates our earthly service to God, something greatly needed in these dark times. Foolish acts of bravado do not prove faith. Rather, they demonstrate irresponsibility and immaturity. Resurrection should only embolden us to responsibly go on in the will of God, knowing that even if we die, we will live.

THE SECOND BIRTH GRANTS A NEW, SOFT HEART

Besides an enlivened spirit, another result of being born again is found in God's promise to "give you a new heart" (Eze. 36:26). Before the second birth, our old heart was a "heart of stone" (Eze. 36:26)—nearly impenetrable. This hardened heart does not respond to anything. If God grants His blessings and protection, such a heart does not answer with praise. If through the gospel God shows how much He loves men, the old heart says, "I'm not interested." If God warns of the judgment to come, it says, "I'll take my chances." This is a heart of stone.

But the promise related to the new birth is that "I will take the heart of stone out of your flesh and give you a heart of flesh" (Eze. 36:26). In this phrase "flesh" means that the heart becomes soft and pliable. It can be moved by God and can respond to Him. This heart finds it easy to love the Lord. Sometimes Christians (myself included) realize how little they love Him. This bothers us because our hearts have been made soft through the new birth. We see the way the Lord loves us and wish we would love Him just as much in return. Unsaved men find such concerns silly.

Two Christians I know, Jeff and Bill, were sitting together in an ice cream shop. Jeff was troubled with himself over not making enough progress in his relationship with the Lord. He wondered out loud if maybe there was something seriously wrong. Bill, known for his sometimes unorthodox shepherding methods, didn't answer. Instead, he turned to two drunken men seated at a table nearby. "Excuse me, " he said, "Are you fellows concerned about not loving the Lord enough?"

"What are you talking about?" they growled, adding some slurred profanity.

Bill turned back to Jeff. "You see," he told him, "you're actually doing fine."

The point was well taken. In the midst of a world where young men meditate over concerns about everything from fast cars to beer, Jeff was an enigma. He was troubled with how things were going between himself and Jesus. That was because his new heart was not only warm towards Christ but convicted over not being warm *enough* to Him. Those who are born again have this characteristic softness within them for the Lord Jesus.

Anyone who has received God's life and been born again, has God's seed in him. When the Bible speaks of "whoever has been born of God" (1 John 3:9), it says that God's "*seed* remains in him" (1 John 3:9). Scripture also points out that we have "been born again, not of corruptible *seed*, but of incorruptible" (1 Pet. 1:23).

In our physical world, every seed bears a genetic code, a set of organic instructions that will guide its future growth. Since God's seed is now in us with its particular "genetic code," we can expect that our growth will not be haphazard. All real Christian development is according to the divine seed that was deposited into us when we believed. What will it grow to look like? For one thing, it will appear holy and righteous—"Whoever has been born of God *does not sin*, for His seed remains in Him, and he *cannot sin* because He has been born of God" (1 John 3:9). God's life has a natural dislike for sin. This is why the Christian cannot settle into sinful behavior and be happy as he once was before salvation. Sin used to feel normal to him. He needed no excuses to commit it. As a sinner, he simply did whatever he wanted. But once the sinner becomes a believer, he starts feeling the need to rationalize and justify his weaknesses. With whom does he argue? It is not with anyone on the outside. It is with contradictory sensations coming from his *inside*. The divine seed in him is coded for holiness and is uncomfortable with sin. As a result, it never gives him a green light for evil.

When a believer wishes to give in to sinful desires, he will find that "he *cannot* sin, for His [God's] seed remains in him" (1 John 3:9b). This does not mean a true Christian loses his ability to do evil things. The Bible recognizes the possibility of a believer committing sins (1 John 1:9; 2:1). The phrase "cannot sin" is related to the part of him that has been born of God—his spirit. That is where the seed of God is located. The newly born spirit hates sin and will not get involved with it in any way. A believer does not need to train himself to dislike wickedness. The life of God within automatically does it for him.

Every life has a nature and a behavioral law to go along with it. We have a cat named Oscar, who is strictly an indoor pet. We had him declawed to keep him from shredding our furniture and curtains. Even so, Oscar regularly goes through the motions of sharpening claws that aren't there. A natural law within him periodically demands that he rub his paws on a chair leg. In the same way, a natural law also governs the dog who cannot resist digging up a flowerbed, or the infant who spits out something bitter but savors something sweet. A life always comes bundled with a nature and a set of predictable behaviors. Eternal life is no different. The day we received it, we became "partakers of the divine *nature*" (2 Pet. 1:4) and got "the *law* of the Spirit of life" (Rom. 8:2). Now we intuitively hate sin, darkness, lies, and the devil, but we love righteousness, holiness, truth, and other Christians.

This is bound to provoke some questions. For instance, we have received a life whose nature is holy. It naturally hates sin and loves righteousness. If that is the case, living a holy life should be as effortless for us as flying is to a bird. Why then, are we still so prone to go astray?

This is where things get complicated, for unlike a bird or any other being in the world, the believer has more than one life and nature. In his outermost part, his body, is sin. Paul said, "in my flesh, nothing good dwells" (Rom. 7:18), and "Sin...dwells in me" (Rom. 7:17). More deeply within him is his soul, which "wills to do good" (Rom. 7:21). This already shows the potential for some kind of struggle. A sinful body and a good soul all cloistered together in one man will produce conflict as surely as shutting up a cat and a dog in a closet. And it does. Paul spoke of the "law in my members [my body], *warring* against the law of my mind and bringing me into *captivity* to the law of sin which is in my members" (Rom. 7:23).

Let's complicate the picture a bit more. Deeper than a believer's body and soul is his spirit, which now has "the law of the Spirit of life" within it (Rom. 8:2). This is an even stranger combination of opposites. The nature of God and the sin nature both indwell a believer. Now there is not only the potential for conflict but the *certainty* of it. As Paul again told us, "the flesh lusts against the Spirit and the Spirit against the flesh; and these are contrary to one another" (Gal. 5:17).

Which life will prevail? It all depends upon which side you take. Receiving the life of God is not a guarantee that you will suddenly begin expressing it to perfection. Our inward situation is not set on automatic pilot. You have the life of God perpetually and for all eternity, but whatever you continue to place your focus upon will become your daily experience. It is written that "the *mind set* on the flesh is death, but the *mind set* on the Spirit is life and peace" (Rom. 8:6 NASB). Mind-set determines our experience. If you choose to ponder filthy things, then that world, with its weakness and darkness, will be what is real to you. But if you "set your mind on things above" (Col. 3:2), then you will be kept in the experience of eternal life.

Just because you have this life does not mean you will be temptation free. Don't be surprised when "the flesh lusts against the Spirit" (Gal. 5:17). I know stories about new believers who were hit with with sudden wild impulses to go do something sinful even as they were attempting to do something for the Lord. Greg, a new Christian, told me, "I can't believe it. I had every intention of reading the Bible with my friend and telling him about Jesus. I was looking forward to it, but somehow I ended up smoking pot with him instead. Wow, that was such a dumb mistake."

Greg may never commit that particular sin again, but rest assured temptation will return in some other form for some other thing. We are in a body of flesh that has been poisoned with sin, one that supplies drives, suggestions, propositions, schemes, fleeting thoughts, and urges that contradict our new life. As believers, our only hope is to continue in the eternal life that we have received. As the Lord said, "Abide [remain] in Me" (John 15:4). But even if you don't remain in Him and end up making a mess of things, don't fall into the second trap of the devil, which is to think that you should just give up. Instead, "If we confess our sins, He is faithful and just to forgive us our sins and cleanse us from all unrighteousness" (1 John 1:9).

Sinners chuckle when they see all these struggles in their "uptight-and-out-of-sight" Christian friends. They say, "I'm glad I'm not religious [which is often their way of saying 'born again']. I can do whatever I want to do. I can go wherever I want to go." The Lord Jesus agreed with this self-appraisal. He said, "Your time is always ready" (John 7:6), meaning that people of the world can do anything or go anywhere they want at a moment's notice. They do not seem to be troubled about things they see in movies. They are seldom bothered about what they hear in popular music. To them, moral issues are matters to be decided based on convenience. Yes, to them it is easier not being a Christian. But this ease comes from the fact that non-Christians only have two natures within them: sin and human goodness. Of course, the sin in them is powerful and always overcomes their frail goodness. As long as a man stays in that conquered position, he will seem to have peace. While Satan has the dominant place in that man's life, there will not seem to be trouble for him. Sinners "go with the flow" because they cannot resist it anyway. They are like lifeless debris—twigs or fallen leaves—being carried downstream to their terrible fate. There is no way for them to overcome the power of their sin nature, so they simply settle back and enjoy the long ride down.

If the unsaved tend to be like debris being carried along, then believers tend to be like salmon, swimming and even leaping against the current. Yes, they often feel a backward drag but only because they are alive and moving forward. The new life they have received is their "swimming power." It is what enables them to combat and overcome the pull of the sinful nature within them. God's life comes bundled with a law and a nature that frees us. That is why Paul could say, "The *law* of the Spirit of life in Christ Jesus has made me *free* from the law of sin and of death" (Rom. 8:2), and Peter says that we are "partakers of the divine *nature,* having *escaped the corruption* that is in the world through lust" (2 Pet. 1:4).

Continuing the salmon analogy, to be "free from the law of sin and death" and to "escape the corruption" just means to leap the falls. Salmon do just that, literally stair-stepping out of the lower pools and water courses. The nature and life law in these fish needs no instructions. When they encounter obstacles to their journey upriver, they automatically launch into an upward ascent. Likewise, eternal life, with its divine nature and life-law enables us to escape and be free from the lower parts of our being.

KNOWING GOD BY HIS LIFE

I suppose one of the reasons I remained disinterested in salvation for so long was the idea that I had to die in order to have it. In other words, I was under the impression that God was primarily a God of the dead. It was not a very attractive selling point for a young man. Happily, in time I found that the concept was mistaken. The substance of the Christian life can be sizably realized today. Jesus prayed to the Father, "this is eternal life, that they may *know* You, the only true God, and Jesus Christ whom You have sent" (John 17:3). Eternal life causes a person to currently know God— on this side of the grave.

Life is the greatest teacher of all. During more than twenty years of marriage I have amassed an incredible amount of knowledge about my wife—her habits, attitudes, likes, dislikes, and what makes her laugh. I can even make predictions about what she will say and think (Now and then, I'm correct.) Yet in the midst of all this knowledge I can still only ask myself "How would Aleisha feel?" "What would Aleisha think?" We have been joined together as "one flesh" for a very long time, but she cannot take her own subjective life and place it within me to be my moment-by-moment firsthand experience. However, this is *exactly* what the Lord Jesus did when we first believed in Him. His life became ours and in some deep abiding way, we immediately began to know Him from the inside out.

God says of born-again people, "None of them shall teach his neighbor, and none his brother, saying, 'Know the Lord,' for *all* shall know Me, from the least of them to the greatest of them" (Heb. 8:11). Formerly, "the least" among men felt that they could not know God because they did not have brilliant religious minds or poetic hearts. Maybe they were simply the worst sinners. Whatever the case, if "the least" receive eternal life, then they can know God along with "the greatest" who have received it. Paul said, "To me, who am *less than the least* of all the saints, this grace was given" (Eph. 3:8). In particular, the grace given to him resulted in over half of the New Testament that we hold today in our hands—very impressive, considering that Paul had been "*less* than the least.*"

No doubt the depth of the knowledge of God will differ according to the relative maturity among Christians. But the point is that real believers are never void of knowing God in some small intuitive way. "Jesus is my Savior!" or "God is my Father!" might not convey any especially deep ideas to scholarly ears, but it is knowledge that comes into a believer along with eternal life. It is within him as a personal realization in his deepest parts. It does not exist in him based on religious indoctrination. Now this is not to say that as a source of knowledge, the Bible is any less important. The Bible is a fail-safe measure. It protects a believer from being deceived by inward thoughts and feelings that do not come from God's life. For as the Christian reads the scriptures, he either sees a confirmation of what he already knows, obtains notice of what he will come to know, or receives correction concerning what he refuses to know. The knowledge of God within him and what is on the pages of the Bible should match. If eternal life is truly spreading through him, then it will look like the God he reads about in scripture.

The prophet Isaiah uttered a comprehensive promise when he said, "the earth shall be full of the knowledge of the LORD as the waters cover the sea" (Isa. 11:9). This fullness of knowledge must come from the surest most profound teacher—God's own eternal life. That is how we learn of His indestructibility and incorruption, His personality, His mystery, and His very nature. Before the knowledge of God reaches the whole earth, it has reached you, the believer. You are a beachhead on this godless world, a first step for true knowledge to spread all over the globe. Believers in Christ have eternal life as the teacher on the inside and the Bible as a check and balance on the outside. God has given them anything they could possibly need to know Him in every way.

7

WHAT IS SALVATION?

BECOMING A CHILD OF GOD

A SHOCKING FACT

After a long hunt in the 1930s, police finally apprehended a particularly monstrous serial killer. Before he went to the electric chair, newspapers splashed the sordid details of his crimes all over their front pages. In the aftermath of all the publicity, the man's children changed their names as soon as they could. It was an obvious statement that they wanted no association with their father's memory. Apparently they knew the stigma that would follow them anywhere they went, to any job they would try to get, to any friends they'd try to make. There would be nervous chuckles, "You wouldn't be related to...." There would be hushed whispers, questions—"You grew up in his house. Didn't you notice anything weird?" And finally there would be idle speculations about whether the murderous father had passed some twisted gene down to his children. Most of us have never needed to deal with such a strange type of shame.

And yet, we have *all* been in those shoes. In fact, our situations were much, much worse, for before we believed in Jesus Christ, we were *children of the devil*. If that declaration seems abrasive to you then it's probably because you are so accustomed to hearing the opposite—that God is the Father of all men. Few beliefs sound so pleasant and inclusive. But the concept is simply untrue that all men share the same spiritual parentage. For the Bible divides the entire human race into "the children of God *and* the children of the devil" (1 John 3:10).

Jesus brought this truth dramatically to light when a group of people told Him "We have one Father—*God"* (John 8:41), and He replied to them, "You are of your father, *the devil"* (John 8:44). That must have been the shock of their lives. If there is a stigma attached to having a murderer for a father, how much more the one who "was a murderer from the beginning" (John 8:44)—in essence, the one who *invented* murder?

The sad fact is that the men of this world who are satanic offspring—"the seed of the serpent" (Gen. 3:14-15), typically do not know it. They mistakenly think that God is their father.

This is like a case I became familiar with a while ago, where a man miserably failed his family and deserted them. His son was left void of a father figure and desperate for anyone to fill the position. So, the little boy began latching onto any likeable male and calling him "Daddy." Though the men good-naturedly allowed it, "Daddy" was neither fitting nor true. This is the situation with unsaved people who refer to God as "Father." Yes, God allows it, but again, strictly speaking, it is not correct. The unsaved have no clue who their real father is, and if they did, they would not want to acknowledge it.

H OW M EN C OULD B E
C HILDREN OF THE D EVIL

The phrase "children of the devil" sounds impossibly surreal. What do these people look like? Perhaps we conjure up images of ghoulish evil-doers, and no doubt in part, those images can very well apply. But "the children of the devil" does not necessarily mean those who behave badly. When Jesus told His Jewish listeners that the devil was their father, He was not talking to a bunch of criminals. These were people who tried to keep the Ten Commandments and serve God.

Behavior was not the major issue Jesus was addressing, so it becomes puzzling when we consider how men could be called children of the devil. If they did not behave themselves into that status, then how did they get there? The Apostle Paul learned something about this from firsthand experience. With all his strength he had sought to be good, even prior to becoming a Christian. What he got, however, was the opposite—"The good that I will to do, I do *not* do; but the evil I will not to do, that I practice" (Rom. 7:19). The problem was not with Paul's lack of trying. He came to realize that the source of his trouble was the presence of an entirely different nature in him—"Sin...dwells in me, for I know that in me (that is, in my flesh) nothing good dwells" (Rom. 7:17-18). Where did this sin nature come from? In order to answer, we must first be aware of the principle that wherever there is a nature, we will always find a father, a source that gave it.

Your human nature, for instance, came from a human father. But where did the sin nature in you originate—that propensity to lie and cheat and hate others? We can't say we got it from a human source. Neither my earthly father nor yours invented sin. In fact, if your dad was like mine, there were some pretty strict house rules *against* evil things. In order to locate the origin of sin in us, we must trace our history all the way back to Adam. Even he, though, was not the father of sin. Romans 5:12 says that, "*through* one man sin entered the world." This means Adam was not the source of the problem. He was nothing more than an "on-ramp" for sin to enter the human race.

The real origin of sin was Satan. As the Lord said, "He is a liar and the *father* of it" (John 8:44). All that is unethical and false had its beginning in him and from the start he sought to pass it on to others. That is why behind the devil's apparently relaxed conversation with Eve was a carefully concealed desperation. His whole plan to infiltrate the human race revolved around her taking a bite of the forbidden fruit. Satan knew that the fruit represented his evil nature, and if the man and woman would just take one small bite, it would enter them. The first human beings would then become children of the devil. Later, the entire mortal race of man would inherit the dark nature Adam had received and an automatic status as satanic offspring. That of course, was exactly what happened.

Now this evil nature in men continually overpowers them, which is why the Lord Jesus said, "the desires of your father you *want* to do" (John 8:44). Later Paul added, "we all once *conducted* ourselves in the lusts of our flesh...and were by *nature* children of wrath" (Eph. 2:3).

Children of the devil definitely exist, and in large numbers. However, they do not come into being through bad attitudes and evil deeds. It was not as if they had been children of God and then lost that status because of severe misconduct. Behavior has nothing to do with it. The components that turned our race into children of the devil were a sinful father and a sinful nature. When humanity got on the receiving end of those two things they became "sons of the wicked one" (Matt. 13:38).

How Men Become Children of God

Though I have made a point of saying that all men according to their fleshly birth are children of the devil, certain Bible passages might sound like they disagree. Luke 3:38 calls Adam "the son of God." A similar thought is found

in Acts 17:28, where men are spoken of as God's "offspring."
Admittedly, there is a sense in which every man can be
considered a son of God, but only according to God's creative
hand, not according to His life.

Consider a literary classic, *The Adventures of Pinocchio*,
by Carlos Collodi. The story begins with Gepetto, an old
carpenter, fashioning a wooden puppet that is then animated
through some miraculous power. Unlike the Disney classic
adopted from Collodi's novel, this wooden boy is heartless
and cruel. In the very first chapter of the book, he smashes
the cricket, who represents his conscience. Then he sets off
on a relentless career of mischief. Still, Gepetto has a bond
of affection with the troublesome marionette and cannot
seem to ever give up on him.

Pinocchio was a wooden boy without real life, but since
he was the created product of Gepetto's hands, the old
carpenter treated him like a son. There is some pertinent
example for us in that fiction, for God can also refer to mortal
men as His sons. Yet, they are only His "sons" in the sense
of being His created image, shaped by His hands from the
dust of the earth. Man is only a "thing formed" (Rom. 9:20),
a "clay...vessel" (Rom. 9:21).

It is a mysterious and wonderful matter then, when the
Bible shows some of these beloved clay "sons" becoming
actual children of God. How could this be? The typical
answer is that they managed to change themselves through
some type of religious efforts—fasting, perhaps, or
meditation, or a program of moral improvement. But to this
the Bible rhetorically asks, "Can the Ethiopian change his
skin or the leopard his spots?" (Jer. 13:23a). Those highly
improbable things would happen before a human being
successfully "willed" himself into the status of a child of God.

We can only be the *actual* children of God by receiving
Christ, for "as many as received Him, to *them* He gave the
right to become children of God" (John 1:12). Believers have
ceased merely being clay mannequins shaped like children,
and have *become* children. Though we could correctly call
this a miracle, it is different from the parting of the Red Sea
and other works of God. Those were miracles of God's power,

but becoming a child of God is a miracle of life. When Christ came into us, the Father gave us life through Him. As John wrote, "He who has the Son has life; he who does not have the Son of God does not have life" (1 John 5:13). Yes, at one time, we did not have a life-link with God and were therefore not His real offspring. But now our situation is different. Things for us have radically changed. As the prophet said, "it shall come to pass in the place where it was said to them, 'You are not My people,' there shall they be called sons of the living God" (Rom. 9:26).

Real Children, Not Metaphors

Perhaps all of this sounds a bit too literal, especially since the phrase "children of God" has been used metaphorically from time to time in our society. The Bible says, "See how great a love the Father has bestowed upon us, that we should be called children of God" (1 John 3:1 NASB). The verse mentions being "*called* children of God" but being called something and literally being that thing can be quite different. Some people call their son-in-law "son." Others even refer to their pets as their "kids" or their motorcycle as their "baby." We understand that they are only using these words as terms of endearment and do not intend to actually mean offspring.

Could this be our case? When God calls us children, is it mainly just a term of affection? Let's return to 1 John 3:1. It says that we are called children of God, but notice the next words: "and such we *are*." We are not only *called* children, we *are* children. The Bible is telling us that "children" is no mere poetic designation. God does not love us as cherished in-laws. "He brought us forth" says James (1:18). He "begets" and has "begotten," says John. Peter says we are "newborn babes" (1 Pet. 2:2), and Paul says "infants" (Heb. 5:13). This is not just language of sentiment, but of *reproduction*.

In various ways, the Bible goes on to demonstrate our real standing as God's children. For one thing, the believers are called "brothers" more than 133 times in the New Testament. No doubt that word has been used to describe members of college fraternities, military units, and close friendships, but *brother* as applied to Christians is meant a different way. It means more than kindred feelings and affections. It refers to a shared life.

Concerning the believers, the Lord Jesus "is not ashamed to call them *brethren*" (Heb. 2:11b). For the Lord to claim us as brothers is not only a matter of how He loves us, but the fact that He and we together share a common life and thus have the same Father—"He who sanctifies and those who are being sanctified are *all of one*" (Heb. 2:11a). He is not ashamed to call us brothers, simply because we are! According to him, "brother" is not an empty label. It signifies an actual child of God.

THE MOST BLESSED PLACE OF ALL

The Bible tells us that we have been born into the family of God. However, we did not begin there. Our first birth was into the family of Adam where there is sin, condemnation, the world, and the devil. A big part of being saved, then, meant escaping our place in one family and getting into another.

Strictly speaking, even if we have the right life, it is not enough without the right position. Just ask Debra Delay. Debra always knew something wasn't right. She was a tall strawberry blonde with blue eyes. Her family, though, was a group of short, dark-haired Mexicans. It took forty years for her to verify that she had been mistakenly switched at birth. As it turned out, she had accidentally been brought home from the hospital by Mexican immigrants while her birth parents mistakenly took the other child, a Mexican infant, home to their Irish family.

It didn't matter that Debra's biological life was Irish, because all it took to change her entire future was where she was *placed*. Debra grew into a world composed of all the thoughts, priorities, views, experiences, and customs related to life in a Mexican family.

This is why the thought of adoption is so important in the Bible (Eph. 1:5; Rom. 8:15). It specifically speaks of placement. The Greek word for "adoption" literally means, "the placing of a son." It is a legal process whereby a person who was born in one family is transferred into another. However, we must be careful, because the biblical thought of adoption is not identical to the human thought. For one thing, an adopted child does not share the same life as those in his new family. That is exactly where the human idea of adoption falls short of biblical truth. Scripture portrays adoption as a transfer, a new placement, but *with* the life of the new family.

This fits the overall composite of both the ministries of Paul and John. It was exclusively John who used the word "begotten," highlighting the believer's life relationship with God. However, Paul often sought to demonstrate the believer's position before God, so he used the word "adoption." Together, the concepts of "begotten" and "placed" exactly portray our relationship to God.

Being set as a child in God's family does not mean we get a place there. No, we get *the* place there. The one valid position in the household of God is that of the Son of God, Jesus Christ. He Himself is the place into which we have been put. "In Him," "in Christ," and "in Christ Jesus," are phrases that occur repeatedly in scripture. All believers are "in Christ," and by virtue of the fact that they have been planted in Him, the Son of God, they have become the many sons of God. When the Father looks at us, He does not see many individual entities, occupying greater or lesser places before Him. He sees us all in the *unique* Son.

This does not mean that since we share the life and the place of the Lord Jesus, we have been elevated to His personal rank. The scriptures always give Him preeminence by calling Him the *"first*born over all creation" (Col. 1:15), *"first*born from the dead" (Col. 1:18), and *"first*born among many brethren" (Rom. 8:29). No one is His equal.

Although compared to Christ, the believers are the "little ones" (Matt. 18:6), they are never portrayed as poor, broken-down sinners who are pretending to be His children. Being in Christ causes the Father to see us as "sons of God" (Rom. 8:14), and standing in that blessed place, we are entitled to all the benefits of "dear children" (Eph. 5:1).

A PLACE OF EXTRAORDINARY CARE

One of the blessings related to being a child of God is that "your Father knows the things that you have need of before you ask Him" (Matt. 6:8). This fact is, in itself, comforting. No need can cross our path that has not already been completely foreseen by the Father. So, even if we cannot accurately verbalize our necessities in prayer, He understands anyway. If this is the case, though, why must we ask Him for anything? If He already knows our need, then why pray? That would be a valid question if prayer were merely informational in nature. That is, if it only functioned to present things to God that He might not have known or that He simply overlooked. In reality, prayer is more relational than informational. In every case, God is already aware of our lack; He only waits for *us* to notice it so that we will come to Him. Without such felt needs, we would go for long periods of time without approaching the Father. This is like the college student who goes away to school, becomes embroiled in campus life, and gets into a bad habit of never writing or calling home. Then one day the money runs dry and he remembers that he has parents out there somewhere. Of course, when he calls home, it is a pleasant occasion for the parents, even if the bottom line is financial need. God also values our "calls home." He enjoys our communication with Him, though it took a mini-crisis to trigger it.

Neither does prayer mean that we must beg the Father to care for us. The Lord said, "If you then, being evil know how to give good gifts to your children, how much more will your Father who is in heaven give good things to those who ask Him!" (Matt. 7:11). In fact, those who are not His children (called "Gentiles") are anxiously seeking their needs (Matt. 6:31-32), because they do not sense that they have a heavenly Father. They pray to Him, but have no compelling reason to believe that He will answer their prayer or help them at all. Deep within, they know that they are not the children of God, so their prayer often resorts to begging, bribing, and sometimes even threatening Him. In a healthy relationship, children never have to do this with their fathers, because they trust that their fathers will do what is right for them.

While my daughter Elizabeth was still a toddler, she would wander through a crowd, see me, and without a word, hold up her arms. That meant "I might recognize other people here, but you are the only one that *has* to pick me up. I trust you will respond to me. Many others are friendly but only you are *Daddy*." She never once had to say, "If you pick me up, I'll pay you" or, "I'll take you to court if you don't feed me!" Good fathers don't require such negotiations or threats. And if they, being imperfect mortal men, can love their little ones so easily, how much more God the Father, whose love is perfect?

Maybe as a child of God, you remember some crushing disappointment when He did not seem to come through for you. But parental care also extends into the area of *not* giving a child everything he asks for. The Lord said, "What man is there among you, who, if his son asks for bread will give him a stone? Or if he asks for a fish, will give him a serpent?" (Matt. 7:9-10).

The question is, what happens when Christians, not knowing what is good for them, ask for stones or serpents instead of bread or fish? We often foolishly pray for items or opportunities, which, if we got them, would cripple our spiritual life (or even our physical life!). We are shortsighted, as children often are, and see no harm in asking for this or that. Many of us are surprised when the Father does not provide what we want, and especially when He provides the opposite. In cases like that, we may have had little or no wisdom, so the Father graciously ignored our requests and provided what He felt was good for us. Think of how many times as a child you wanted toys but parental wisdom gave you clothes. You wanted candy but got broccoli. You wanted television but got homework. To the juvenile mind it was all unfair. But where the love of a parent is concerned, there is no such thing as unfair. In the interests of the health, care, and training of a beloved child, a parent might withhold all kinds of pleasures and comforts. God the Father would do no less for us. He protects us even from our own foolish desires.

A PLACE ALWAYS WATCHED OVER

The children of God are never left alone, unguarded and unobserved. We are told that "the very hairs of your head are all numbered" (Matt. 10:30). God the Father notices everything about us and monitors with loving concern every tiny detail of our lives. And this is not only restricted to outward matters. Even our inward meditations do not escape His notice:

> "O Lord, you have searched me and known me...you understand my thought afar off...there is not a word on my tongue, but behold, O Lord, you know it altogether." (Ps. 139:1-4)

So, the child of God cannot escape unobserved, even into some inner recess of the brain, because the Father can follow him there.

Some Christians aren't always excited about this "everywhere" Father. They feel the same way that teenagers do about a parent who always seems to show up and crash the party. I was one of those "blessed" teenagers. One day while I was in high school, I decided to cut class and walk home. It was easy. The school was a short distance from my house, and both my parents were at work. I would relax in a big easy chair, eat snacks, and listen to music for the rest of the day. But as I was beginning to do just that, and congratulating myself on how smart I was, my dad pulled up in the driveway. Presumably, he was taking a rare home lunch break.

What followed was one of those adrenaline-filled

moments when you have to do something, even if it's crazy. So, seconds before he opened the door, I dove into the tiny crawl space behind our couch. He had shown up at the worst possible time but surely, I thought, I'd be safely hidden in that sliver of carpet between the couch and the wall. For the second time I congratulated myself on how smart I was. No one would ever dream of looking in that dark little spot...or so I thought.

At that moment a random chain of events began to occur. The phone rang. Through the couch I could hear a muffled conversation. "Yeah, I'll help," my dad said, apparently talking to my mother. Then the vacuum cleaner started at the back of the house, working its way through all the rooms down the hallway to the living room and the area around the back of the couch. It was almost as if my dad had followed a trail of bread crumbs straight to me. But I was still okay. He wasn't at the right angle to see behind the couch. Before I had a chance to breathe a sigh of relief, though, he leaned over to pick up a piece of lint and there the two of us were, looking full into one another's faces. I can laugh about the whole thing, now that twenty-five years have passed, but needless to say, being discovered that afternoon was not a very "comfy" experience. Afterwards I didn't tell myself I was smart again for at least a week.

The best parents always seem to have a penchant for finding their kids, for looking out the window at the right moment, and for passing by in a car at precise times. Kids hate it, but it is just what they need. Rest assured that God would do no less with His own children. Volumes could be written about how He showed up in the lives of His children when they least expected it—or wanted it. For example, as Sam is in the middle of a sin, the telephone rings. It is a call from another Christian who wants to pray with him. Brenda is headed somewhere that she shouldn't go, when, for some reason, she fixates upon the Jesus bumper sticker on the car in front of her. Mel is in the middle of a wild party when his friend suddenly wants him to explain what this God "stuff" is all about. In each case, the Father somehow made His presence known to the wandering, hiding believer.

Nothing is concealed from Him, even the things we wish to conceal.

Some new Christians sometimes flirt with their sinful past, going back to indulge in it again. Don't think the Lord won't notice a "vacation" of that kind. Our heavenly Father never loses sight of His children. There will never be a time in your Christian life when you will be unaccounted for. Perhaps according to your short experience as a believer, you have already felt lost, but, in fact, you have never been lost, even for a second. In low times it is easy to start thinking that "the Lord has forsaken me, and my Lord has forgotten me" (Isa. 49:14). God's response to this mistaken thought is to tell us, "Can a woman forget her nursing child, and not have compassion on the son of her womb? Surely they may forget, yet I will not forget you. See, I have inscribed you in the palms of my hands..." (Isa. 49:15-16a).

A PLACE OF PROTECTION

It is common knowledge that you shouldn't get between the young of certain animals and their mothers. A harmless pig, for instance, can quickly turn into a three-hundred-pound battering ram if she thinks someone is threatening her piglets. It works the same way with a bear and her cubs, a hen and her chicks, and even the beloved family dog, who may become irate with someone handling her puppies. The protective instinct of a parent is in all of them, and in human beings as well.

God Himself possesses the purest and most powerful concern for His children. To Him we are not adherents of the Christian religion, subscribers to the teachings of Jesus, or followers of the Judeo-Christian ethic. The moment we are placed in His Son, He sees us as "dear children" (Eph. 5:1). That is why He desires to protect us and sometimes even to avenge us.

We do have examples of God's parental outrage in the Bible. One revolved around the way the Jews treated the Lord Jesus. In a parable (Matt. 21:33-41), God was symbolized as the owner of a vineyard who leases it out to vinedressers (the Jewish leaders of the day). Later, when the owner (God), sent His servants (representing the prophets) to the vineyard, they "took his servants, beat one, killed one, and stoned another" (Matt. 21:35). Seeing the futility of sending servants, the owner (God), "sent *his son* to them, saying, 'They will respect my son.' But when the vinedressers saw the son, they said among themselves, 'This is the heir. Come, let us kill him and seize His inheritance.' So they took him and cast him out of the vineyard and killed him" (Matt. 21:37-39). At this point in the parable, the Lord Jesus paused and asked His Jewish listeners, "When the owner of the vineyard comes, what will he do to those vinedressers?" (Matt. 21:40). The audience supplied the verdict: "He will destroy those wicked men" (Matt. 21:41).

Then, "the chief priests and Pharisees...perceived that He was speaking of them" (Matt. 21:45). Upon realizing this, these men should have been warned about mistreating Christ. The parable had indicated that the Almighty Father was fully behind Him, had called Him "My Son," and had sent Him to Israel. And if anyone laid violent hands upon that Son, the offended Father would penalize their unrepentant hatred. They should have listened, but didn't.

History tells us that approximately thirty-seven years after the Lord Jesus was crucified, the Roman army marched into Jerusalem and destroyed it, killing thousands and leveling the Jewish temple. Don't think, though, that God was some vindictive Person, who vented His wrath right away. Remember that the destruction of Jerusalem occurred thirty-seven years *after* Christ's crucifixion. During the intervening time, the gospel of the forgiveness of sins was preached in the city continually. God offered a chance to repent for those who would listen. At the time the gospel was, for the most part rejected, then retribution came— "When they made light of it...he sent out his armies, destroyed those murderers, and burned up their city" (Matt. 22:5, 7). The point is that God highly esteems His Son, and it is very risky to abuse Him. There are definite consequences, as the example of Jerusalem demonstrates.

Since God's favor rests so strongly upon His Son, judgment always comes to men as a result of how they treat Him. Now the believers are those who have been placed in this Son. Because of their standing in Him, the Father favors them with the same jealous care. This will be graphically proven at the end of the age. Then, the nations remaining on the earth will be judged based upon how they treated Christians, even in the smallest details—"Whoever gives one of these little ones only a cup of cold water to drink in the name of a disciple, assuredly, I say to you, he shall by no means lose his reward" (Matt. 10:42). To all those who have done things to us, both good and bad, the Lord Jesus will say, "Inasmuch as you did it to one of the least of these, My brethren, you did it to Me" (Matt. 25:40).

It seems fantastic that the eternal destinies of nations are being decided not only based upon their attitudes toward the Son of God, but according to their treatment of the *sons* of God. Outwardly, Christians do not seem any more special than anyone else. They are not smarter or richer, and they certainly don't wear halos. Making them the grounds for any kind of judgment, then, sounds funny. However, God is not joking. When it comes to us, He is dead serious. We find that it is not advisable even to *neglect* the welfare of a believer. As the Lord told those He judged, "Inasmuch as *you did not do it* to one of the least of these, *you did not do it* to Me" (Matt. 25:45). The resultant penalty for indifference to the children of God is "everlasting fire" (Matt. 25:41). The sentence is shocking, but indicative of God's heart towards even the smallest believer.

Often there are deliberate attempts from others to obstruct the progress of a new Christian. The people doing it might think they are only playing around, seeing if they can shake the new believer's faith with questions or arguments. Some folks have even tried to bait new Christians back into sin by using alcohol, drugs, or sex. But stumbling them is foolish, for, in many cases, God has worked long years to save them. He has loved them and drawn them to faith, has begotten them, and placed them in His Son. Where God is concerned, hurting that person's spiritual life is like confusing and killing a little child. The Lord Jesus warns, "Whoever causes one of these little ones who believe in Me to sin, it would be better for him if a millstone were hung around his neck and he were drowned in the depth of the sea" (Matt. 18:6).

Still, poor treatment of believers often escalates from "just playing around" and gets into malicious acts—things like violence or threats or other kinds of intimidation. Reports regularly emerge from different quarters about Christians being beaten or murdered. We believers are not guaranteed immunity from suffering for our faith in this world. However, the Bible solemnly testifies that "It is a righteous thing with God to repay with tribulation those who trouble you" (2 Thess. 1:6) and "'Vengeance is Mine, I will repay,' says the Lord" (Rom. 12:19).

The physical world is not the only place where God's children experience His protection. The spiritual world is also fraught with danger. Take Job, an Old Testament character, as an example. While he was down here on the earth worshiping God, he was totally unaware of what was going on in the spiritual realm, where the human eye cannot see. The Bible pulls the curtains back on a scene that might have filled him with dismay had he witnessed it. For there we find that Satan was familiar with the man and despised him in the worst kind of way. That is why he threw his best efforts into assassinating Job's character and moving the Lord against him. Satan said to God, "Stretch out Your hand and touch *all that he has*, and he will surely curse you to Your face!" (Job 1:11). Then later, he added, "stretch out Your hand now, and touch *his bone and his flesh*, and he will surely curse You to Your face!" (Job 2:5).

Each time, God allowed the devil to bring trials into Job's life, but with careful limitations. First, "the Lord said to Satan, 'Behold, all that he has is in your power; only *do not lay a hand on his person*'" (1:12). Even when the trials were about to become increasingly fierce and painful, the divine protection was not completely withdrawn—"the Lord said to Satan, 'Behold, he is in your hand, *but spare his life*'" (Job 2:6).

These examples show that the devil is not free to act however he pleases with the Lord's people. The Lord must grant him permission. It's a very sensitive matter to discipline someone else's children. About twenty-five years ago in the south, paddling was still used in the school system. But before teachers could do it, they had to obtain a signed permission slip from the parent. In a similar way, before the devil can do anything against the children of God, the Father must allow it. He must grant permission, and even then, he sets stringent limitations. In Luke 22:31, the Lord Jesus warned Peter, "Satan has *asked* for you, that he may sift you as wheat." Satan could not simply take. He could not bypass the looming, all-powerful Father and simply make off with the children.

Neither Peter nor any of the rest of the disciples could be touched without permission. And when permission is granted and the believers enter trials, they often find that their faith ends up established in a far stronger way. Peter wrote that "After you have suffered a while, [God] will Himself perfect, establish, strengthen, and settle you" (1 Pet. 5:10). Though the devil always hopes to destroy us, the Father knows how to bend or limit satanic persecution so that we would actually benefit from it. We are told, "You have been grieved by various trials, that the genuineness of your faith, being much more precious than gold that perishes, though it is tested by fire, may be found to praise, honor, and glory, at the revelation of Jesus Christ" (1 Pet. 1:6b-7).

One of the greatest blessings that we have as children of God is an almighty Father who is so much for us. As the verse asks, "If God is for us, who can be against us?" (Rom. 8:31). The endless stream of His care, watchfulness, and protection makes us able to say, "how precious...are your thoughts to me, O God! How great is the sum of them! If I should count them, they would be more in number than the sand" (Ps. 139:17-18).

MATURING IN GOD'S FAMILY

God's love for His children is not random and aimless. He cares for us in such remarkable ways for a reason—so that we would grow into fully mature sons of God. The problem is that we have no idea what that means or how to get there. What should a spiritually mature "you" look like, anyway? It's very hard to say. This is a question that doesn't even come easy in the physical life. Sometimes when kids try to imagine themselves thirty years older, they draw a blank. What will they look like or sound like or how will they think about things? They don't know. Even their best guesses can sound pretty humorous. "When I grow up I'm going to spend all of my money on toys and candy" or "I'm going to live in a treehouse with my dog, Spot" are the types of things said. At the beginning stages of Christian life, there can be just as many clueless ideas about what the future holds. What does God do to facilitate our arrival at maturity, when we hardly even know what it looks like? The answer, again, is placement. God takes ignorant sinners and positions them in the unique Son of God. Why? So that they may "learn Christ" (Eph. 4:19). This is very similar to the idea of an apprenticeship, where an inexperienced person is placed next to an expert, so that he can properly develop in his field. We have been placed in such close proximity to the unique Son of God so that we can learn how to be sons of God. This is both an experiential and an educational process that all Christians must go through.

The Lord Jesus Himself went through a learning process while here on earth. Concerning His own relationship with the Father, He said, "I always do those things that please Him" (John 8:29b). He had no sin and never made a mistake, yet still He "*learned* obedience by the things which He suffered" (Heb. 5:8). The Lord already knew what it meant to be the Son of God in heaven with glorious immortality and no pain or limitation. But upon becoming a man, He entered the experiences of being the Son of God on the earth. This meant living in a world manipulated by the devil, filled with weak, ignorant companions, and all the infirmities and limitations of the human life. He successfully passed through this process with "loud crying and tears" (Heb. 5:7 NASB), to become a mold into which all the believers would be cast. Now since He is the very definition of what it means to be called "Son," we are all destined to be sons "*through Jesus Christ*" (Eph. 1:5 NASB). All of God's newly born children are placed in Him to "grow up in all things into Him" (Eph. 4:15).

This growth will continue until a time in the future when we reach full conformity to Christ (Rom. 8:29). Then we will look exactly like the Son of God in every part of our being. As of now, we do not. Any honest believer will admit that in terms of his thoughts, behavior, attitudes, and priorities he does not always resemble Jesus. In fact, he may look more like a child of the devil!

This very problem necessitates another area of divine parenting—the Father's discipline. Due to our tendency to stray and settle into bad habits, chastisement of some kind is needed. It is just like the biblical principle states: "Foolishness is bound up in the heart of a child; the rod of correction will drive it far from him" (Prov. 22:15). Now admittedly, this doesn't sound like fun. "All discipline for the moment seems not to be joyful, but sorrowful" (Heb. 12:11 NASB). You never appreciate discipline until you look back to see where you might have ended up without it.

Yet not all discipline is punitive. Strictly speaking, discipline is a guided exercise of learning and correction with a positive end in view. In any healthy family, the process of growing up is discipline oriented. I was born into the Myer family. Naturally, I had no idea what it meant to be a Myer son except through parental rewards, reinforcement, encouragement, and responsibilities. I remember certain specifics that made profound impressions upon me. Once while I was still very young, I saved my brother from drowning. This was highly praised, impressing upon me that a Myer son should value the life of another Myer son. According to my father, other lessons were needed as well, like learning how to treat younger sisters, properly addressing adults, and even caring for an overweight cocker spaniel. Table manners were enforced, and I was not allowed to escape from chores like washing dishes. It was all the process of becoming a son, though for a while, the positive effect of it would only show up in glimmers. The moment I was not under a guiding hand, I would revert to behaving like a wild boy raised by wolves. It took a long time to conform me to the image of a "Myer."

As children of God we will pass through innumerable lessons related to growing in Christ. Some of these will involve God withholding things we really wanted but did not need. Others will have to do with allowing us to get our way in order to find out that our way was the worst thing for us. Other lessons deal with bad attitudes and areas of life where we do not allow God to lead us. There are also those related to handling rejection, misunderstanding, forgiveness, service, healthy judgment, and holiness in all things. Even the Apostle Paul had to learn these lessons. For instance, apparently, his many glorious revelations of Christ had the tendency to make him proud. What could God do about such a problem? Paul needed to see great revelations in order to help us all, yet if his pride went unchecked, his Christian life would have been ruined. The answer was discipline. Paul later wrote, "to keep me from exalting myself, there was given me a thorn in the flesh, a messenger of Satan to buffet me—to keep me from exalting myself!" (2 Cor. 12:7). Paul hadn't intended to become proud, but it is a habit of fallen human nature to become that way. The "thorn," therefore, was a correction and a protection to him. No one knows what his "thorn" actually was, whether physical, psychological, or spiritual, but the suffering it caused reminded Paul that he was still a weak mortal man who was dependent upon grace. Thus Paul learned to despise any form of self-glory. This was God conforming him to the "mold" of Jesus Christ, the One who had said, "I honor My Father...I do not seek My own glory" (John 8:49-50) and "If I honor Myself, My honor is nothing..." (John 8:54).

God the Father employs everything great and small to complete our growth—"All things are yours: whether Paul or Apollos or Cephas or the world or life or death, or things present or things to come—*all are yours*" (1 Cor. 3:21-22). The world and even the universe itself revolves around God maturing His children—*"All* things work together for good to those who love God, to those who are called according to His purpose" (Rom. 8:28).

GROWING PAINS AMONG GOD'S CHILDREN

When the Bible says that "all things work" toward our maturation as sons, that includes God's correction. I'm well aware that the concept of punitive discipline is likely to draw some winces. Maybe you had an authority figure in your life that was abusive. The limitation of human fathers is that "they disciplined us for a short time as seemed best to *them"* (Heb. 12:10 NASB). Sometimes due to human weakness a parent will lash out and deliver some type of punishment that only acts as a release valve for his own anger. I made it an early practice never to spank my daughter while I was angry. This was sometimes difficult, but I knew that discipline had to be something good for her, not me. So, I would wait for every bit of negative emotion to leave me before I did anything. Of course, then there was another problem. After I had gotten over my anger, I found myself not wanting to discipline her anymore. Why bother now that I wasn't mad? Again, I had to realize that discipline was not for the sake of my emotional release, but for her learning and training. I found that it took the strongest kind of self-discipline to consistently discipline someone else, especially if they had big, blue eyes and pigtails and said "Daddy" in the most charming way.

God, of course, is the model of a Father who measures out discipline according to whatever is "for *our* good that we may share His holiness" (Heb. 12:10 NASB). So, before we curse certain circumstances or begin to hate certain people, it is good to stop and ask ourselves, "Is it not from the mouth of the Most High that woe *and* well being proceed?" (Lam. 3:38). God Himself says, "I make peace *and* create calamity" (Isa. 45:7). The point is that, as we negatively respond to life's many situations, we should be careful, for we may be unfavorably responding to God Himself. To this attitude the scripture says, "My son, do not regard lightly the discipline of the Lord, nor faint when you are reproved by Him" (Heb. 12:5).

I have made a strong point of discipline here, since it is so terribly misunderstood in the new believer's experience. Some arrive at the conclusion that hardships occurring right after salvation must mean God has placed a curse on them or abandoned them. This is exactly the opposite of the biblical view which states, "Those whom the Lord *loves* He disciplines, and He scourges every son whom He *receives*" (Heb. 12:6). In fact, discipline is so strongly related to being God's child, that the Bible warns us concerning the *absence* of it: "If you are *without* discipline, of which all have become partakers, then you are illegitimate children, and not sons" (Heb. 12:8). In other words, if God's disciplinary hand is missing from someone's life, it is an indication that such a person is fatherless.

I like the old story of two boys who were fighting. A man rushed out of the house and grabbed one of them by the collar. As he disciplined him, an onlooker pointed out that the other boy was more at fault. The man shouted back, "I don't know about that other boy, but this one is *mine!*" The other boy escaped not because he was more highly favored. He escaped because he *wasn't* a son.

If we only understood this principle, then the inequity of life wouldn't bother us Christians so much. For instance, we notice certain evil people prospering, people that cheat and steal and lie and do dirty things with impunity. Instead of catastrophes falling upon them to punish their wrongs, their bank accounts seem to increase. Nothing bad ever seems to happen to them, so a believer might begin to envy their "peace," that is, their lack of divine discipline. Even characters in the Bible were tempted to do this. One was a psalmist named Asaph, who wrote Psalm 73. In it he said, "I was envious of the boastful, when I saw the prosperity of the wicked...They are not in trouble as other men, nor are they plagued like other men...Their eyes bulge with abundance; they have more than the heart could wish...Behold, these are the ungodly, who are always at ease; they increase in riches" (Ps. 73:3, 5, 7, 12). Later, Asaph came to understand the pitiful fruit of lives that grow without God's loving restriction. He described them with words like "destruction," "desolation," "consumed," and "terrors" (Ps. 73:17-19).

A lack of heavenly discipline is a negative matter, marking people who do not belong to God. That is why in relation to the wicked we find phrases like "God gave them up" (Rom. 1:24, 26, 28) to do whatever they wanted, and in relation to pagans that He "overlooked" their idolatry (Acts 17:29-30). When sinners seem to get all the breaks, it doesn't mean they're lucky. It means they're spiritually illegitimate.

Children always seem to complain when those from other families have more liberties than they are allowed to have. So-and-so always gets to go here or there...*and I don't.* So-and-so always gets to wear this or that...*and I don't.* Most parents simply say, "What those other kids do is none of my business." There's a lot packed into that response. Roughly translated, it means, *"You* are my business. I will never stop raising you. I will never abandon you to find your own way in this world. Even if I pity you and would like to see you stay up late and have candy anytime you want and watch whatever television programs you want and skip piano lessons and let your grades dip lower than they ought to be, I won't allow these things, because of the harm they might bring to you."

Now, if a sinful parent feels this kind of responsibility toward his child, it must be infinitely more so with God. "I will not leave you orphans" is His promise to us (John 14:18). God never begets people and then leaves them to raise themselves. "He who has begun a good work in you will complete it until the day of Jesus Christ" (Phil. 1:6).

It is written that "he who spares his rod hates his son, but he who loves him, disciplines him promptly" (Prov. 13:24). The "rod" of discipline is an integral part of growing up in God's family. It literally shapes our character, direction, outlook, and attitude. That is exactly why the child who does not receive it is said to be "hated"—because he is doomed to have an unshaped, ill-prepared, or even warped future. God would never be so remiss with His children. An all-wise hand is resting upon us, one that is driven by the depths of parental love.

The question arises concerning Christians who do not respond to the "rod" of the Lord. Even after God disciplines them, they continue living a sinful life. In fact, discipline only seems to make them angrier and more determined to resist Him. What happens to these believers? Some have arrived at the extreme conclusion that God will "unsave" them by withdrawing His salvation, and then that child will no longer be His child. But as I stressed in the earlier part of this chapter, we are not God's foster children. We are His *begotten*. We belong to Him by birth and not only by legal arrangement. Therefore this limits what can legitimately be done about a "problem child." He cannot be returned as though he were a department store purchase. He cannot be disposed of as if he were the kitchen trash. His birth cannot be undone as if loosing a knot. (For a much more detailed analysis, see the chapters dealing with eternal security.)

What then can the Father do with children who resist growing up? This is a larger problem than what we realize. It is a fact that at the time of their deaths, many Christians are still spiritually immature. The solution to this dilemma is for God to continue their maturing process *in the next age*. A number of Bible verses portray the discipline that can come upon lazy, sinful believers at the time they stand before Christ. The Lord whips one (Luke 12:47-48), sends another to "outer darkness" (Matt. 25:30), and shames another (Matt. 24:48-51). These verses present such a stern picture that it might seem confusing. Would the Lord deal with His beloved children in such a way? Some Bible readers who confront these passages feel that it could not be. "God loves us," they say. "He would never be so harsh or strict." Then they offer alternate explanations—that those dealt with so strongly must not be real Christians. They must be unsaved people. But there is little evidence to support such a view. And we need not adopt it, either, in order to preserve the concept of God as the loving Father of the believers.

Even the best father might resort to extreme methods in order to deal with a child who was out of control. For example, under normal conditions, a household with a few children is generally peaceful. However, if the kids begin using drugs, destroying the house, or hurting each other, the disciplinary approach of the parents will change. For one thing, the father will no longer appear to be kind and gentle. If He does not get through to the unruly children after initial efforts, he may adopt even harsher measures. As the situation requires it, his severity will escalate.

This is what is happening in the Bible when God seems to behave in an uncharacteristically strong way toward some believers. He is simply rising to their need. Thank God that our stubbornness cannot make Him give up. The Father will at last overcome all the obstacles in our dispositions and will bring us into maturity. Though some believers resist His work in this age, the Bible does not show any resisting it in the next.

This may be an unsettling thought for Christians who have been assured that no matter what they do on earth, all will be comfortable in the future. But God has chosen us for maturity in Christ and He intends to complete that process, either now or later.

THE FUTURE GREATNESS OF GOD'S CHILDREN

Richie Rich was a comic book character who was a child of fabulous wealth. He had his own helicopter, motorcycles, a butler, and parents who lavished a fortune in weekly allowance upon him. Young readers of that comic eventually dreamed of being in Richie's shoes. It was thought that a child of such privilege could have anything he wanted and do anything he wanted, whenever he wanted.

Real life, however, is another story. Very often children from families with a long tradition of wealth and power are treated with the strictest discipline. They have meals that don't always include pizza or cheeseburgers (try flaming duck-kabob or swordfish ala-something). Their social functions don't always involve parties and hanging out (except maybe with folks fifty years older than they are and to music from another century). Their extracurricular activities might involve more than basketball (fencing or equestrian lessons, anyone?). Their schedules include bedtimes (sooner than they'd like), and wakeups (earlier than they'd like). And if the child of privilege strays from parental expectations in any of those areas, discipline will come to correct his attitude. Why? Not only because he needs to mature, but because of his future responsibilities. This child is being groomed to inherit a huge fortune or a giant business or perhaps even a throne. His great future requires careful training in the present.

Now it is true that some children of wealth and privilege end up living however they please with little or no restraint. They are the ones who squander the family fortune. Since they have not been made to understand the concept of self-sacrifice, suffering, and hard work, eventually, they cannot run the family business or oversee its interests.

There is an application in all this to the children of God. We are "those who will *inherit* salvation" (Heb. 1:14) and it is "an *inheritance*, incorruptible and undefiled and that does not fade away, kept in heaven for you" (1 Pet. 1:4). Inheritance comes only after we have grown into fully mature sons. That is because without maturity, we cannot handle it. In this world there are children who scheduled to inherit a gigantic estate. Before they can receive it they must grow up so that they can properly manage it. A six-year-old, for instance, who prematurely received a one hundred million-dollar inheritance would be cheated out of it by any scoundrel who could get near him. Even without "help," the child himself might squander his fortune on frivolous things. Observe what happened in the parable of Luke 15. The prodigal son decided to receive His inheritance before he was ready. The outcome was that "he squandered his estate with loose living" (Luke 15:13).

As a rule of thumb, the greater the inheritance, the greater the training needed to receive it. God's training is the most thorough of all because He wishes to give us an awesome inheritance. Paul said, "I consider that the sufferings of this present time are not worthy to be compared with the coming *glory* which shall be revealed in us" (Rom. 8:18). No one is exactly sure of what this will look like, but John gives the mysterious assurance that "we are children of God; and it has not yet been revealed what we shall be, but we know that when He is revealed, we shall be like Him, for we shall see Him as He is" (1 John 3:2). At some point in the future, a marvelous thing will happen and "we shall be" something far more glorious and wonderful than we are now. Currently, in outward appearance, we look like all other men; our status as children of God is somewhat hidden. But at the point of maturity, the glory hidden inside of us will be manifested, it will be "the *revealing* of the sons of God" (Rom. 8:19). At that time, the Lord will "transform our lowly body" (Phil. 3:21), manifesting to everyone that we are His sons. Our current state is that we are "eagerly waiting for the adoption, the redemption of our *body*" (Rom. 8:23), because when it happens, our physical mortality with all its ailments, injuries, limitations, birth defects, and genetic problems will be "swallowed up in victory" (1 Cor. 15:54). We will, in a very real sense, inherit the glory of God *bodily*.

This state of maturity will enable us to handle some lofty responsibilities. We will rule over cities (Luke 19:18-19), reign as kings (Rev. 22:5), have authority over all the Lord's possessions (Matt. 12:47), judge the world and angels (1 Cor. 6:2-3), and be the eternal city in which God dwells (Rev. 21:10-11, 1 Pet. 2:4). Think what would happen if an immature believer somehow managed to attain any one of those things. Chaos would result if such great matters fell into the hands of a self-indulgent believer. How could a Christian judge fallen angels if he himself had not learned to hate sin and love the holiness of God? How could he be placed over all the Lord's possessions if he had hardly learned to care about the things of God? Only maturity could enable us to adequately handle the privileges and exalted rank God wishes to bestow upon us.

Everything changed for us in the moment we believed the gospel of Christ. We became "little children" (1 John 2:1, 28), people born of God and therefore entitled to all of His care and protection. And now, during this short earthly existence, we are silently, invisibly being prepared for a glorious tomorrow full of things which "eye has not seen and ear has not heard and which have not come up in man's heart..." (1 Cor. 2:9).

8

HOW TO BE SAVED

No Shortcuts, Please

In case you thought about skipping this chapter since you're already saved, *don't* do it. When people ignore or fly through instructions because they think they don't need them, the results can be pretty lousy.

One night I tried to help out with dinner by making a side dish—stuffing. It was the boxed kind with directions that had to be scrupulously followed. Of course, smart guys don't need that kind of guidance. They can get by with common sense and a few looks at the pretty picture on the front of the package. I raced through the directions, doing a few creative modifications along the way. The stuffing was ready before I knew it, but we couldn't dig it out of the pot—not with conventional tools, anyway. It's amazing how a few altered directions and a low flame could produce something so...strange. The "stuffing" didn't look like the picture on the box, although it did resemble a very dense car wash sponge.

Likewise, if you and I don't slow down and absorb the directions related to being saved, then we'll ignore or "improve" them. That would mean ending up with a Christian life quite different from the kind shown in "the picture." What the New Testament describes and what we would have would not match very much at all.

B E W A R E   O F   T H E   G A L A T I A N   T R A I L

Knowing how you were saved is incredibly important. The way that you think you became a Christian will forever influence how you will continue as one. You should understand as clearly as possible how you began, otherwise your Christian journey will take you to places you really don't need to go, and inflict a lot of unnecessary hardships.

This was the case with the Galatian believers. Paul asked them, "Are you so foolish? Having *begun* in the Spirit, are you *now* being made perfect by the flesh?" (Gal. 3:3).

A Christian's "beginning" and his "now" are supposed to be an interwoven whole, not two disconnected experiences. The Galatians didn't see that. They thought salvation came one way, but the Christian life continued another way. According to them, their beginning had little or no bearing on their present. How they had begun was something behind them. Now it was time to roll up their sleeves and get busy being religious. Paul called such thinking "foolish." He knew that if a person's Christian life departed from its healthy beginning it would become dysfunctional.

When the Galatians set off in a direction that was different from their glorious start, their Christian lives degenerated. "The sense of blessing" among them disappeared (Gal. 4:15 NASB). Where they had once received

Paul "as an angel of God, even as Christ Jesus" (Gal. 4:14), they later began to see him as their opponent (Gal. 4:16). These believers, "before whose eyes Jesus Christ was clearly portrayed...as crucified" (Gal. 3:1), traded that focus for something else. They fixated upon slavish religious commandments, becoming people "who desire to be under the law" (Gal. 4:21).

Paul's solution to the complicated mess they had made was to remind them how they had *begun* the Christian life— "This only I want to learn from you: Did you receive the Spirit by the works of the law, or by the hearing of faith?" (Gal. 3:2). In essence, that rhetorical question asked, *Do you see all the useless things you've subjected yourselves to in the name of being a good Christian? Now look back to the beginning of your life with Christ. Consider the simple, joyful faith you began with and tell me if it matches where you're at today.*

Unfortunately, many Christians have taken the "Galatian trail" and been led into spiritual poverty. Feeling hopelessly mired in their dull condition, they try all kinds of new experiences and practices to get out of it. When the dust settles, though, the new "stuff" has compounded the problem. It has only made a lengthier list of things the believer "ought" to be doing.

The key to our current spiritual problems is often found in understanding our beginning. Suppose we were to tell the Apostle Paul, "I cannot go on being a Christian. It is too hard keeping up with all the things Christians are supposed to do." He would very likely ask in return, "How were you saved? That is how God wishes you to continue." It stands to reason then, that the more clearly we understand our start, the better equipped we will be to follow Christ until the end.

GRACE—NOT SO EASY TO UNDERSTAND

A believer reading instructions on how to be saved might

appear as redundant as a fellow in New York trying to learn how to get to New York. Of course he already knows, doesn't he? Well, maybe not. And neither, necessarily, does a saved person clearly know how a person gets saved. History assures us of this. One of the earliest debates in the church revolved around how a man is saved. Right in the midst of Christians in the first century, "Certain men...taught the brethren, saying, 'Unless you are circumcised according to the custom of Moses, you *cannot* be saved'" (Acts 15:1). From that point on for two thousand years, there have been constant repeats of such confused teachings. Many have warned that salvation cannot come without special activities, practices, or ceremonies. Others have held the idea that self-reform is the key to being made right with God. Some from the fringes of Christendom have tried to introduce blatantly weird ideas that are little more than sheer superstition. For some reason, confusion continues to endure, despite the fact that the New Testament clearly tells us how a person is saved. Written there in different ways almost one hundred times, we find that salvation comes by believing in Jesus Christ. Faith in Christ is what makes human beings right with God.

It doesn't take a genius to read and understand the phrase "a man is justified by faith" (Rom. 3:28). The problem comes when we read it, understand it, and do not quite believe it. "By faith" sounds too good to be true. It couldn't be that simple. There's got to be more to it than that. We find it hard to accept that something as great as salvation could be received so easily. If forgiveness of sins and eternal life can be obtained just by believing in Jesus, then it would be virtually *free*.

That's right. We were "justified *freely* by His grace" (Rom. 3:24). The words "justified," "freely," and "grace" always go together. They cannot be separated. God will only *give* His salvation. He will not sell it or bestow it as a reward. If someone will not take it for free, then God will not give it. If a man offers to do something for salvation, God will refuse to give it because under those circumstances, it would not be given freely out of His grace. This is a critical New

Testament truth. It is just as important to understand how salvation is given as it is to understand the content of salvation itself. In fact, if anyone turns away from the gospel of the *grace* of Christ to another gospel—one that requires human effort, will power, or works—they are, in effect, turning to a false gospel (Gal. 1:6-7).

Why would anyone turn away from a free gift? Well, I do it all the time and so do you. Think of the occasions when you entered a store and there was a special table set up where someone was offering a "free" gift. Most of us have walked right past it because the sign said "Free kitchen utensil," but the small print said "Upon completion of credit card application." I've become desensitized to anything with the word "free" on it, especially mail. In my house, "free!" printed on an envelope guarantees it a trip straight to the trash. Any worldly offer of grace is suspicious. As the old saying goes, "If it sounds too good to be true, it probably is."

So, we wonder if anything is truly free. Even though God offers eternal life as a " *free* gift" (Rom. 6:23 NASB), our minds, so accustomed to being deceived by the world, still wonder if there are hidden costs. Maybe the Bible has concealed them. Of course, that view would make salvation resemble a very long contract with a *lot* of fine print. You sign your name at the top and then later, upon closer scrutiny, you find out what you really owe. But when God says "Free," He does not go back and erode the meaning of the word with a multitude of small qualifications. In fact, the Bible avoids the principle of "Yes, Yes and No, No" (2 Cor. 1:17). Since God says, "Yes, yes, salvation is free," then we can trust He will not say, "No, no it's not really free."

Once we've established that something *is* truly free, the next question is whether that item is worth having. For instance, you may somehow get a free alarm clock, but it needs to be stomped in order to stop ringing in the morning. The free egg flipper melts right in the skillet. The free wallet bends and fractures like a piece of particleboard. After experiences like those, we find ourselves preferring *not* to have anything free. In fact, convince the average guy that salvation is free, and he will wonder if "all that spiritual stuff" is really worth the fuss. He suspects that if it truly had worth, it would be harder to get.

That is our human difficulty in grasping the concept of grace. If something is said to be free, then it's a lie. If it is free, then it must be garbage. But God's grace is no gimmick. It is truly a "free gift" (Rom. 5:16, 18), and all of salvation's blessings are things "freely given to us by God" (1 Cor. 2:12). There are no strings attached. And as to the worth of it, the Bible uses the phrase "the *riches* of His grace" (Eph. 1:7), indicating the highest kind of value.

God is called "the God of *all* grace" (1 Pet. 5:10), and for good reasons. The Lord Jesus Himself was a free gift, therefore the Bible says that He was "full of *grace* and truth" (John 1:14). Since "God does not give the Spirit by measure" (John 3:34) but gives Him generously, the Spirit is called "the Spirit of *grace*" (Heb. 10:29). We also find that since the gospel message contains the promise of free salvation, it is called "the gospel of the *grace* of God" (Acts 20:24). If we cannot learn to appreciate grace, then we will have a very difficult time appreciating the entire New Testament. We will tend to misunderstand God, Christ, the Spirit, and the gospel, and to put it bluntly, that would be missing the whole "ball game!"

Grace sets the Christian faith apart from all world religions. The main belief systems today have prescribed courses of action that allegedly lead to spiritual health. The Jewish religion has its law, and says that one must keep it in order to become acceptable in God's eyes. Similarly, Muslims have their fasts, feasts, and religious rules. The Hindu teaches karma, and the Buddhist, the eight-fold path. The whole religious world either instructs or demands. It tells the sinner to become someone or do something in order to satisfy God or achieve spiritual transcendence. Yet the gospel of grace does not impose religious pre-qualifications on a lost soul. Neither does it ask a man for anything; instead, it offers to give him everything. Grace truly makes the gospel of Christ unique.

Not everyone is thrilled at the prospect of free salvation. Some religious minds are horrified at the thought. "If there were an effortless way to be right with God, wouldn't all the lazy, evil people purposely take advantage of it?" they ask. The answer is yes. That is exactly what God wants. The Lord Jesus said, "I have not come to call the righteous, but *sinners* to repentance" (Luke 5:32). The people He called—prostitutes and tax collectors—could not ever have hoped to upgrade themselves. Even if they had tried, they would have fallen far short of the moral energy to achieve it. So, as religious failures they stayed away from the temple and the Ten Commandments. But when they detected the grace that was in the Lord Jesus, they came to Him like moths to a light. And this is the principle of grace—a gift being given regardless of the recipient's condition. It is God calling all the wrong people, those who are without religious energy, behavioral success, will power, or hope.

RECEIVING WITH YOUR SPIRITUAL HANDS

With God so willing to give salvation, it would be a shame if we didn't know how to take it. The Apostle Paul revealed the secret in Romans 5:2: "we have access *by faith* into this grace." Grace describes the gift and the attitude of the giver, but the word "faith" relates to the receiver and the means of receiving. We "*receive* the promise of the Spirit"—how?— "through *faith*" (Gal 3:14). Faith is the set of spiritual hands that we use to receive salvation. Grace says, "I will give you something regardless of who and what you are." Faith reacts to that offer by saying, "I will accept it." Faith is the only proper reaction to God's offer of salvation. The prophet Isaiah asked, "LORD, Who has *believed* our report?" (Rom. 10:16), because believing God's "report" is the best honor that a person can give it and the only way that the contents of the "report" can be received.

WHERE DOES FAITH COME FROM?

Mark Twain once wrote, "Faith is believing what you know ain't so." Unfortunately, this rings true for a lot of people. They have a hard time receiving the gospel because—as one college student said—"It all sounds like a fairy tale." Well-meaning Christians advise them to drop their doubts and "Just believe." But are people without the hands of faith supposed to invent a set of them? Those that try will find that they can't seem to work up one gust of lasting faith because faith does not come from self-effort. It is not a personal accomplishment, like learning to play the violin. Neither is it a native quality of certain personalities who are just more trusting by nature. No one is born with faith.

Where then does faith come from? Romans 10:17 is one of the clearest verses in the Bible on this subject. It says, "Faith comes by hearing" the Word of God. The ability to believe the gospel does not originate within us, it must *come* to us. Faith is communicable. It rubs off on us just by hearing "the word of faith" (Rom. 10:8). That is why the Word of God and the preaching of it are so important. A sinner's continued exposure to it will give him the "hands" needed to receive God's salvation. Of course "hearing" in the biblical sense means more than picking up audio vibrations with the eardrum. It means to give heed, to be open and receptive. It is as simple as that. In order to have faith, no one needs to work up a mighty blast of "I think I can, I think I can" or even "I think *God* can, I think *God* can." It all comes down to hearing. Even if a person is barely open to hear one verse in the Bible, at least an eyedropper full of faith can get into him. At that rate, it will take time for him to accumulate faith. But eventually, his spiritual hands will develop to the extent of receiving Jesus. The good news is that they will not need to attain gigantic size. Like an infant's hand, as small as it is, can grasp objects, "little" hands of faith can take hold of God's great salvation.

Apart from the supply of faith available in God's Word, men find it impossible to believe in the Lord Jesus. They complain that it is too hard, and are frankly amazed at those who do believe. Looking inside themselves for faith, they find nothing but doubts, suspicions, and skepticism. This inward search is like a bucket lowered into a dry well that comes back up empty every time. Faith never originates within the unsaved. It must come by hearing the Word. This is why the Bible says that Jesus is "the *author* and finisher of our faith" (Heb. 12:2). The source lies in Him and His Word, not in us.

WHAT IS TRUE BELIEF?

The results of my early gospel preaching efforts often left me feeling disturbed. I would approach someone, share God's plan of salvation, and then help that person pray. In many cases the outcome was depressingly anti-climactic.

"Greg!" I would say, ten times as excited as he was, "You're saved!"

"Uh-huh."

"You've just received Christ!"

"Uh-huh."

"You've been born again!"

"Yup, guess so."

Sometimes, even worse, people argued with me.

"Ernie, you're saved!"

"I am not."

"But you are, you believed in Jesus!"

"Maybe so, but I ain't saved."

What happened? On my part, the gospel had been preached, and on the other guy's part there had been a prayer to "seal the deal." Yet deep within I knew, and so did the other fellow, that he was no more saved than a block of cement. In cases such as those, what went wrong was that the people in question failed to receive anything. Their acknowledgement of the gospel was not a receiving of the Lord Jesus. They were cordial. They agreed. They nodded. And they were not saved.

It is important to know that while only belief in Christ will save a man, not everything that we call "belief" will save us. For example, James wrote that "the demons *believe*—and tremble!" (2:19). Their belief is so strong that God frightens them, yet they are not saved by their faith. Even the most intense belief (or at least what we call belief) can amount to nothing.

With so much talk about faith going on today, it is easy to become confused. Many people, for instance, have come to the conclusion that bare mental acknowledgment automatically counts as saving faith. It is as though an admission that Jesus existed must trigger salvation. Logic of that kind will not even work in the secular world. If a man offered you a new car for free and you merely acknowledged it and walked off, it would still not be yours. You would have failed to *receive* it. Real belief in Christ causes us to receive Him (John 1:12).

Then what is a faith that receives? The Apostle Paul simply said "Believe in your *heart*" (Rom. 10:9), meaning, first of all, that receiving Christ is an inward matter. The human heart is a composite of different, but closely related functions inside of us. It includes our mind. In Matthew 9:4 the Lord asks, "Why do you *think* evil in your *hearts?*" and Genesis 6:5, speaking of man, mentions "the *thoughts* of his *heart.*" Our heart also includes our emotions. The Lord told the disciples, "*Sorrow* has filled your *heart*" (John 16:6) but then said, "Your *heart* will *rejoice*" (John 16:22). Additionally, our heart wills, chooses, and decides. Hebrews 4:12 talks about the "*intents* of the *heart*" and Acts 11:23 mentions "*purpose* of *heart.*" Finally, our heart includes our conscience, as we are to have "our *hearts* sprinkled from an evil *conscience*" (Heb. 10:22). All these functions of the heart—thought, feeling, will, and sense of right and wrong—are engaged to some extent when a man believes in his heart.

BELIEVING WITH YOUR MIND

Believing in the heart, is first of all, a matter of thought. That means when we believe in Jesus, we acknowledge and agree with the fact that He is the Son of God. We drop our contentions on the subject, our clever counter arguments, and our wise sayings that circumvent the truth about Him. We banish the fashionable views that place Christ on the same level as Buddha and Mohammed and others. We dismiss attempts that try to recreate Him as a lesser being— a prophet perhaps, or simply some sage. Ultimately, faith concludes that "Jesus Christ is Lord" (Phil. 2:11). Faith agrees that "first of all...Christ died for our sins according to the scriptures, and that He was buried, and that He rose again the third day according to the scriptures" (1 Cor. 15:3-4). Those are the facts, and as long as they are in dispute, a person cannot be said to have believed in his heart.

Before believing, our minds were full of other thoughts. Part of believing in one's heart, therefore, is a rethinking of things. This is called "repentance," a biblical word that literally means "to think again." Once upon a time I thought that Jesus was Lord of a building down the street with stained glass windows and uncomfortable benches. When I *thought again*, I realized that Jesus was Lord of *all*, including me. Once I thought that the only people who got involved in the Christian "racket" were losers who were not very smart and did not have a very exciting social life. But when repentance came along, I thought again and realized that *everyone* is a loser and needs salvation regardless of his IQ and social life. Yes, that meant me, too.

Repentance is an acknowledgment that you were mistaken in what you thought of yourself, your life, salvation, Christ, and God. It is like a sick man finally facing reality and admitting that he is truly sick. Obviously, by itself, repentance will not save anyone. Merely acknowledging you are sick will not make you one bit better. But before you are willing to receive a doctor's care, you must admit that you need it. That is how thinking again is vitally important.

Real repentance is an upheaval that leaves an indelible mark upon a person. Prior to Paul's salvation, he was "breathing threats and murder against the disciples of the Lord" (Acts 9:1). He "persecuted the church of God beyond measure and tried to destroy it" (Gal 1:13). He said, "I myself thought I must do many things contrary to the name of Jesus of Nazareth. This I also did in Jerusalem, and many of the saints I shut up in prison, having received authority from the chief priests; and when they were put to death, I cast my vote against them. And I punished them often in every synagogue and compelled them to blaspheme; and being exceedingly enraged against them, I persecuted them even to foreign cities" (Acts 26:9-11). This was a person with an extreme case of anti-Christian feelings. He not only hated Christ, but also tried to destroy the Lord's disciples. Yet, when Paul met Christ on the road to Damascus (Acts 9:3-5), his thinking went into a stunning reversal. Concerning all his previous life's work, he later wrote, "I did it ignorantly in unbelief" (1 Tim. 1:13). Paul's repentance caused the early Christians to say with wonder, "He who formerly persecuted us now preaches the faith which he once tried to destroy" (Gal. 1:23). The day Paul "thought again" was a vivid landmark in his Christian life.

That is why *"repentance* toward God and *faith* toward our Lord Jesus Christ" always go together (Acts 20:21). Without rethinking anything, we will not see the need to believe in Christ, nor will we see any beauty in Him. So God "now commands all men everywhere to *repent"* (Acts 17:30), an important component of believing in the heart.

BELIEVING WITH YOUR EMOTIONS

Critical as it may be, analyzing the facts of the gospel and acknowledging the truth of them is not enough. Since the mind is only one part of the heart, then mental agreement is only a part of believing in the heart. If we do not go beyond the intellect, then we will be left with a "head faith," something that still falls short of receiving Jesus. People who fit into that category don't disagree with anything in the gospel, but they didn't necessarily want it, either. So this brings us to the next critical component of believing in your heart—appreciation and desire. Suppose a woman wants to bake a cake for her husband. He is indifferent to the idea, so she tries to describe it to him by saying that it will have eggs, flour, sugar, and milk in it. The man agrees that the recipe does call for those ingredients. She goes on to say that it will have three layers and chocolate frosting. He acknowledges that such a thing exists because he has seen photos of it in cookbooks. What is missing from this picture? Some type of emotional response to desire the cake. The man's mind is engaged, but not his emotions!

The Lord Jesus never intended for His death and resurrection to just become news. He wanted it all to be the gospel, that is, the "*good* news." Real good news never becomes mere academic information. When an expectant mother hears, "It's a girl!" she doesn't respond by requesting a history of ultrasound technology. When a woman says "Yes!" to a man's marriage proposal, he doesn't sit down and logically sort through why she said it.

Neither should men, upon hearing of salvation, treat Jesus with the detached interest of a scientist studying an insect. The Lord desired to be a magnet to the world. He said, "And I, if I am lifted up from the earth, will *draw* all peoples to Myself" (John 12:32). Drawing people means attracting them. It means that men would not only agree with the doctrinal truths about Jesus, but that they would also want Him.

In the Gospel of John, a Samaritan woman heard Jesus say that He had the living water of salvation. She did not respond with, "Sir, I believe you are correct when you say that you have living water. I would like to go meditate under a tree and consider the subject." Instead, she said, "Sir, *give* me this water" (John 4:15). Her true belief was proven by her desire for what Jesus had. And for all of us, at some level and in some way, such emotion must be involved when there is real heart belief.

BELIEVING WITH YOUR WILL

Procrastination can be a disease, especially when it comes to things like paying taxes, cleaning house, or doing homework. For me it is replacing old shoes—an ordeal that can take up to a year. First, I have to admit that I need them. That usually doesn't happen until the shoes look like a dozen horses have stepped on them. Then, there's the months during which I still wear them, knowing they're well past retirement age. Finally, I see a pair that I really like and then, for some strange reason, that's when I hesitate for weeks or months longer. My annoyed wife usually asks, "Why don't you just *get* them?" Then I say, "Well...not this time."

There are a lot of people out there doing the same thing with salvation. More than a few atheists can recall a time when they were definitely attracted to Christ, but didn't make a decision to receive Him. They agreed with the gospel, felt some drawing to the message, and yet something still failed to click.

This exact experience happened in the New Testament to a corrupt politician named Agrippa. He heard the gospel directly from the mouth of the Apostle Paul. Not too many people in history have had such a privilege, and yet Agrippa could only say, "You *almost* persuade me to become a Christian" (Acts 26:28). That little remark speaks volumes about what might have happened in the man. Agrippa apparently found Paul's gospel convincing and even attractive. His mind and emotion both said "Yes" to Jesus. His human will, however, silently said, "No." That one red light was enough to stop salvation's progress. As a result Agrippa *almost* believed in his heart and was *almost* saved. Of course, that is not good enough. Real belief in the heart goes beyond agreeing with the gospel and liking it. Heart belief crosses over into *taking* the gospel.

This reminds me of Blondin, a man who had a tightrope - walking act across Niagara Falls. The crowds would cheer him wildly, especially when he pushed a wheelbarrow full of bricks across. One day he asked his fans, "Do you think I can wheel a man across like this?" "Yes!" they cried. To this he asked them, "Who then will volunteer?" A hush fell over the crowd. They believed in Blondin's ability, but not if it was applied to any one of them. In a similar way, the heart that really believes in Christ chooses to entrust itself to Him for eternal salvation. It not only says, "Christ can save people" but also "Christ can save *me*." That heart is personally willing to stake its eternity on the Lord. It does not trust self, works, religion, or anything else. It says, "Yes" to salvation.

BELIEVING WITH YOUR CONSCIENCE

It's normal for a believer to have registrations of regret for where he has been, how he has acted, and all the time he has wasted being separated from Christ. This is generally called repentance. Though repentance is mainly a matter of thoughts, feelings are involved as well. These come from a stricken conscience. This does not mean, however, that extravagant outward shows of emotion are necessary for salvation, nor can they save us anyway. Judas Iscariot found this out firsthand. After betraying Jesus, he realized he had sinned. Then, filled with remorse, he went out and hung himself (Matt. 27:3-5). There was no doubt that the man was upset over what he had done, yet his anguish alone could not help him. His grief actually *eclipsed* any opportunity for salvation. It was a case of regret run amuck.

In the book of Acts, we find a healthy example of the sorrowful conscience at work. When the crowds realized that the lowly Nazarene that they had crucified was Christ the Lord, they were "cut to the heart" (Acts 2:37). There is no indication from the passage that they fell on the ground weeping. Sorrow stung them within, but it drove them to desire salvation. That is why they said to Peter, "What shall we do?" (Acts 2:37). That is the true benefit of regret. "Godly sorrow produces repentance *leading to salvation*" (2 Cor. 7:10).

Feelings of abject sadness aren't necessary for receiving Christ. However, if a person doesn't have some measure of regret for his previous sins, then it's difficult to understand why he'd want to be saved anyway. The heart that receives Jesus at least faintly knows unhappiness over its own dark past. The delicate workings of conscience goad it on to salvation.

The Bible says that you will be saved if you "Believe in your *heart* that God has raised Him [Jesus] from the dead" (Rom. 10:9). We typically pay attention to the word "believe" but not the word "heart." Yet, it is hard to know what believing really means without defining the heart. Heart belief in Jesus encompasses agreeing with the facts concerning Him, having a desire for Him, making a decision for Him, and regretting our past ignorance of Him. Added together, these key components make up a faith that receives Christ.

DON'T MAKE IT COMPLICATED

After hearing about what it means to believe in Jesus, some Christians might become flustered and begin to second-guess their faith. They start asking themselves whether they have desired Christ enough, or felt sufficient regret for the past, or made a strong enough decision for Christ. The question of "how much" is paramount to us. The twelve disciples were also concerned with that. They said to the Lord, *"Increase* our faith" (Luke 17:5), but He responded that they only needed "faith as a *mustard seed"* (Luke 17:6).

Where salvation is concerned, it is authenticity and not quantity that carries the day. Even a speck of real faith can be enough to receive Jesus. The problem is that sometimes the more we think about an elementary matter, the more complex it becomes. So, along with a clear view of what belief in the heart actually means, we simultaneously ought to hold onto its simplicity. If faith were supposed to be something great and mysterious, many simple, common people would find it impossible to receive Christ. But thankfully, God has ordained child-like belief in Jesus as the means through which we all are saved. Even the feeblest, trembling hands of faith can receive salvation.

THE POWER OF SALVATION

Regardless of how little expectation there is upon our faith, I've met individuals who frankly say, "This might work for others but not for me." One reason I think they feel that way is due to the kind of sins they have committed. Some deeds, like those of a sexual nature, are embarrassing and degrading. After people commit them, they feel so stained that even the gospel's promise of forgiveness gives them no hope. Maybe they have committed crimes of violence or they are addicted to drugs. Then again, their reluctance to believe may be related to the sheer volume of sin in their life—the thousands of things that come out of general godless living. Whatever the case, the person in question will feel that he cannot be saved, and that if he could be, it would certainly not come through simple faith in Christ.

Such pessimistic feelings, though, are not based on the truth. Consider the crowd that listened to Peter's gospel on the day of Pentecost. Some who were present there had, just fifty days prior, spat on Christ and cried out for His crucifixion. If any group of people ever had doubts about whether they could be saved, it would have been them. But, "The gospel of Christ ...is the power of God to salvation for everyone who believes" (Rom. 1:16). In light of the gospel, those who were directly involved in killing Jesus were not hopeless. They could hang onto the phrase "*everyone* who believes." Theoretically, even the Roman soldier who pounded the nails through the Lord's hands could have been saved if he had believed.

Now if "everyone" includes those who supervised, cheered, or otherwise carried out the crucifixion of Jesus, then who is excluded from the possibility of salvation? What man has done something worse than those who brutalized the Son of God and pinned Him to a piece of wood? God had come as a man to help us and they had killed Him. Yet many of these same people were saved a short time later. They believed in and began to pray to the Person they had murdered. If this sounds surreal, it is only an indication of the power of the gospel through faith in Christ. Salvation is truly for "everyone who believes"—Satanists, prostitutes, sorcerers, blasphemers, and, yes, even those who killed Christ Himself. People today rarely realize this. They imagine that Christ only offers His salvation to semi-good guys and that He rejects those who really need it. But Jesus said, "the one who comes to me I will by no means cast out" (John 6:37). Anyone who approaches Him with the open hands of faith will not walk away with them empty.

Salvation is so powerful that there is no such thing as a case that is too hard for it to handle. Let's consider an Old Testament picture. In Numbers 21:6-7, we find the account of some Israelites who sinned. "So the Lord sent fiery serpents among the people, and they bit the people; and many of the people of Israel died. Therefore the people came to Moses, and said, 'We have sinned...pray to the LORD that He take away the serpents from us.'" There were several key components—sinners, a deadly snake bite, and a desire for salvation. In response, God then told Moses, "Make a fiery serpent, and set it on a pole; and it shall be that anyone who is bitten, when he looks at it, shall live" (Num. 21:8).

The way of salvation was simplicity itself: *look* upon the serpent. Maybe a few of the people had problems trusting that. Would looking at something cure a snakebite? Simple first aid would have made more sense. Why would looking at anything be a cure for snake venom? Perhaps "logical" Israelites died because they supposed there was a more trustworthy way of being saved. There were possibly even those who thought that they had a more deadly snakebite than others, and were hopeless, so they decided not to bother looking. All would have died. What about the ones that took the God-appointed way of salvation? The passage continues, "So Moses made a bronze serpent and put it on a pole; and so it was, if a serpent had bitten anyone, when he looked at the bronze serpent, he lived" (Num. 21:9). As it turned out, a look was all that was required, just as God had promised. Salvation came instantaneously, regardless of the severity of the snakebite.

This story is even more striking when we see the connection between the brass serpent and the salvation we are promised today. Jesus said, "As Moses lifted up the serpent in the wilderness, even so must the Son of Man be lifted up, that whoever believes in Him should not perish, but have eternal life" (John 3:14-15). A look at the bronze serpent brought immediate salvation, and so does a look of faith at the Lord Jesus. So, for us to think that we are too evil to come to Jesus makes as much sense as thinking that we are too sick to go to the hospital.

There is another very notable picture of salvation. According to the Old Testament arrangement, if a person committed a sin, he brought an animal—a bull or a sheep—and laid his hands upon its head (Lev. 4:2-4). By doing this, instantaneously, the man's sin was put upon the animal. All of his evil deeds and his entire evil personality were transmitted (symbolically) to the innocent creature. The sinner's identity had been joined with that of the lamb or bull. Then, a priest would come and kill the beast. Following that, the sinner could walk away sinless (symbolically, that is). In the eyes of God, he was free and clear, because the death of the animal could be counted as his own death. His sins could therefore be counted as dead, too—wiped out. And all this took place because of one touch.

Eventually Christ came "to put away sin by the sacrifice of *Himself*" (Heb. 9:26). When this happened, all of the Old Testament animal sacrifices were finished. God no longer required them or even wanted them. This is why Jesus said to God, "Sacrifice and offering You did not desire, but a *body* You have prepared for Me" (Heb. 10:5). The body of the Lord Jesus is the unique sacrifice of the New Testament. When we believe in Him, we reach out in faith and place our spiritual hands upon Him.

The result of "laying hands" on the sacrifice of Jesus goes far beyond dealing with our sin problem. It brings us into such an immediate oneness with Him that His entire work becomes our own. Now whoever believes in Him can say, "I have been crucified *with* Christ" (Gal. 2:20). He died for me, but when He died, *I* died as well. Not only this, but when He rose from the dead, *I* rose—"Even when we were dead in trespasses, [God] made us alive *together* with Christ (by grace you have been saved), and raised us up *together*" (Eph. 2:5). Finally, a believer can say that Christ ascended to heaven and sat down there *and so did I*—God "made us sit *together* in the heavenly places in Christ Jesus." (Eph. 2:6). This union with Christ and all of His mighty work is the strongest kind of salvation, yet a mere touch of faith was all it took to make it ours.

There are no complications in God's simple way of salvation. It only takes a believing look at Christ or a believing touch to "destroy the works of the devil" (1 John 3:8) in a man's life, even when those works are quite serious and have greatly accumulated. This is why Paul said, "where sin abounded"—that is, where it was stacked up in a great pile—"grace abounded *much more*" (Rom. 5:20). No sinner should think that he has "outsinned" grace. Neither should anyone think that he is a particularly difficult person for the Lord to save. When Paul spoke of sinners, he said, *"I* am chief" (1 Tim. 1:15). You are not the chief sinner. Paul was. And if the chief of sinners could find himself completely immersed in salvation, then you are no trouble at all to save.

WHY FAITH AND NOT WORKS? —
WORKS BRING GLORY TO MEN; FAITH GIVES IT TO GOD

With all the talk of grace, faith, and being saved, the mortal human mind still wonders why God is not interested in people doing a little something to earn their salvation. The idea of human works for justification does not even enter God's mind. His first and last answer as to how a man gets saved has nothing to do with "going dutch," that is, Him doing His part and us doing ours. A man asked the Apostle Paul and his traveling companions, "Sirs, what must I do to be saved?" (Acts 16:30). Suddenly, right there was a "fill-in-the-blank." Anything could have been said. Because the question was so clear and direct, the answer would also need to be clear and direct. It would unavoidably become something of a text-book response that men would reference for thousands of years to come. If there were anything additional concerning how to be saved, it was the Holy Spirit's golden opportunity to insert it there.

Put the typical person in Paul's shoes at that moment

and you might have heard plenty of supplemental requirements: "What must you do to be saved? Well, let's see, first of all, get your life straight. Then, believe in Jesus and follow the Ten Commandments. Then, go to church. That's how to get saved." These responses are actually very popular today. None of them, however, were given by the Apostle Paul. He and his companions told the man, *"Believe on the Lord Jesus Christ and you will be saved"* (Acts 16:31). Faith in Christ was how the Holy Spirit, through Paul, filled in the blank. Given the chance, He did not add anything to what we needed for salvation beyond simple faith.

The New Testament continually exalts the thought of faith as the sole requirement for salvation simply because it must. God knows that human beings have an incurable desire to work for everything. Lurking in the mind of every person is the concept that if we want to be saved, we must earn it. "God helps those who help themselves," we say, thinking we are quoting the Bible (it's actually Benjamin Franklin).

In a world where no one is giving out free lunches, humanity has been forced to develop a strong work ethic. It is an outcome of Adam's fall: "Cursed is the ground for your sake; in *toil* you shall eat of it all the days of your life" (Gen. 3:17). Obviously in this physical setting, work is a must for our survival. There is nothing wrong with that. Work-consciousness only becomes a problem when it inflates the ego and causes us to despise and reject necessary grace. Unfortunately, this is exactly what tends to happen in the minds of men.

One Christian youth group conducted an experiment to illustrate that truth. They stood in the center of a shopping mall with quarters, handing them out for free to the shoppers. As they were distributed, nothing else was said, except "Free, please take one." Some predictably received the gift, even circling around for another. Surprisingly, others were downright rude. They rejected the quarters and brushed past the kids as though the offer of free money had been a personal insult.

It all demonstrates that the proud only value what they

work for.   They find it terribly humiliating to receive anything apart from their own efforts.   This attitude might be commendable in human society, where everyone ought to bear his own share of the workload, but it fails miserably in spiritual affairs, especially where salvation is concerned. "God resists the proud, but gives grace to the humble" (1 Pet. 5:5). He causes all His blessings to descend upon those who are lowly in heart and poor in spirit. Just like a torrent of water rushes down a slope, so grace can only go downward to those who humbly receive it.   It cannot flow upward to the proud who wish to work for it.

The impossibility of salvation through works is graphically illustrated in the Gospel of Luke.   There, as Christ died on the cross, a thief died on a cross next to Him. "He said to Jesus, 'Lord, remember me when you come into Your kingdom" (23:42). The Lord could have said, "You must first go and repay the things you stole, then I will remember you," or "Change your ways," or some other command.   But this would have been quite impossible for the man to do. The fact was, the thief was attached to a cross and could never move again.   He had found the audacity to hope for salvation free of charge, even though he had probably never spent five minutes serving God,in his whole life.   There was no time for pride, for cutting deals or offering payment. All this thief had left was faith.   As it turned out, that was all he needed. "Jesus said to him, 'Assuredly I say to you, today you will be with Me in Paradise'" (Luke 23:43).

Faith represents the humbling of a person under God. Faith is the sinner's declaration that he cannot do what God asks, nor become what God wants, so he must take salvation for free.   That eliminates any possibility of human pride. When you receive a gift that you don't deserve, one whose worth outweighs anything you could ever earn, thus the appreciation (or, glory) rightly goes to the giver, *not* to you. If a father gave his son a car, would everyone gather around the son and admire him for the way he received it? No. If we noticed the son at all, it would only be to acknowledge him as fortunate. All the admiration and appreciation would go to the giving father instead. This is also what happens in salvation. God gives and is glorified; we receive and are blessed.

Men are often known for their hard work and devotion toward what they think is holy. I once read a report from India about a fellow who made a religious vow. It involved holding his arm up in the air and not lowering it...*for years.* Incredibly, he was successful. In fact, at the time I read the report he had already managed to do it for decades. Of course the attainment came with a price. The man's arm had shrunken and atrophied to a considerable extent. This sort of extreme act demonstrates the lengths to which people are willing to go in order to win divine favor of some sort. We do these things because we want God to be happy with us and give us a decent afterlife. Somewhere deep inside of us, we hope that He is saying, "Thank you for doing your best. Next time try harder and ask for My help so that you will be more successful." What God actually says, though, is nothing of the kind. To all our works He simply says, *"Stop!"*

In the Old Testament there was a commandment dealing with the complete cessation of work. It was called the Sabbath. At prescribed intervals, it required men to stop all their efforts at helping themselves (Ex. 31:12-18). One symbolic use of the Sabbath was to stem the amount of sin on earth. It seems that the more men work to establish their righteousness before God, the more sin they actually produce. Romans chapter 7 shows us that powerful efforts to save oneself only issue in powerful failures. Sin is like sweat. The more the sinner moves around, the more it seeps out of him. If he works much, he sins much. Even if he finally achieves some sort of religious victory, that very victory will produce sin. The sinner's successful work is just as bad as his failure. Why? Paul tells us that salvation is "not of works, lest anyone should *boast*" (Eph. 2:9). Even if a man's best efforts were victorious to save him, he would immediately fall into the sin of pride and pat himself on the back. God's way of saving the fallen man, who is a sin-producing factory, is not to call for greater efforts. Instead, His way calls for a *halt* to all activity.

The physical Old Testament Sabbath was a picture anticipating that God would one day dispense with all human effort. The Lord Jesus Himself announced the arrival of that day to those who were weary with failure: "Come to Me, all you who labor and are heavy laden, and I will give you *rest*" (Matt. 11:28). The beginning of salvation is not with working, but with resting. Salvation comes not with mortal energy but with the true Sabbath, who is Jesus Christ Himself. He seemed to be telling the religious Jews at that time, "All your works have left you worn out. The very mention of God makes you feel tired and guilty. *Stop!* Drop everything and come to Me."

WORKS INSULT THE GIVER; FAITH HONORS HIM

Jesus once compared Himself to a man "who when he had found one pearl of great price, went and sold all that he had and bought it" (Matt. 13:46). The pearl symbolized a salvation so costly to the Lord that it took "all that he had" to obtain it. If salvation cost Him His glorious, sinless life, then nothing in the sinner's pockets could ever buy it. Still, men attempt to do this all the time. It is extremely difficult for us to understand the priceless nature of salvation.

There is an old story that portrays this point exactly. A missionary in India, David Morse, had been fruitlessly trying to convince his Indian friend, Rambhau, to trust in Jesus for salvation. Rambhau appreciated religious works far more than the idea of faith and grace. One day he pointed to a man on the road.

"Do you see that man over there? He is a pilgrim, perhaps to Bombay or Calcutta. He walks barefoot and picks the sharpest stones—and see—every few steps he kneels down and kisses the road. That is good. The first day of the New Year I begin my pilgrimage. All my life I have planned it. I shall make sure of heaven. I am going to Delhi on my knees."

Morse said, "Man, you're crazy! It's nine hundred miles

to Delhi. The skin will break on your knees and you'll have blood poisoning and die before you can get to Bombay."

"No, I must get to Delhi. And then the immortals will reward me. The suffering will be sweet."

The missionary pleaded with Rambhau and told him that Jesus had died and that salvation was free, but to no avail. The old man was determined to conduct his pilgrimage. Finally the day came when it was scheduled to begin. Rambhau called his missionary friend to his house for a last good-bye. He then pulled out a box. "I have had this box for years," he said. "I keep only one thing in it. Now I will tell you about it. I once had a son."

"A son! Why, Rambhau, you have never said a word about him."

"No, I couldn't. Now I will tell you, for soon I will leave, and who knows whether I ever shall return? My son was a diver, the best pearl diver on the coasts of India. He had the swiftest dive, the keenest eye, the strongest arm, and the longest breath of any man who sought for pearls. What a joy he brought me! He always dreamed of finding a pearl beyond all others. One day he found it, but when he found it he had already been underwater too long. He died soon after."

Rambhau bowed his head and for a moment his whole body shook. "All these years I have kept the pearl," he continued, "but now I am going, not to return...and to you, my best friend, I am giving my pearl." The old man drew from the box a carefully wrapped package. Gently opening the cotton, he picked up a mammoth pearl and placed it in the hand of the missionary. It was one of the largest pearls ever found off the coast of India, and it glowed with a luster and brilliance never seen in cultured pearls. It would have brought a fabulous sum in any market.

For a moment the missionary was speechless. "Rambhau," he said, "this is a wonderful pearl, an amazing pearl. Let me buy it. I will give you ten thousand rupees for it."

Rambhau stiffened his whole body. "Friend, this pearl is beyond all price. A million rupees could not buy it from me.

I will not sell it. You may only have it as a gift."

"No, Rambhau, I cannot accept that. As much as I want the pearl, I cannot accept it that way. I must pay for it or work for it."

The old man was stunned. "You don't understand at all. Don't you see? My only son gave his life to get this pearl, and I wouldn't sell it for any amount of money. Its worth is in the lifeblood of my son. I cannot sell this; I can only give it to you in token of the love I bear you."

The missionary could not speak for a moment; then he gripped the hand of the old man. "Rambhau, don't you see? That is just what you have been saying to God." Rambhau looked searchingly at the missionary, and slowly he began to understand. Great tears rolled down his cheeks. "Friend," he said, "I see it now. Jesus gave Himself for me. I accept Him" (Pearl 133).

Payment for a gift that is priceless, no matter how great the sum that is offered, only insults the giver. Since nothing could ever buy salvation without cheapening it, the "pearl" can only be given away.

If we were able to purchase our salvation by behaving according to God's law, then it would create a very serious matter, "for, if righteousness comes through the law, then *Christ died in vain*" (Gal. 2:21). To make something vain means to make it worthless and meaningless. That would be the ultimate devaluation of the Lord's sacrifice. If you could free yourself through behavior modification, then why was His suffering and death necessary? Giving His life for us on the cross would be little more than a contingency for weak people, and all but meaningless for the strong.

When we stop behaving, trying, and working to earn salvation, and simply receive it, we are saying that the life of the Lord Jesus is valuable beyond measure. Freely receiving it honors God the giver and preserves the worth of the gift itself.

Why God Gave the Law

Even as we are drawn to thoughts of faith and grace, we can't help but cast a nervous eye on God's law. The imposing phrases "Thou shalt" and "Thou shalt not" literally demand our attention. What are we to do with them? Even seasoned Christians can become confused over this topic. In an attempt to reconcile the Old and New Testaments, some conclude that salvation comes through believing in Jesus and also trying to keep the Ten Commandments. Otherwise, why would God bother to give the law at all? This is an important question, and until it is answered, we Christians will credit our salvation to faith but suspect that our works were somehow involved as well. We will always confess Jesus as Lord, but in some way believe that the co-commander is Moses.

"What purpose then does the law serve?" (Gal. 3:19). It actually fulfills a very important function. In ancient times God made a promise to Abraham that "In your seed all the nations of the earth shall be blessed" (Gen. 22:18). That seed was to be Christ (Gal. 3:16). But before all the nations of the earth could be blessed in Christ, there was one big problem. A Savior will not be welcomed with open arms, unless someone wishes to be saved. And for people to want salvation, they must first understand that they need it.

That is where the complication really lies. It is not easy for human beings to see their ruined moral and spiritual condition. We think our sins are simply harmless expressions of doing what comes natural to us. As long as we continue under that illusion, believing we are healthy and not sick, there will be no need of a "doctor." The idea of a Savior will seem quite unnecessary.

Humanity continued in that blinded mind-set for a very long time, until the world had accumulated a great number of transgressions against God. Still, "sin is not imputed where there is no law" (Rom. 5:13), so mankind failed to have any real anxiety over its evil deeds. Hence, the coming of Moses and the Ten Commandments. The law "was added *because* of transgressions" (Gal. 3:19). When that happened, the "light" came on. God's written standard began to illuminate man's condition so that they could see how far they had wandered from Him. In a sense, it was a divine thermometer to show us all that we were truly sick and running a high fever.

Paul wrote, "I would not have known sin except through the law. For I would not have known covetousness unless the law had said, 'You shall not covet'" (Rom. 7:7). Without God's commandment against coveting, Paul would have lived out his lustful desires, thinking that they were okay. But he was introduced to the law and saw that his condition was actually condemned. At one point he might have minimized his situation, but under the magnifying glass of God's Word, his sin began to look "exceedingly sinful" (Rom. 7:13).

The law was meant to operate this way for everyone. The Lord tells us in the law, for instance, "You shall have no other gods before me" (Ex. 20:3). Honestly bringing that standard to bear upon our lives may expose some startling things. For one, we might realize that we rarely ever put God first. Many other activities, things, and persons routinely come before Him. They are important, but God is not. Thus, much of what we innocently call priority conflicts (that put God in second place) may actually be subtle forms of idolatry. We also have the commandment not to covet, that is, not to desire things that belong to others. Yet, we often cannot rest when our neighbor has something better than we have. Greed and jealously make it hard for us to be at ease until we have gotten that item, or at least gotten something comparable to it. By exposing those feelings as the sin of coveting, the law literally tells us the truth about our real condition. As David said to God, "The entrance of Your words gives light" (Ps. 119:130).

This leads us to the shocking conclusion that God did not give His law to us so that we would successfully keep it and stop sinning. Instead, "The law entered that the offense might *abound*" (Rom. 5:20). God gave His written standard so the sinner could actually see the abundance of sin in his life. "The law is spiritual" (Rom. 7:14) and "the commandment holy and just and good" (Rom. 7:12), so what happens when this standard is given to unholy, unrighteous, fleshly men? There can only be one outcome—a multitude of sins. It is all according to plan, so that the Lord can prove to us our inability to match Him. In effect, when the law is successful, we begin to realize that we are hopeless. Only then will a person be ready for the Savior.

While God is attempting to show us our lost condition, some well-meaning people have the tendency to misunderstand. The law works to prove their sinfulness but they work to prove their holiness. They try very hard to keep God's commandments. Like the Israelites of old, they declare, "Whatever God has said, we will do!" (Ex. 19:8). This good but misguided attitude completely misses the deeper purpose of the law.

The fact is that God wants men to realize their utter weakness and to cry out, "O wretched man that I am! Who will deliver me from the body of this death? I thank God—through Jesus Christ our Lord!" (Rom. 7:24-25). Men should give their lives over to the Savior, not throw more energy into succeeding without Him. If we disagree with the law's verdict that our offenses abound and instead, seek to prove that our righteousness abounds, then we are ignorantly issuing a challenge to God. We are saying, "Your standard is not too hard for me. I do not need to be forgiven of my sins or receive a new life. I only need to keep trying in order to be as perfect as you are!" This attitude, of course, does not impress God in the slightest. On the contrary, it literally *dares* Him to further prove a person's sinfulness.

Christ came at a time when the human race had broken God's law in every way. In a sense, He arrived at the midnight of human failure. Thankfully, it was the end of one age and the beginning of another—"The law was given through Moses, but grace and truth came through Jesus Christ" (John 1:17). Now, did Christ bring in grace because the way of law failed? No. Grace was brought in because the law had successfully proven its point. After thousands of years, the law made it unequivocally clear that humankind could not match God. As a race, we were then ready for the Savior. That was the entire point of the law—

preparing us for Christ. Grace was not an addendum, a patch to mend the broken system of law-keeping. In fact, grace was God's primary thought from the very beginning. Paul speaks of the "grace which was given to us in Christ Jesus *before time began*" (2 Tim. 1:9). This means that God's grand intention from eternity was that we would freely receive from Him, *not* try to earn things from Him.

The person who tries to work for eternal salvation will get results, but only wrong ones. His efforts at perfection will be riddled with failure. Even his small successes will turn into deficits, as they fuel his pride. The more he does, the more he seems to fall. The sinner may be aware of the Lord's work of salvation, but his dogged persistence to earn it demonstrates how little he understands the value of it. His determination not to receive God's free gift of salvation insults "the Spirit of grace" (Heb. 10:29). Hence, the sinner who works for eternal life will not get it, but for the trembling, faltering one who, like the dying thief, can only say, "Remember me, Lord Jesus," salvation comes immediately. Only faith can receive the riches of grace and give glory to the Lord Jesus Christ.

NEW TESTAMENT PRACTICES CANNOT BRING SALVATION EITHER

Old Testament law can't save anyone, but how about New Testament practices like prayer and baptism? These have, at different times, all been held as necessary for salvation. The result is that spiritual exercises get elevated to an importance that they were never intended to have. It also essentially transforms the New Testament into another kind of Old Testament—full of commands to "do this" and "do that" in order to be right with God.

PRAYER IS NOT A REQUIREMENT FOR SALVATION

An overwhelming majority of people think that salvation comes by praying for it. That is why the formal sinner's prayer is such a standard piece of equipment for those who share the gospel. Getting someone to pray is said to be "closing the deal." Prayer, not faith, is thought to be the last word on salvation. I am well aware that many great gospel preachers utilize prayer at the end of their gospel messages. I am not dismissing it as unimportant, but we must be clear about what it accomplishes. Does prayer convince God to save us, or does it function as a new Christian's first attempts to commune with his Father? The scriptures lean toward the latter.

If we must pray before receiving Christ, then the assumption is that God wishes to withhold salvation until a formal request is made. But who desires salvation more— men or God? The Bible tells us, "God our Savior...desires all men to be saved." (1 Tim. 2:3-4). Men, however, do not desire to be saved. They must be convicted and convinced by the Holy Spirit. God must appeal to them often for years, even decades, before they will receive Him. Otherwise they would happily and ignorantly go to hell. If God implores men to receive His salvation, then how much does a man, in turn, have to plead with God for it?

The Gospel of Luke describes a man who was in the worst kind of condition. He was impoverished, feeding hogs, and secretly hoping that he could eat some of what he fed them. Coming to his senses, he decided to return to the father he had run away from. But before he went back, he rehearsed to himself a speech: "Father, I have sinned against heaven and before you, and am no longer worthy to be called your son. Make me like one of your hired servants" (Luke 15:18-19). What the runaway didn't know, was that his father had been waiting and watching day after day, anticipating his return. This must have been the case, because, "A great way off, his father saw him, and had compassion, and ran and fell on his neck and kissed him" (Luke 15:20). The son did not need his rehearsed begging speech. He tried to recite it, but there is no indication that the father paid any attention to it. Instead, the old man began pronouncing blessings on his son: "Bring out the best robe and put it on him, and put a ring on his hand and sandals on his feet.

And bring the fatted calf here and kill it, and let us eat and be merry" (Luke 15:22-23). Did "prayer" convince the father to take the son back? Indeed, did the father need any convincing at all?

Some of you reading this book were saved not long ago, perhaps a few weeks or a few months back. You may be thinking that you were saved when you prayed the special prayer at a gospel meeting or at church or with a friend. I don't mean to imply that you were not saved, but only that it was not the prayer that saved you.

In Acts 10, while Peter was preaching the gospel, the Holy Spirit fell upon his audience, saving them. Conspicuously missing was any kind of sinner's prayer. Yet, if these people did not ask for salvation, how did they get it? The Bible tells us: "The Holy Spirit fell upon all those who *heard* the word" (Acts 10:44). Romans 10:17 says, "Faith comes by hearing," so it must have been that as they heard the word, faith came to them and as a result, salvation came as well. Yes, in your case you may have prayed for salvation, but you were not saved by it. Salvation comes the moment you hear the word of Jesus Christ and accept it. Such a transaction is usually invisible, silent, and instantaneous. Actually, by the time you bowed your head to pray for salvation, you were *already* saved.

Watchman Nee, a noted Christian teacher, understood this very clearly. He once told the story of a man to whom he preached the gospel. When the man indicated that he believed, Nee said, "Now let us kneel and pray." "Will we pray for God to save me?" the man asked. "No," Nee said, "We are going to thank Him for saving you already."

Prayer is one of the most important Christian exercises. If you don't do it, you can forget about spiritual growth or enjoying the Lord's presence. However, this book, and in particular this chapter, only deals with our entrance into salvation. When that is the issue, prayer is not a primary matter; only faith in Christ.

SALVATION IS NOT THROUGH SAYING "LORD JESUS"

Peter tells us in Acts 2:21, "Whoever *calls* upon the name of the Lord shall be saved." Paul also says, "If you *confess* with your mouth the Lord Jesus and believe in your heart that God has raised Him from the dead, you shall be saved" (Rom. 10:9). These verses appear to identify our mouths as highly instrumental for salvation. However, this is a teaching that can be taken to unbiblical extremes. Some people for instance, have been led to think that simply repeating the Lord's name can save a person.

Consider Sam and Joe, two Christians who walked into a hardware store. Sam, being something of a gospel preacher and hoping to see some "action," told the cashier to say "Lord Jesus."

"Lord Jesus," the young man said, a little bewildered. Sam instantly became elated and told him, "You're saved!"

The cashier rolled his eyes, bagged their purchase, and got them out of there as fast as he could.

In the parking lot, Sam and Joe began talking about their encounter.

"Do you really think that guy was saved?" Joe asked.

Sam was miffed at the suggestion that the "salvation event" was not real. "Of course I believe he was saved. I stand on the Word of God. Romans 10:9 says to confess with your mouth that Jesus is Lord and you will be saved. That's what he did. He's saved."

If we take a closer look at Romans 10:9, however, we will find that Sam really wasn't standing on the Word of God. He was standing on one misunderstood verse, which had been isolated from its surrounding context. As a result, he thought that just because someone says the words "Lord Jesus" it means a true confession of the Lord has been made. But if Sam had read a few verses farther into the chapter, he would have found that real confession has a root. If this root is authentic, then the confession and the salvation are also. If it is not authentic, then saying "Lord Jesus" even one hundred times will not do anything for a man. Romans 10:14 brings us to the core issue: "How then shall they call on Him in whom they have not *believed?"* According to the verse, true calling or confessing is not possible without faith underlying it. Faith is the central matter, the root. Without faith, the statement "Jesus is Lord" cannot and will not save anyone.

We have to pay attention to the particular terminology the biblical writers used. Peter uses the word "call," and Paul uses the word "confess." Both terms are strongly backed by the concept of faith. Picture a man sitting in the living room, calling for his wife in the kitchen. Obviously, he believes she is in the kitchen or else he would not call her. He expects to get a response. His calling is backed by a belief that she will answer from the other room. If he sat there and repeatedly said his wife's name while not believing that she was there, then that would be both strange and empty.

The scriptural concept of calling upon the Lord is always attached to faith. Confessing the Lord's name is also. The word "confession" itself means that we verbally admit something that we know to be true. If I say something with my mouth that I don't believe is true, then that is not a confession; it is a lie. A real confession that "Jesus is Lord" comes from the deep conviction that it is the truth— therefore confessing His name is the result of real faith spilling out of our mouths.

Salvation cannot come from invoking the name of a person that you don't believe in. Neither will repetitively saying "Lord Jesus" even help you to believe. "Faith comes by hearing" (Rom. 10:17), not by calling, shouting, or chanting. That means our friend Sam, from the example above, should have spent his time speaking the word of faith to that cashier and not telling him to "Just say this."

BAPTISM IS NOT A REQUIREMENT FOR SALVATION

Baptism is another New Testament command which is often thought to be necessary for salvation. The idea that physical water somehow protects us from the lake of fire is nowhere to be found in scripture, but it has become entrenched in the religious mind. As a result, those who have been dunked or sprinkled think that they are eternally okay. They count water as more important than faith. From the sentimental standpoint, there is something quite special about the act of descending into a tub of water while others sing and pray. Perhaps the event is marked with special clothing and impressive surroundings. Unfortunately, the whole ceremony can eclipse the need for faith.

The Bible must be consulted for a balanced understanding. We read in Mark 16:16 that "He who believes *and* is baptized will be saved; but he who does not believe will be condemned." Notice that this verse has two parts. The first part puts baptism and faith together; the second part speaks of faith by itself. In the first part, baptism and faith are necessary for salvation, but in the second part, faith alone is needed for deliverance from God's condemnation.

John 3:18 agrees with this when it says, "He who believes in Him is not condemned, but he who does not believe is condemned already, because he has not believed in the name of the only begotten Son of God." Faith in Christ frees us from condemnation. So when God looks at us, He cannot see anything that calls for His judgment. That means we are saved before Him.

When faith is accompanied *with* baptism, then that is a different matter. It refers to being saved before men. It is a visible act, a statement to everyone that you have been put into the death of Christ (Rom. 6:3), that you have left this crooked generation (Acts 2:38, 40), that you have been placed into the body of Christ (1 Cor. 12:13), and that you have been "submerged" in the Divine Trinity (Matt. 28:19). All believers should be baptized. It is their testimony of the invisible things the Lord has done to them as a result of believing in Jesus. Baptismal water is meaningful from the standpoint of representing something in the spiritual world. But the water itself confers nothing. Without faith, whoever gets baptized only gets wet. With faith, whoever gets baptized gets saved before men. But when it comes to being saved before God and escaping His condemnation, which is the subject we are currently addressing, baptism is not a requirement, only faith.

SALVATION DOES NOT REQUIRE A CONFESSION OF SINS

How many sins did you commit before you met Jesus Christ? Maybe you can remember twenty. A more actual count, factoring in unclean thoughts and bad attitudes might number in the hundreds of thousands. These ride a sinner's back like a monkey. In fact, when we first considered Christ in a favorable way, that "monkey" was quick to whisper in our ears, "What about *me?*" Indeed, what *about* all the sin history that a person carries around? Before a man can expect to be saved, shouldn't he apologize, at least to God, for those things?

I John 1:9 says, "If we confess our sins, He is faithful and just to forgive us our sins and to cleanse us from all unrighteousness." This would seem to verify that confession of sins is necessary before a man can be forgiven and saved. The problem with that interpretation is that John's letter was written to those already saved. His intended audience was Christians, not non-Christians. In telling the believers to confess their sins for cleansing, he was giving them an important key to experiencing a good fellowship with God. But he never meant for those instructions to be taken and applied to the unsaved.

Then what should a sinner do with the monkey on his back? Forget about it and believe in Jesus! There are simply no instructions in the Bible for naming or tinkering with past indiscretions before we can be saved. We are never charged to revisit old sins, mull over their gory details, and beg pardon for them. Now, perhaps *after* salvation, the Lord Jesus will lead you to right certain wrongs and make restitution for some things, but that is purely a post-salvation experience.

There are cases in scripture that show this happening. In the gospels, a man named Zaccheus had swindled a lot of people. Later, touched by God, he received Jesus into his home. But when the swindled people saw the Lord going into Zaccheus's house, they "complained, saying, He has gone to be a guest with a man who is a sinner" (Luke 19:7). God had forgiven Zaccheus, but obviously his victims had not forgiven him. Therefore, the Lord moved Zaccheus to right his wrongs and say, "Lord, I give half of my goods to the poor; and if I have taken anything from anyone by false accusation, I restore fourfold" (Luke 19:8). In another passage, some who had practiced sorcery brought together their magic books after they were saved and burned them (Acts 19:18-19). God had already forgiven these people, but He led them to go on and dispose of all their sinful possessions.

Neither restitution nor confession of sins is wrong. There is nothing improper about an outpouring of honest apologies toward the Lord or toward people we have hurt. Regardless, we must keep in mind that salvation's lone requirement is simple faith in Christ, and nothing more. This frees sinners from the burden of trying to reconstruct their evil past and confess hundreds of dirty details, one by one.

If salvation did come through confession, it would be terribly risky—especially for those who have a bad memory. Perhaps such people would find themselves in a constant state of anxiety. Because of their absentmindedness, they would never know if they had remembered to confess everything. Even those with excellent recall might still overlook a handful of trespasses. Imagine appearing on Judgment Day with a cluster of unforgiven sins hanging over you, all because they had just slipped your mind.

And memory is not the only problem. When the unsaved approach Christ, they rarely perceive how sinful they are. They might confess five hundred sins, but fail to mention the other eight thousand of which they are guilty. Their ignorance of God's holiness blinds them so that they hardly know what counts as sin. That is why eternal salvation does not rest upon apologies. Being washed of our filth does not come that way. Rather, the Lord deals with those who approach Him, "cleansing their hearts *by faith*" (Acts 15:9 NASB).

All too often, man's response to God is to do something.

It is like the scene in John 6:28, where a crowd had been touched by the Lord's words. He moved them—inspired them—and the old predictable response arose. "They said to Him, 'What shall we do that we may *work* the works of God?'" It seems that men are always so willing to do something, as though they were able, and are always so willing to give, as though they had something. The Lord's response did not recommend the keeping of laws or spiritual practices of any kind. He answered them, "This is the work of God, that you *believe* in Him whom He sent" (John 6:29).

THE PLACE OF WORKS

Without a word of balance to what we have been discussing, we could all become like a pendulum and swing too far to one side. That is, we might become Christians who despise works. God does not hate good works, "for we are His workmanship, created in Christ Jesus *for good works*, which God prepared beforehand that we should walk in them" (Eph. 2:10). Actually, God worked so hard to save us so that we indeed would work. He prepared and fashioned us to fit the particular deeds that He tailored for each one of us.

Everywhere in the New Testament good works are commanded. You are charged to *"work out* your own salvation" (Phil 2:12) and to "let your light so shine before men, that they may see your *good works* and glorify your Father who is in heaven" (Matt. 5:16). None of those charges, however, are given to the unsaved. They are only given to the saved. Why must the saved do them? So that they can glorify God, manifest their obedience to Him, advance His work on the earth, and remain in fellowship with Him. Still, all of the believer's work is considered a "work of *faith*" (1 Thess. 1:3). That is, they never depart from a life of receiving. As they work for the Lord, they must continue to hold out the hands of faith to Him. This is so they can receive the grace necessary to do all the things He requires of them. The saved will find that grace multiplies many good works in their lives.

What the unsaved will find is exactly the opposite. The gospel of grace eliminates all their works and orders them to "Stand still, and see the salvation of the Lord" (Ex. 14:13). Never was a charge more contrary to the human concept. It is very common for people to speak of trying to be saved or trying to be born again but this is completely inconsistent with God's way. Have you ever attempted to be a cheetah? Perhaps if you tried running faster, it would happen. Have you ever wanted to be an eagle? Maybe if you jumped off a roof and flapped your arms hard enough it would happen. Those who are trying to be saved will shortly find that they will have an easier time trying to become a cheetah or an eagle. After some brave attempts, these hardy souls collapse. "I tried the Christian thing," they say, "And it was too hard." Yet the idea of such an uphill battle is misleading. God has not ordained an elaborate, taxing process to become a Christian. In fact, it may be harder *not* to be saved than it is to *be* saved.

After the Lord Jesus ascended to heaven, He poured out the Spirit "on all flesh" (Acts 2:17). Now human beings are walking around under a vast flood of "spiritual water." The Lord is all around them. It is not a challenge to find Him, much less receive Him. Water always looks for a crack or an opening, however small. Deep-sea salvage crews are always carefully aware of this fact. At great depths, a pin-sized hole in their submarine might spell disaster, for the sea might end up in the submarine with them! Keeping something airtight can be a feat, especially when it is surrounded with water.

Today, as the Spirit surrounds us, if there is the slightest opening of faith in a man, He has a way to get in. People that seem hermetically sealed off from Christ often experience this. Though their lives are fully rigged to keep God out, they inadvertently make friends with one committed Christian and begin to hear things about Jesus. While channel surfing, the couch potato who hates "all those church hypocrites," accidentally finds and watches a Jesus movie. The guy who attends a church function for the pizza and to check out the women, hears a twenty-minute talk on the death of Christ. In all these cases, without their even being aware of it, the "water" may have begun to seep in. Ultimately, the tiny opening in their heart will lead to the whole ocean of the Spirit no longer being outside of them but inside as well.

Men only agonize over the difficulty of being saved because they fail to take God's way. Jesus said, "I am the door. If anyone enters by Me he will be saved" (John 10:9). This door has not only been opened, but has been *bolted* open for two thousand years. The difficulty comes when men attempt to open what is already opened. They bustle around trying to prepare things when God's invitation has sounded out for a long time: "Come, for all things are now *ready*" (Luke 14:17). When we pay attention to that invitation, then we will find that being saved does not require what we thought. Salvation does not need the works and practices and personality strengths that world religions require. New Testament salvation involves a God who freely gives (grace) and a humbled sinner who joyfully takes (faith). As long as these two things are present, being saved is neither mysterious nor difficult.

Reference Notes

"The Pearl." *Echoes of Grace*. (Substantially adapted). Addison, IL: Bible Truth Publishers.

HOW TO KNOW FOR SURE THAT YOU ARE SAVED

A LEGITIMATE CONCERN

He was the "man of steel." He was billed as being faster than a speeding bullet, more powerful than a locomotive, and able to leap tall buildings in a single bound. It was all true, at least on television. But there came a time when the 1950s actor who played Superman, George Reeves, was found in his home dead of an apparent suicide. All it had taken to end his life was one small bullet. Decades later, another actor named Christopher Reeves played "the man of steel" on the big screen, but in real life he fell off of a horse and was paralyzed from the neck down. Cinematic special effects had made both men look invulnerable in their day, yet in each case the man of steel proved to be no more than a man of flesh.

Claiming to be saved is about as dramatic as claiming to be Superman. Consider it: when a person says, "I am saved," it means that he has received God's indestructible, eternal life. Nothing can even come close to destroying him—"though he may die, he shall live" (John 11:25). The question is, can anyone really know whether or not he is saved? Can we be assured of our salvation, or must we walk around blindly trusting that we are "men of steel" until Judgment Day, when some of us will be tragically proven wrong? Some say yes, we can know. But they proceed to tell us how, based upon guesswork. Their assurances are derived from personal opinions and religious assumptions. This is a dangerous gamble. A man can believe anything he wants on this side of the grave. But on the other side he may find out that he trusted in things that couldn't have guaranteed him a cup of coffee, let alone eternal blessings. Still, wrong ideas are recycled daily, every time someone is asked why he thinks he has salvation. Here are a few of them:

I am saved because I go to church.
I am saved because I am a good person.
I am saved because I had an unusual experience.
I am saved because one of my close relatives is a minister.
I am saved because I made some religious improvements.
I am saved because a God of love wouldn't condemn me.
I am saved because I was raised in a Christian family.
I am saved because I believe in a god.
I am saved because I try to follow the Ten Commandments.
I am saved because I just know it.

The Bible will not validate any of these assumptions. Though some of them might sound reasonable, the truth is, all together they don't add up to anything thicker than an eggshell. That's hardly a foundation you'd want to rest your eternal future upon.

Perhaps you unconciously believed some of those statements yourself. Now that I've called them all into question you might feel a little threatened. This is not bad.

Being concerned about the authenticity of our salvation is a normal and even necessary thing. The Lord Jesus Himself deliberately stirred the disciples to consider it. In a parable that He spoke to them, He compared true Christians—"sons of the kingdom"—to wheat (Matt. 13:30, 38a). Then He compared false believers—"sons of the wicked one"—to tares (Matt. 13:38b). Tares are noxious weeds, which in the early stages of growth closely mimic wheat. Even an experienced field hand has a hard time telling them apart from the good crop. This parable is a stunning portrayal of today's situation, where false Christians often stand shoulder to shoulder with real ones in the home, in the workplace, and yes, even in professing churches. They assume that since they share some of the same values as true believers, then that means they must also be saved. These "tares" have no idea that they are only religious mimics of the Christian life, "having a form of godliness but denying its power" (2 Tim. 3:5). They are such good copycats of the wheat, that they themselves don't know they are false. Many of them will continue to confidently affirm that they are Christians all the way up to the final judgment. At that point, the true situation will be brought to light. The wheat (genuine believers) will be gathered into God's barn, while the tares (the false ones) will be gathered and thrown into a furnace for burning (Matt. 13:40).

In the world today, some criminals go to great lengths learning to produce false items. They counterfeit money or forge art masterpieces. But fakes are eventually discovered. The consequences for creating them range from fines to jail time. However, a forged salvation is the most serious of all because it ends with "the furnace of fire" (Matt. 13:42). That warning should create in all of us a desire for what is genuine. It should remind us of the necessity of having what is real.

When the Lord Jesus warned His disciples that one of them would betray Him, "they were exceedingly sorrowful, and each of them began to say to Him, 'Lord, is it I?'" (Matt. 26:22). Even then, at that late time, they were aware of the possibility of self-deception—of being false but not knowing it.

True believers tend to be those with the most concern about having an authentic relationship with the Lord. False ones, on the other hand, dismiss the question. They never seem to need the assurance of salvation. If asked whether they are saved, they often will say yes with no proof to corroborate their answer. Some even become defensive, as though being asked the question was a personal affront. Typically, real Christians like to talk about their salvation experience, and when they say, "Yes, I am saved," they can back it up with evidences provided by God.

You Can Know That You Are Saved

I am not suggesting that believers ought to linger in doubt—far from it—but they should pass through a healthy stage of self-check. Without going through that phase and entering into a firm assurance of salvation, the Christian will always seem to be marooned on an island of uncertainty. In that state, it will be hard for him to have the joy and boldness needed to follow Christ and sometimes suffer for Him.

The Bible can provide help in reaching the personal assurance of salvation, because it is full of certainty and knowing. The Apostle John told the believers that "you may *know* that you have eternal life" (1 John 5:13 NASB). He specifically selected the word "know," not "guess" or "hope." John also said, "we *know* that we are in Him" (1 John 2:5), "we *know* that when He is revealed, we shall be like Him" (1 John 3:2), and "We *know* that we have passed from death to life" (1 John 3:14).

This type of assurance was also the bottom line in Paul's gospel when he said, "Let it be *known* to you brethren, that...by Him everyone who believes is justified" (Acts 13:38-39). All who believed could then go on "in full *assurance* of faith" (Heb. 10:22).

Knowing That You Are Saved **Now**

Being assured that you are saved has a lot to do with knowing that you are saved at this very moment. This is where people balk. They think that salvation is a matter only belonging to the future. After you die, it is thought, then you will be saved. In particular verses, the Bible does speak of salvation as related to the future, but that is only in respect to its maturity—its final stages.

For example, when a farmer plants seed, he begins looking forward to the end of the growing season with a certain kind of hope. It's not a hope that the seed will be in the ground on harvest day. No, the initial planting phase is long past. He now looks for its full development. Similarly, believers should be people who *know* that they have already "been born again not of corruptible seed, but incorruptible" (1 Pet. 1:23). By knowing that the seed is currently planted within us we can then hope for its complete development. That is why God "has begotten us again to a living *hope*" (1 Pet. 1:3). It is not a hope that we will be born again. According to the verse, God has already done that. The "living hope" is unto a further experience of the salvation that we already have, to "an inheritance incorruptible and undefiled and that does not fade away, reserved in heaven for you" (1 Pet. 1:4).

Our positional, once-for-all salvation is something we have presently. An enduring (but incorrect) concept is that only when we stand before God will we know whether we have been forgiven by Him and have eternal life. When does God decide whether we are sons or devils? Many of us see ourselves as standing on a trap door the day that we appear before Him. If we are approved, then we will be His sons. If we are disapproved, we will fall through the door into the lake of fire. But the Bible makes a very strong case for salvation *now,* not then:

> "Having *now* been justified by His blood, we shall be saved from wrath through Him." (Rom. 5:9)

"There is therefore *now* no condemnation to those who are in Christ Jesus." (Rom. 8:1)

"And because you *are* sons, God has sent forth the Spirit of His Son into your hearts, crying out, 'Abba, Father!'" (Gal. 4:6)

"But *now* in Christ Jesus you who once were far off have been brought near by the blood of Christ." (Eph. 2:13)

"Beloved, *now* we *are* children of God..." (1 John 3:2a)

HOW TO KNOW THAT YOU ARE SAVED—
THE BIBLE SAYS SO

It is possible for people to deceive themselves. You can want something so badly that you'll sell yourself on the idea of having it, even if you don't. Take all the folks who think they look like celebrities or those who believe they have the best ways to cook certain dishes. The embarrassing reality might be otherwise. John Doe may no more resemble a movie star than he does Mister Potato Head. Jane Doe's beloved chili recipe might produce a plate of something that tastes no better than dog food with beans. John and Jane both believe things about themselves, but their beliefs rest on a layer of wishful thinking. This is not where we want to stand with the issue of salvation—telling ourselves and everyone else that we are saved without a shred of evidence to substantiate it.

In order to confirm our new birth, we need an objective, unchanging witness that can't be clouded with bias or imagination. That means we need it in writing, just like a contract. This is exactly where the scriptures provide an invaluable service. Nothing can settle the question of our salvation more definitely than the concept of "the Bible says."

"These things I have *written* to you who believe in the name of the Son of God, in order that you may *know* that you have eternal life." (1 John 5:13 NASB)

Even with written assurances, though, our feelings might still not agree. They could tell us a different story altogether. For instance, since you don't exactly spring out of bed in the morning, you may not feel very eternal. Furthermore, when you got a flat tire, or lost your wallet, or caught the stomach flu, you didn't particularly feel Christian at those moments, either. If, in the early part of my Christian life, I had continued gauging my spiritual status based on random feelings, it would have been disastrous. The mixed signals I received would have driven me mad with uncertainty. It was not until I believed the truth of God written down on paper, that I felt safe to discard all conflicting sensations, all bouts of depression, and all torrents of doubt. "The just shall live by *faith*" (Rom. 1:17), the Bible says, not *feeling*. Real faith only needs to know whether God has said something. That is good enough.

How often on a trip have you "felt" you were headed north or south, east or west? Navigating by an emotional compass will result in driving straight into the Gulf of Mexico (when you were hoping to arrive in Minnesota). It always takes an objective source to rescue us from inner turmoil. That's why we have roadmaps. My roadmap shows me that when I am traveling on Highway 71 north and passing 480, I am headed straight for Cleveland. I could be seized with a sudden deep personal fear that I am just about to hit Houston, Texas, instead, that I am terribly lost, and that I have somehow gotten turned around on the U.S. interstate system. A mere glance at the map would tell me that my feelings were rubbish. I might need to take a nap at a rest stop, but I am certainly not lost.

The Bible acts just like a roadmap to help us regain our bearings. In the midst of a confused emotional landscape, we will find nothing more stable than the printed Word. It is outside of us and therefore immune to moods brought on by gloomy weather, stock market crashes, weight gain, head colds, and "the blahs." Since it never changes, the Bible will steadfastly tell us the truth when our own hearts will not.

Regardless, there will always be people who tell themselves that because of who they are and how weak they are, assurance verses could not possibly apply to them. But when John wrote "that you may *know* that you have eternal life" (1 John 5:13), he issued a massive blanket statement. It would apply to any believer who read the New Testament for at least two thousand years. From the human standpoint, that was a very risky thing to do. John was not personally acquainted with all the problematic people down through church history who would read his writings. But then again, he didn't need to know them. The Holy Spirit, who guided his writing, knew all of our cases, yet still issued the same promise that if you believe in Jesus, then you can know you have eternal life. Apparently, none of us could be so messed up as to invalidate that written guarantee.

In order to settle the issue of whether or not you are saved, only one question remains: Did you do what God has told you to do? Romans 10:9 says "that if you confess with your mouth the Lord Jesus and believe in your heart that God has raised Him from the dead, you will be saved." *Did* you confess with your mouth and believe in your heart? If so, you are saved, even if you have not registered anything impressive on the emotional Richter scale.

But, you may wonder, aren't we staking a lot on the Bible? It seems that entrusting our eternity to a few verses is like hanging on a thread over a volcano. It looks like anyone who trusts the Word to such an extent must have great faith.

Let's look at it another way. When I was ten years old I knew a kid named Wilbur who had a reputation for lying. He told us that he had rode his bike in a demolition derby, that his navel was actually an old gunshot wound, and—well, you get the picture. Finally Wilbur became one of those people who fit the old saying, "I know he's lying because his lips are moving."

Now you *would* need to be a giant of faith to believe Wilbur if he told you that salvation came just by believing in Jesus. No one would blame you for hesitating and then holding out for more proof. But in order to believe God's Word, our faith only needs to be reasonable, not great. "It is impossible for God to lie" (Heb. 6:18), therefore to believe Him makes perfect sense.

That's why it sounds strange when Christians *try* to believe the Bible's assurance of salvation. It is as though they are trying to believe the promises of a street hustler or the claims of a television commercial. They don't realize the nature of their illogical struggle, which is to doubt the Word of One who has never lied and never will. Yes, the dilemma is peculiar. Because of God's track record alone, He should be entitled to unreserved trust.

Not everyone has the same reason for balking at God's written assurance. Another form of disbelief actually comes wrapped in reverence. Some people refuse to believe in the certainty of salvation, because to them it sounds too presumptuous. It is best, they think, to remain lowly and *hope* that they *might* be saved. At first the sentiment sounds humble. But nothing could be more proud than seeing the plain assurances of God and then refusing to agree with them. Knowing we are saved is not a matter of arrogance. It simply means we agree with the Bible. When the scriptures say, "Whoever believes is saved," then we can stand on that God-given fact. There is nothing egotistical involved.

The new Christian does not need to be a spiritual giant in order to find the assurance of salvation. God has made it easy for us to verify, since it is plainly written in the black and white letters of the Bible. One does not need to feel or experience. He only needs to read and believe.

HOW TO KNOW THAT YOU ARE SAVED—THE SPIRIT SAYS SO

Scripture is the primary source of the assurance of our salvation. However, God has been kind enough to multiply further proofs. He is not a silent spectator as we process doubts and battle uncertainty. He does not sit back and watch while the poor mixed-up Christian thumbs through Bible verses. Romans 8:16 tells us, "The Spirit *Himself* bears witness with our spirit that we are children of God." According to this verse, all real believers have an inner witness assuring them that they are indeed born of God.

The word "witness" calls to mind a court trial. During the proceedings, if there is any doubt about the truthfulness of a matter, a good witness can help clear it up. When we put ourselves "on trial" to determine whether we are saved, a witness is available to us that can provide expert testimony—the Holy Spirit. If there were ever a person who was clear about our status before God, it would be Him. He is "the Spirit of truth" (John 14:17), so when He testifies to the validity of our salvation, we can trust that it will be the true story.

I had a firsthand experience of this. After being saved, it wasn't long before I settled down and thought about what had happened to me. People typically do this kind of thing. After an incredible thing happens to them, they disassemble it, scrutinize it, and ask if it isn't a bit too good to be true. My brother once ran into this very thing when he found thirty dollars in a ditch. A few minutes later when his euphoria faded, he wondered if the bills weren't counterfeit. That's exactly what I was doing. Sitting on the edge of a bed, weeks after my salvation event, I wondered if I wasn't being a little presumptuous. Had I been too fast in applying the Bible's assurances to my own case? Maybe I was still unsaved and didn't know it.

I told a more seasoned Christian about my misgivings and he gave me a peculiar set of instructions. "Go back to your room," he said, "and say firmly, 'I am *not* a child of God.'"

I was puzzled. How would that help anything? On top of suspecting I wasn't saved, I would be affirming it out loud. That could only make a bad situation worse.

But I did it. Alone in my barracks room, I said out loud with as much sincerity as possible, "I am *not* a child of God." What followed was very interesting. There was a slight but immediate sense of disagreement in me, as though I had just told a lie. Up until that moment, my mind had been confused and my emotions a bit troubled, but some deeper recess within me was apparently quite clear about my relationship with the Lord. It was my human spirit and the Holy Spirit together, jointly witnessing that I was a child of God, even as I claimed that I was not.

I am not saying that what I did is the only way to realize the Spirit's witness. After all, we are not told *how* the Spirit witnesses—only that He does it. Not every way that He works will be so simple and how-to oriented as what I described. Consider what is involved. Your human spirit is your very deepest, most subjective part. The Holy Spirit is divine and invisible. When these together witness to the truth of our standing before God, it will no doubt be deep, spontaneous, and somewhat mysterious.

New Christians often talk about how difficult it is to describe this inner testimony. They can be utterly defeated in debates with atheists, stranded without any further arguments, made to look like superstitious fools, and yet the Spirit continues witnessing. If the frustrated Christian resorts to describing inward feelings as proof of being a child of God, the atheist laughs and says that it is only part of a religious delusion. Words are weak in explaining the Spirit's internal testimony. A person must have it in order to understand it.

HOW TO KNOW THAT YOU ARE SAVED—YOUR EXPERIENCE SAYS SO

Since our new birth is spiritual, it would be reasonable to expect spiritual evidences to accompany it, like experiences of some kind. However, any time we broach the subject of spiritual experience, some caution is needed. Not all feelings and occurrences described in the Bible were meant for duplication in the lives of every believer. The scriptures tell us of special events accompanying the salvation of some people, but not with others. In various places, some who received Jesus spoke in tongues (Acts 10:44, 46)[1] , but the 3,000 who were saved in Acts chapter 2

---

[1] A miraculous gift of the Holy Spirit that enables a person to speak in another language—one he previously did not know.

did not. Saul of Tarsus saw a vision from heaven the day he was saved, but his experience was unique to him. No one else in the New Testament claimed a repeat of the Damascus-road event. Other Christians have professed extraordinary circumstances, even miracles, attached to their salvation, but these are not a standard part of the born-again "package." Not everyone who believes in Jesus will receive them. Expecting such special phenomenon to come with salvation will do us more harm than good. Many a new Christian has ended up in a labyrinth of confusion, searching for signs of new birth that the Bible actually never promised.

If we look for experiences that definitely accompany salvation, we must search the Bible for those that are common to *all* believers. And they do exist. Any new life, shortly after being born, will automatically begin to exhibit certain native tendencies. Human infants, for example, have a natural suck reflex, cry a lot, and spit out bitter things. In a similar sense, your new spiritual birth will also produce certain emotions and experiences. These will mostly be related to peace, joy, and love.

Even so, we must not go to extremes. Some people find it easy to become overly subjective (into themselves) and concerned about the duration and intensity of feelings. They may begin to ask questions that are impossible to answer. If salvation brings peace, for instance, then how much peace should we have in order to know that we are saved? If a truly saved person is joyful, then should he be joyful all day long without ceasing? How intense should the joy be? Does it come along explosively, or gradually, like the warmth you feel as you drink hot chocolate? Experiences will vary in their intensity from one believer to the next. Due to our personalities and individual needs, the Spirit decides when, how strong, and how long these feelings should be.

THE PROOF OF PEACE

Peace with God is a sign that some major spiritual event has transpired in a person's life. The Apostle Paul said, "Having been justified by faith, we have *peace* with God through our Lord Jesus Christ" (Rom. 5:1). A justified person is at peace with God on *God's* terms. Plenty of people try to establish peace with God on *their* terms. They use many excuses to make themselves feel better about their sins. Only a self-deceived peace results from that approach. It is a fake tranquility that comes from dodging the issues and not looking God straight in the eye.

Let me digress for a moment and relate an example from my early work history. I'll never forget the first time I got a paycheck. Up until then I had almost no experience managing money. So, after an intense four-day splurge, I was shocked to find myself broke for the rest of the month. This actually continued every payday for a while, until I learned some things about budgeting. But in the meantime as a young ignorant guy, I started doing what some of the other young ignorant guys were doing—borrowing. We would find some soldiers who (incredibly) still had money after the first week of the month and we would beg them for loans.

I never knew how much a little debt could change how you feel toward the person that you owe. It starts practically the minute after you borrow that twenty-five dollars and gets worse with every passing day. Each time you bump into the fellow who loaned you the money, you're wondering if he's thinking about it. Is he thinking that you're a bum for needing to borrow it? Is he regretting having loaned it to you? Is he suspicious that he'll never get it back? This is what I thought that the other guy thought, so it was hard for me to laugh with him, work with him, or even look him in the eye. I had no peace. I tried doing a few things to alleviate the awkwardness, like leaving the room when he entered. That gave a shaky, momentary comfort, but it wasn't real. I was in debt, plain and simple. Nothing but clearing that debt would bring me any rest.

Since their many sins are like a mountain of debt before God, "'there is no peace,' says the Lord, 'for the wicked'" (Isa. 48:22). This is why the justified person is such an anomaly in this sinful world—he has peace with God. Though he was a debtor, he has claimed Christ's payment for sin. Instantly, God justified him, declaring him to be debt-free. The resulting deep-seated relief within him now comes from the fact that the holy requirements of God upon his life have been satisfied. Though the Lord "has appointed a day on which He will judge the world in righteousness" (Acts 17:31), the new believer is at peace about it.

You may say, "*What* peace? I haven't had any beyond five minutes of being saved. Since I've come to Christ, my problems have only seemed to multiply." The Lord Jesus Himself knew something about this. He had experienced "the Spirit of God descending like a dove and alighting upon Him. And suddenly a voice came from heaven, saying, 'This is My beloved Son, in whom I am well pleased" (Matt. 3:17). It was a high point for Him, yet directly following this glorious experience "Jesus was led up by the Spirit into the wilderness to be tempted by the devil" (Matt. 4:1). Furthermore, "He was with the wild beasts" (Mark 1:13) and "He was hungry" (Matt. 4:2). God had publicly confirmed that Jesus was His Son and that He was well pleased with Him, yet the circumstances immediately following seemed to suggest the opposite. Where was the peace that should have belonged to Jesus?

The question arises from our misunderstanding of the word "peace." We popularly think of it as meaning the calm of the world around us. But the peace that comes from salvation is not like that. As the Lord Jesus said, "My peace I give to you; *not* as the world gives..." (John 14:27). The tranquility He provides is deep and abiding and we're liable not to notice it if we're paying attention to all the "noise" around us. Yet, when we consider the justification we have in Christ, peace is there. It is peace with *Him*. We have not been guaranteed peace with our clunker cars or with our work situations. Peace with Him means rest connected to the giant issues of sin and death, of judgment and punishment. It is a calm related to our eternal destiny. It says, "justified." The cloudless sky in the depths of our hearts assures us that now, at long last, our standing before God is righteous.

The Proof of Joy

C.S. Lewis was an Oxford Professor, an atheist who, for many years, thought that there was nothing to the Christian life. Later, after finally coming to Christ, he wrote a book about the experience entitled *Surprised by Joy*. The chief point, of course, stands out in the title. Lewis was simply not expecting anything delightful in salvation. It was as though he had expected Jesus to be a lemon, but biting down, found sweet instead of sour.

Because of preconceived notions, a lot of people have shared Lewis's amazement. Most of their lives they assumed that the Lord was a jumble of boring services, hard pews, incomprehensible teachings, and judgmental people. They confused the most uninspiring elements of the Christian religion with Christ Himself. But sorting through things and eventually touching the Christ of faith, they found themselves saying to Him, "In Your presence is fullness of *joy*" (Ps. 16:11). They discovered a small miracle, as Peter wrote—"Though now you do not see Him, yet believing, you rejoice with joy inexpressible and full of glory" (1 Pet. 1:8).

This peculiar joy was a promise to the disciples. The Lord Jesus said, "I will see you again and your heart will *rejoice*, and your *joy* no one will take from you" (John 16:22). Such gladness subsequently becomes a proof that you have seen Christ from within, with the eyes of your heart (Eph. 1:18).

I mentioned in the beginning of this book that when I was saved, I was in the midst of an emotional pressure cooker. Even after believing in Jesus, nothing in my environment changed for the better. I was still agitated about certain things and sorrowful over others. However, some significant factor had changed *internally*. I was now strangely happy about Christ. He had not answered any prayer to dissolve the hardships in my life. So, this was not a joy that emanated from being freed of discomforts. Instead, it had sprung from seeing someone, or rather, being seen *by* Him. The promise had come true for me: "I will see you again and your heart will *rejoice*" (John 16:22).

Saved people find a deep vein of joy even when little or nothing is going right on the surface of their lives. Isaiah said, "With *joy* you will draw water from the *wells* of salvation" (12:3). In arid regions, water is seldom found at surface level. It is usually out of sight, hidden deeply within the ground. A well might look like a dark empty hole in the earth, but drop a bucket in there and listen. Eventually there will be a splash.

Watchman Nee was a Christian from China who became a source of spiritual help to many thousands of believers. The last years of his life were spent in a communist prison. During his incarceration, he lived under the most spartan conditions, experienced the loss of his wife, was denounced by Christians he had discipled, and endured the chronic pain of angina until it killed him. Nonetheless, his last known correspondence to the outside world said clearly and simply, "I still remain joyful at heart." Nee's life tested and proved the truth of the promise that "No one will take your joy away from you."

I have known believers who endeavored to be joyful because they read that real Christians ought to be. They tried so hard to be happy that it began to look forced. But the joy of salvation needs no human energy to churn up. Genuine spiritual joy comes from Christ, not self-effort. If you work too hard to get something that the Bible says you already have, then it will end up looking and feeling artificial. The joy of salvation is not a commandment that we must try to carry out; it is a normal response. Even the apostle's call to "Rejoice in the Lord" (Phil. 3:1) does not mean that we need to manufacture the happiness needed to do it. We can rejoice because the joy of salvation is there already.

If you are a Christian who can't seem to find the joy I've described, try something extreme: *Forget* about it. Instead, put an emphasis on "Looking unto *Jesus*" (Heb. 12:2). A good percentage of the time, spiritual drought occurs because of a Christian's preoccupation with feelings. His problem is that while he is hunting for joy, he has more than likely looked *away from* Jesus. A simple redirection of his attention to Christ will do a lot to solve the problem. Remember that God has not merely conferred some happy feelings upon us from heaven. Joy is in your heart for a reason—Christ is there.

Salvation is not a famine, as the unsaved suppose. The Bible characterizes it as a feast (Luke 14:16-17), a celebration, a happy occasion. After the prodigal son returned, the father said, "bring the fatted calf here and kill it, and let us *eat and be merry"* (Luke 15:23). The centerpiece of the celebration came down to one simple item shared between the prodigal son and his father—that slain calf. Today Christ has been slain and the Father shares Him with us. "You were called into the fellowship of His Son, Jesus Christ our Lord" (1 Cor. 1:9). Now He is not only God's delight (Matt. 3:17), but ours as well. This simple newfound joy, in itself, is an assurance of our salvation. We can say together with the prodigal son, "Once upon a time I thought I could only be happy without my father. But something has changed. Now I am merry *with* him."

THE PROOF OF LOVING THE BROTHERS

In my pre-Christian days, I felt that a person who was born again was to be avoided as if he were someone with head lice or the stomach flu or bad breath. I had known a handful of Christians. It wasn't that they were unpleasant or unlikable. In fact, some of them were great guys, so the problem wasn't them at all. They simply had something that I didn't love. Whatever it was (I called it religion at the time) made me feel uncomfortable. It was as if they were functioning in life with five fingers while I was trying to get by with four. And that was fine with me. I would have rather kept my handicap than accept anything "the God Squad" (as we called them) had to offer me.

That was why it was so strange after believing in Jesus to find myself seeking these same people out. In fact, following my salvation, I couldn't think of anybody in this world I would have rather been with. They did not necessarily have backgrounds or personality types that were compatible with mine. The only explanation was that the eternal life in them had also gotten into me. It was just as John had written—"We know that we have passed from death to life, because we love the brethren" (1 John 3:14).

Love for other Christians is a characteristic of the new birth: "Whoever believes that Jesus is the Christ is born of God, and...loves him who is begotten of Him" (1 John 5:1). The new life within you always recognizes and loves the new life within others.

By saying this I am not suggesting that we will love everything about other believers. In fact, I quickly found that the very Christians I loved had an unlovable streak in them as well. No believer is just a big bundle of spirituality. The new birth is sheathed in all the flaws and quirks of human personality. You may begin to notice that the Christians you absolutely loved for a period of time in the beginning are bossy, overly talkative, too passive, temperamental, and so on.

After dealing with these dispositional challenges for a while and not doing very well at it, some of us have begun to wonder if there is really *any* love in us. Some might even say, "You'd better find a stronger proof of salvation than loving the brothers. If anything important rides on *that*, I'm in trouble."

However, Paul tells us, "Concerning brotherly love...you yourselves are taught by God to love one another; and indeed you do so toward all the brethren...but we urge you, brethren, that you *increase* more and more" (1 Thess. 4:9-10). Obviously "increase" means there's room to grow. So, if you have discovered that you're low on love for the brothers, you're right. If you think you're *void* of love for the brothers, you're wrong. Being born of God means that you will love all others who have been born of Him. You won't be able to help it.

Occasionally, I hear about people who discover that they are adopted and who then mount a search for their biological family. They can't seem to rest knowing that strangers are walking around out there who physically resemble them and share their DNA. So, they hope to shake hands with these unknown persons and maybe even forge a relationship with them. This type of thing is what drives us to seek out other Christians. It is more than an "ought to" or a "should" that draws us together with others of the faith. The presence of a new inner sense demands that we find them. And when we do, we will love them, difficulties notwithstanding. This affection is a universal sign of the second birth, an assurance that we have been saved.

Spiritual experiences were never meant to supercede the truth of scripture. God has provided help to us in a certain order. First, He gives written assurances of salvation in the Bible as our primary touchstone. Only afterwards does He point us toward felt assurances. These secondary confirmations, though, are like butterflies. If we make them primary issues and chase them around trying to obtain them, then they will elude us. If we stand still, however, and make the facts of the Bible our primary emphasis, then salvation's feelings will tend to light upon us. Sensations like peace, love, and joy will then testify that our negative situation with God has been cleared up and a new life has begun.

The Proof of a New Family Likeness

Allen, a recently saved thirty something, sat across the lunch table from me genuinely puzzled. "I can't figure out what's wrong," he said. "It seems like something is frustrating my relationship with the Lord."

"What do you think it is?" I asked.

"I'm not sure, but a couple of times I thought it might be my girlfriend."

"What about her?"

He gave me a knowing glance. "Well, I *live* with her."

"Allen," I said, "It sounds like you may have already figured out what's wrong."

Like thousands of other new Christians, Allen had encountered a heightened inward sense of righteousness brought on by his new birth. Although he was still relatively unaccustomed to it, he had found it quite real. Thankfully, a short time after our conversation, he married that live-in girlfriend, and now they are a strong couple for Christ. I don't think Allen knew it then, but the subjective righteousness welling up in his heart was a proof that he was truly a child of God. His aversion to living in a sexual relationship outside of marriage was evidence of his membership in "the household of the faith" (Gal. 6:10).

You see, not only physical features, but also behavior runs in families. Some children sound just like their parents when they talk. They even laugh like them. But the behavior that characterizes the family of God is righteousness— "...You know that everyone who *practices righteousness* is born of Him" (1 John 2:29b).

This does not mean a state of instant behavioral perfection is bestowed on you when you believe. In fact, nothing is more boorish than a Christian who thinks he is perfect when the rest of the world knows better. We are never promised to become sinless on this side of glory. Nor does the Apostle John tell us that we are false Christians if we sin. He says that the new birth brings with it an instinct for righteousness that motivates right behavior. Since "He [the Father] is righteous" (1 John 2:29a), those born of Him, will in part always have a certain discomfort with sin. It's like cats avoiding water. They do not instinctively seek to swim, but *can* they do it? Yes, and occasionally they do, although something in them does not like the experience and feels miserable when the whole thing is over.

Righteousness, or at the very least, disgust with sin, is evidence of the new life within. It means that in some deep way, we have obtained the divine family likeness. And, true to form, it keeps coming out both in the things we do and in the things we don't do.

ANSWERING DOUBTS—
THAT TERRIBLE THING IN YOUR NON-CHRISTIAN PAST

During a casual conversation, a young fellow named Parker told me how that he had believed in Jesus. But he went on to say, "I just can't shake the idea that when the

Lord sees me, it's going to be like this—" and he turned a thumbs-down. There was no denying that Parker had done something that was bookmarked large and ugly in his past. Whether it was related to sex or violence or some kind of crime was hard to say. For sure it was continuing to haunt him. I shared some verses with Parker, hoping to strengthen the assurance of his salvation, but he shook his head sadly as if to say, "You just don't understand. You don't know what I've done."

Like Parker, new Christians frequently stop and wonder how they could possibly be saved. Could God have really forgiven all of their past evil deeds, including "the big one?" (whatever it was). These people may have genuinely believed in Jesus, but they are swamped in doubt whenever the specter of some past sin visits their memory. It seems to say, "Before you get used to thinking you're saved, just recall what you did." Under that kind of discouragement, even a vivid salvation experience can start looking a bit like a mirage. The affected Christian will begin toying with the idea that maybe he celebrated prematurely. Perhaps in a fit of self-delusion he has only imagined being in the river of life. Maybe the reality is that he is still sitting in a sandbox. Past sins can inflict those doubts and paralyze new faith.

Let's consider what the Bible says about the very worst forms of wickedness. No doubt any sin, regardless of how small, introduces a person to spiritual death. But there is such a thing as "great sin" (Ex. 32:30), "greater sin" (John 19:11), and sin that is "very great" (1 Sam. 2:17). We also find "great abominations" (Ezek. 8:6), and "greater abominations than these" (Ezek. 8:15). Apparently, there are differing degrees of sin. For example, some transgressions are beyond self-destructive; they are also ruinous to other people. Sins in this category require the Lord's forgiveness *and* punitive action such as prison or even the death penalty. Murder is one of them. It is a very serious offense, but is it unforgivable? Is that where God draws the line and rejects faith in Christ as not sufficient? Though most of us have not committed murder, the answer is still important, because it will have a direct bearing upon how

God deals with all lesser sins.

I John 3:15 says, "No murderer has eternal life abiding in him." This seems to indicate that murder is the sinner's point of no return, the place where even divine forgiveness cannot go. But John didn't say, "No murderer has been forgiven" nor did he say, "No murderer has eternal life." Instead, John wrote that "No murderer has eternal life *abiding* in him." "Abiding" is not a term that describes being born again. It refers to the ongoing relationship between God and a person who is already born again. For eternal life to abide in a person means that it continues to exert a positive influence upon him. First John 3:15, therefore, has nothing to say about whether a murderer can be born again. Neither does scripture prohibit a repentant murderer from being saved.

In 1983, after years of prostitution and heroin use, a young woman named Karla Faye Tucker murdered several people with a pickaxe. Shortly after she was arrested and sent to prison, a traveling ministry group came to the penitentiary. They preached the gospel that night and Karla received Christ.

For fifteen years following that day, she sought to follow the Lord and minister to her fellow inmates. Though for the rest of her life she was sorry for what she had done, she believed that the Lord Jesus had saved her, even up until the last day of her life when she was executed by lethal injection.

David Berkowitz, the infamous "Son of Sam," went on a killing spree in the seventies, taking the lives of six people and wounding others. He was sentenced to three hundred and fifty years in prison. When he eventually encountered the gospel through another inmate, his first reaction was to reject it. He believed himself too evil for God's love. But rejection slowly turned to acceptance. Berkowitz finally gave in to the Word, believed in Christ, and was saved.

More than twenty-five years have passed since that time, and today Berkowitz serves as an assistant prison pastor. His conversion was no ploy to gain sympathy from the parole board, either. He himself has steadfastly turned down opportunities for parole, because he believes his crimes are too serious to ever deserve freedom. He does not feel that society owes him forgiveness but believes that he has certainly received God's forgiveness in Christ.

The next time your questionable past rises up to challenge whether you could ever truly be saved, think of Karla Faye Tucker and David Berkowitz. Their sins were far more destructive than yours, yet the grace of Christ embraced them both.

According to our human estimation, where some sins are the size of pellets, others are the size of boulders. Thankfully though, even offenses that great cannot prevent God from extending his salvation to us. But according to the feeling of some believers, there are sins larger than boulders. These are the size of mountains. They are evil deeds intentionally aimed at God Himself. The Bible calls them blasphemies— acts or words that degrade something holy to the level of the ridiculous or profane. Christians who, in their unsaved past were involved with things like Satanism, witchcraft, or certain forms of paganism have almost certainly fallen into this sin. Many groups associated with those things have initiation rites involving blasphemy. They require new members to swear allegiance to devilish spirits or utter dark oaths against Christ. Even a person not associated with an evil group could just as easily do some of those things. In a fit of anger he could curse God or out of carelessness might tell a filthy joke about Jesus.

These acts can leave an enduring mark of darkness on the conscience. Blasphemy is not a sin against another person here on earth; it is a clenched fist rising up to strike the face of God. So, it is not hard to understand why the believer who has done such may now find it difficult to say, "Praise the Lord, I'm saved."

Yet there is good news about these discouraging satanic blots. Jesus said, "*Every* sin and blasphemy will be forgiven men" (Matt. 12:31). We have from His mouth the final word concerning all the attempts to disgrace Him and dishonor God. *Every* blasphemy will be forgiven. This greatly reduces the number of possible past sins that might forbid salvation.

Not only can men be forgiven of doing the worst things to one another, but for doing the worst things to God as well. Whether it is the size of a pellet, a boulder, or a mountain, no sin can withstand the grace of Christ.

But suppose a sin in your past looms even larger than a mountain. Maybe it is the size of an asteroid. Would anyone have to worry about an evil so enormous? Again, some say yes. I just quoted the verse where the Lord Jesus promised that all sins and blasphemies would be forgiven. I didn't quote all of it, though. The rest of the verse contains a qualifier—"the blasphemy against the Spirit will *not* be forgiven men" (Matt. 12:31). Of course, the possibility of having committed an unforgivable sin is serious. It could leave us all open to endless doubt.

Some believers have wondered if, in the days before salvation, they blasphemed the Spirit without realizing it. The more they meditate on the question, the more elusive the answer seems to be. The past can be such a blur of sins that maybe blasphemy against the Spirit is sandwiched somewhere in the middle, unnoticed and unknown.

If the slightest possibility exists for an unforgivable sin in our past, then we will find it hard to have any assurance of salvation. How can we know that we have not committed "the big one"? Let's start by identifying what the Lord meant when He spoke of blaspheming the Spirit. In the gospel of Matthew, we find Jesus casting out demons. This He did "by the Spirit of God" (Matt. 12:28). But antagonistic religious observers said, "This fellow does not cast out demons except by Beelzebub, the ruler of the demons" (Matt. 12:24). They wanted so badly to discredit the Lord, that they condemned the power He wielded—the Holy Spirit—as being satanic. In doing so, they blasphemed the Spirit.

Before a believer ransacks his past to see if anything fits that description, he should be aware of something: there is no evidence to suggest that the sin of blaspheming the Spirit can be committed today. If it were possible for anyone to commit it, then the apostles did a terrible job of warning us. Neither Peter nor Paul placed a clause in their preaching that promised forgiveness to all except for those who had blasphemed the Spirit. John wrote of a "sin leading to death" (1 John 5:16), but this appears to be a sin (which he does not identify) that brings physical death. "Sin leading to death" was apparently the type of judgment at work in Corinth. Paul warned the believers there that because of their divisive ways "many are weak and sick among you, and many sleep [die]" (1 Cor. 11:30). But blaspheming the Spirit is not a sin whose judgment stops with punishing the body. It is a sin that will never be forgiven, meaning that its penalty stretches well past physical death and keeps going into eternity.

The Lord Jesus spoke of this unforgivable sin, but the apostles chose to say nothing about it. If it were a danger to all of us, they should have amplified His solemn warning in all of their gospel addresses. As it stands, however, they did not. The apparent reason for their silence was that they did not see the unforgiveable sin as being a threat during the time of their ministry. They must have viewed it as a sin of a very confined nature, only committed by certain people at a certain time during the Lord's earthly ministry.

Blaspheming the Spirit, then, would be a sin that not many people have had the opportunity to commit. In order to do it, a person would need to see the Lord Jesus in the flesh and condemn his ministerial work as being satanic. Obviously, no one reading this book would qualify, even by accident.

However, on a strange note, I personally know of two people who tried to blaspheme the Spirit on purpose. They were God-haters who wanted to demonstrate their complete contempt for salvation. So, they bitterly cursed the Spirit and abased Him with all kinds of crude and irreverent words. What happened to them? Later in life, both repented and came to Christ. One of them today is a church elder and an example to the entire congregation of love and service to Christ. Another is a minister who teaches the Bible and has led many people to the Lord. These two *tried* to commit "the big one" and were not able. The grace of forgiveness still found them. So, when I hear of new believers being afraid that they might have accidentally committed the unforgivable sin, I am skeptical. Neither scripture nor personal observations tend to support that possibility.

Our unsaved past is a dangerous place to idly mull over. Sprinkled amongst the good memories are plenty of dark ones. It's not long before you find yourself revisiting, reconstructing and even reliving the guilt of sins that you previously fell into. Some of them, or maybe just one of them, will stand out in terms of severity. Then nagging doubts can begin to develop about how such a thing could ever be forgiven. This is partly why Jesus said, "Abide in *Me*" (John 15:4). He did not tell us to abide in our past. Although we should never forget what great sinners we are before God, our sinful past is gone. Don't treat it like a horror movie that you keep rewinding and watching repeatedly. God said, "their sins and their lawless deeds I will remember *no more*" (Heb. 10:17). If He refuses to let our past be a problem, then why should we?

ANSWERING DOUBTS—SINS AFTER SALVATION

Nothing casts a more serious shadow of doubt on our salvation than the sins we commit after receiving Christ. Some believers stop following the Lord when they notice that sin is still with them—not only the evils they used to commit but ones they have just recently invented. Being overcome with disappointment, they succumb to the idea that they must not have been truly saved after all.

No Christian should be careless concerning sinful deeds or think of them as inconsequential. However, there is an obsession with faults and failures that can drive us into a crisis of faith. If we look for the assurance of our salvation based on behavioral perfection, we will never find it. Clashes between the new life we allegedly now have and old, resurfacing sins will become hard for us to understand. The result will be lots of questions and no assurance.

A sinning Christian partly welcomes the opportunity to go back to the dark life he left behind and have some "fun."

At the same time, however, he feels grieved. These contradictory feelings can actually make a believer aware of something new about himself—not that he no longer sins, but that a deeper part of his being *hates* it. This makes him something peculiar in a world of unsaved people, because the hope of the unsaved is to vent, to gratify, to gain at others' expense, to be funny at all costs, to feel good. The unsaved hate it if they *cannot* sin. The situation is not so easy with those who are born again. Their flesh loves to sin at the same time as their inward parts despise it.

We find this curious internal conflict typified in the life of Lot. This Old Testament man made a very unwise decision to move into the ancient evil city of Sodom. Genesis 13:10 indicates that he saw the area as being attractive like "the garden of the LORD." Our old external life always sees sin that way—as a Garden of Eden, a paradise of delights. Yet, the Bible describes Lot's experience living with the people of this "paradise." It says that he was "oppressed by the filthy conduct of the wicked for that righteous man dwelling among them, *tormented* his righteous soul from day to day by seeing and hearing their lawless deeds" (2 Pet. 2:7-8). The lost people in that immoral city were quite happy with life there. But Lot was different. He might have been temporarily satisfied with Sodom, but certainly not in his heart of hearts. Apparently, a deeper part of him was neither fooled by it nor fulfilled.

Don't be surprised if your old, corrupt nature is at home committing sins. It always wants to return to that kind of life, just like "A dog returns to his own vomit and a sow, having washed, to her wallowing in the mire" (2 Pet. 2:22). But simultaneously another nature is in you—that of a sheep which loves Christ and longs to follow Him (see John 10:11, 14-16). Sheep do not like their own vomit nor do they wallow in the mud. It is not in their nature to do so. This is why there often seems to be such a struggle within us.

As in Lot's case, a righteous man can still fall into sinful situations. His flesh is like a dog or a pig, while his spirit is like a lamb. When he wallows in the mud of sin or eats the vomit of wickedness that does not mean he is a false believer.

It only indicates that he has wandered from his spirit to the base, external parts of his being. Such lapses require a Christian to return to his fellowship with the Lord. They should not, however, plunge him into doubt over whether he has been saved.

An eloquent atheist once spoke to a crowd, presenting reasons why it was foolish for a modern man to believe in God. When the talk concluded, the young intellectuals in the audience applauded him enthusiastically. An older man stood up at the back of the room. His weathered face and clothes were evidence of a hard past life.

"Excuse me, Mister Speaker," he said.

The room quieted.

"You said that there is no God. I don't know how to argue with all of your smart facts. I just have one question. If there is no God, please tell me who or what it was that came into me when I believed in Jesus, and stopped my drinking, healed my marriage, and turned my whole life around?"

Every eye in the audience looked at the floor. No one said a word. It was an awkward moment for Mister Speaker.

Many believers can readily identify with such dramatic testimonies, especially those of us who have come from very dark backgrounds. Just as many, however, have no idea what is meant by "Jesus turned my life around." They can't quite relate to a night-and-day conversion experience. A number of these people are from Christian homes and were saved at a very early age. They haven't accumulated the same feelings and experiences because young children typically do not have a sense of being "delivered...from the power of darkness and conveyed...into the kingdom of the Son" (Col. 1:13). Due to their limited maturity, kids simply lack the deep contemplation of things like the horrors of sin or the emptiness of a life without Christ.

Later on, these same Christian kids grow up and find that they cannot give a powerful before-and-after salvation testimony. In many cases, they cannot even say when they were saved. This often becomes a source of frustration to them, as they try to figure out with calendar certainty when it happened. If they can't, then they wonder if they are really Christians at all.

The truth is, we can't always know with scientific precision when every person gets saved. This is the case even in the lives of notable New Testament examples. Although it is clear that Paul was dramatically saved, what about Peter? He was around Jesus for years, and we can only guess when salvation came to him. There was the time that Peter first came to Christ (John 1:40-42) and a time when he claimed to believe (John 16:30). There was a first time Peter called Jesus "Lord" (John 6:68), and a first when he confessed that Jesus was "the Christ, the Son of the Living God" (Matt. 16:16). Of course, there was also the first explicit mention of Peter receiving the Spirit (John 20:22). Now, on which of these occasions was Peter saved? It is very difficult to say.

Sometimes the life of people raised "around Jesus" mimics Peter's experience. It seems that the things of Christ are part of their earliest memories. During their growing up years, they had many shades of responses to the Lord. For example, there was the time little Susie called Jesus "Lord," and then there was the moment she asked Him to come and live in her heart. Many years later, Susie (now wanting to be called Susan) goes to a youth camp where a preacher asks her if she is saved. Susan confidently says, "Yes." He asks her when that happened and immediately her head swims with recollections of Christ that stretch back before kindergarten. Confused, she says she has been saved all her life. The preacher correctly responds that no one is a Christian *all* life long. We can only become Christians through receiving Christ. "Now," he restates, "*When* did that happen?" Susan is frustrated. She knows she is saved, but can't give the day or the hour.

Before her frustration reaches a crisis point, she really only needs to answer one question. This is the question that everyone must answer—"Have you *now* or *ever* in the past believed in your heart that Jesus Christ is the Son of God and that God has raised Him from the dead?" If this is in doubt, then the thing to do is believe right now and call upon His name. However, if the answer is definitely "Yes, I believed in Jesus Christ," then there is no need to allow uncertainty to continue riddling the assurance of salvation.

Due to poor hospital records, some people in this world are uncertain of when they were born. But a questionable birth date should not cause them to doubt that they had been born at all. In the same fashion, the assurance of our new birth does not lie in knowing specific times and dates. it depends on faith in Christ.

ANSWERING DOUBTS—HOW MUCH FAITH IS ENOUGH FAITH?

Faith is important, but the more it is stressed, the more a new believer is prone to wonder if he has enough of it to be saved. He may have truly believed in Christ, yet at the same time be concerned that the measure of his faith is an ounce or so short of the required amount.

Going down the road of focusing on faith, measuring it, comparing it, and second-guessing it, invariably leads to making your faith the *object* of your faith. This is a mistake. Faith is not our Savior, it is only the means of receiving the Savior.

A strange reversal takes place when we are more faith-conscious than Christ-conscious. For one thing, the means and the object switch places. I knew a man who was in his late thirties and still single. For a while he had felt the desperate tug of "Get married-or-die-alone." Then he met a woman. The problem was that whenever he talked about her, I got the impression that he wasn't marrying to get the woman; he was getting the woman so that he could get married. It was a clear case of elevating the means over the object. Eventually, the woman saw through it and the relationship ended.

Christians can fall into the same trap when they elevate the means of receiving Christ (faith) over Christ Himself. We feel the need to do this when we notice the smallness of our belief and then desperately try to help it by obsessing over it. We reason that any faith less than perfect means our salvation is still in question. But the Bible does not specify how much we need to believe in order to be saved. Scripture seems to indicate that it only takes faith the size of a mustard seed to be justified forever.

Doubt is actually less of a problem than what we make of it. For a Christian, doubt is faith that realizes its gaps and shortages. In fact, real faith often cries out, "Lord, I believe, help my unbelief!" (Mark 9:24).

Flawless believing is something of a myth, even in the lives of seasoned spiritual people. The Apostle Paul once wrote that in order to speak of all the good examples of faith, "time would fail me" (Heb. 11:32). But if I tried to portray all the difficulties of faith in those same people, time would fail *me*.

Sarah, the very aged wife of Abraham, found God's promise of her future pregnancy so ridiculous that she laughed at it (Gen. 18:11-12). She didn't soberly struggle with believing the promise; she dismissed it outright. Then she got caught. "The Lord said to Abraham, Why did Sarah laugh, saying, 'Shall I surely bear a child, since I am old?' Is anything too hard for the Lord?...But Sarah denied it, saying 'I did not laugh,' for she was afraid. And He [God] said, 'No, but you did laugh!'" (Gen. 18:13-15).

Sarah doubted, laughed at God, and then lied about it. That certainly qualifies as a limping faith, yet we find her remembered in scripture this way: "By *faith* Sarah herself also received strength to conceive seed, and she bore a child when she was past the age, because she judged Him faithful who had promised" (Heb. 11:11).

This glowing appraisal of Sarah's faith is not some New Testament idealized version of her story. It simply demonstrates that even a faith that hiccups and limps is glorious.

Sarah was no aberration. We find definite signs of faith temporarily breaking down in other famous lives. John the Baptist, for instance, was the one to see Jesus and declare, "Behold! The Lamb of God, who takes away the sin of the world!" (John 1:29). Sometime after that statement of faith, this same John visited the valley of doubt. Locked up in prison and shaken because Christ did not come to his rescue, he sent a question to Jesus: "Are you the Coming One, or do we look for another?" (Matt. 11:3). It was a shocking reversal for John. His faith had flattened out. Yet in the very moment of John's crisis, Jesus said, "Assuredly, I say to you, among those born of women, there has not risen one greater than John the Baptist" (Matt. 11:11). John's doubt did not dissolve his standing with Christ. The Lord could appraise him positively, even when the man's faith was beset by weakness. In another case, Paul commended the Thessalonian believers, saying, "your faith grows exceedingly" (2 Thess. 1:3). But this could only mean that they had begun the Christian life with a faith that was much smaller and less mature. If it had grown by leaps and bounds as the apostle indicated, then it must have been tiny at the start. Like those Christians, when we received the Lord Jesus, we did it with an imperfect faith. This is not a problem, for our salvation is not according to the might of our belief, but according to the might of the One we receive.

STRENGTHENING THE ASSURANCE OF YOUR SALVATION — *BY FEEDING ON THE WORD*

Some Christians still find the assurance of salvation and the blessed rest that comes with it impossible to obtain. There are reasons for this. One of them has to do with the kind of things we feed our minds.

Greg was a brother that had been delighted to meet Christ. He devoured the Bible, but it wasn't long before he began to devour every other book that had something to say about Jesus, too. A number of those publications contradicted the truth of scripture. They did it by subtly and repeatedly hinting that Jesus was not the Son of God and that the Bible was not divinely inspired. Greg took it in stride, thinking that if he really wanted to learn anything, he needed to hear all viewpoints. His desire to educate his new faith had driven him to teachers who had no faith of their own. All they had to give was doubt, and that was exactly what began to grow in him.

It wasn't long before Greg suffered a downturn in his Christian life. Others warned him the same way that Paul had warned Timothy: "Guard what was committed to your trust, avoiding the profane and idle babblings and contradictions of what is falsely called knowledge—by professing it some have strayed concerning the faith" (1 Tim. 6:20-21). But the allure of knowledge, even though it was false, was too much for Greg. As a result, the "wiser" he became, the less assured he was that he had ever been saved at all. His confidence had suffered erosion by things the Apostle Peter had warned of —"there will be false teachers among you, who will secretly bring in destructive heresies" (2 Pet. 2:1).

As a believer, Greg should have taken the Bible's charge to "let that abide in you which you heard from the beginning" (1 John 2:24a). This is no meaningless command, for "If what you heard from the beginning abides in you, you also will abide in the Son and in the Father" (1 John 2:24b). That blessed condition would have filled Greg with joy and assurance, but since he wasn't interested in that, he became a believer who found it difficult to ever be happy. His heart still feebly told him of the glories of Jesus, however his restless intellect would not settle down to abide there.

If you want to strengthen your assurance of salvation, the first rule of thumb is very simple: don't *weaken* it! Learn to abide in the truth of God's Word and not in every opinion that crosses your path. A turning point occurred in the life of Billy Graham when he decided to do that very thing. While his friend and fellow evangelist, George Templeton Strong, immersed himself in liberal religious ideas, Billy set himself to abide in the Word. The outcome was quite telling. George ended up terminating his evangelistic service and denying that the Bible was the Word of God. Billy, on the other hand, was strengthened in his assurance and has since brought millions to faith in Christ.

Moments of doubt, as I have said before, don't invalidate

our faith. But that doesn't mean we should feed doubt, either. Carelessly reinforcing uncertainty can cause it to harden into unbelief. Feed faith instead, with a steady diet of the Word of God in the Bible, good spoken messages, and healthy spiritual books. "As newborn babes, desire the pure milk of the word, that you may grow thereby" (1 Pet. 2:2). That kind of diet will feed faith, which in turn will feed the assurance of our salvation.

STRENGTHENING ASSURANCE— BY LIVING A LIFE IN THE LIGHT AND DEALING WITH OUR FAILURES

In the first months of my Christian life, I was with a little group of young, single guys who were seeking the Lord. We tried to look out for each other. If anyone began to wander into a spiritual danger zone, the others would exhort him and try to bring him back. We generally had a high, positive morale—everyone, that is, except for Wayne. Wayne was our resident "Eeyore." A big part of his chronically ho-hum attitude was his lack of assurance that he was saved. I never could understand why his faith in that area was so anemic. He had believed in Jesus. He read the Bible and went to church meetings. Yet, if anyone suggested to him that he was saved and entitled to all the privileges of a child of God, he would hang his head. Sometimes in our Bible reading, we would come across promises of grace that would cause our group to get excited, everyone that is, except for Wayne. He would say, "Yeah, right" or some other sarcastic remark that registered his disbelief. None of us knew why he did that, because none of us knew about Wayne's other life—at least not at the time. It was another life that he lived with a whole different set of friends on the nights that we didn't gather for fellowship.

Rumors began to get back to us about Wayne's foul mouth and poor attitude on the job. When we approached him about what we had heard, he confirmed the rumors and let us know much more than we wanted to hear.

No wonder Wayne had such trouble believing he

was saved. He was attempting to live in darkness and light at the same time. The result, at least according to his experience, was a gloomy twilight where it was too dark to sing praises, but too light to enjoy sin with total abandon. In either realm, he felt like a hypocrite. In the bar, he had to hide the light that was in him. In our gatherings, he had to hide the darkness he was pursuing. He was in the same dilemma that the Apostle John wote about: "If we say that we have fellowship with Him [God] and walk in darkness, we lie and do not practice the truth" (1 John 1:6). Wayne was a true Christian according to the second birth, but a liar according to his daily walk. That was why he would sit in the middle of our joyful Christian meeting, feeling that he was a Judas Iscariot. The contradiction between his professed faith and his behavior was seriously eroding his assurance of salvation.

Many children of God stand in those shoes. They have become so burdened with sins that although they agree with the truth of God's salvation, they can't *sing* of it. They may solemnly nod their heads to the doctrine of grace, but cannot *raise* their heads to praise the Lord for it.

The Bible tells us to "Draw near with a true heart in *full assurance of faith*" (Heb. 10:22a). But how does the troubled Christian arrive at full assurance? The answer comes from the very next phrase of the verse: "Having our hearts sprinkled from an *evil* conscience" (Heb. 10:22b). A heart that wishes to be true and fully assured cannot be shackled to a conscience that is stained with evil. In fact, an evil conscience only seems to bring the assurance that a person is *not* saved. It stands to reason, then, that if we wish to distance ourselves from doubt and have the full assurance of faith, we must do something about the "dead elephant"— the evil conscience—tied to our hearts.

The secret of doing this lies in being *sprinkled* from an evil conscience with "the *blood* of sprinkling" (Heb. 12:24), that is, the blood of Jesus. We believed, were washed in the blood of Christ, and were forgiven of our sins once for all, but sins have a way of resurfacing in our daily lives and damaging our walk with the Lord. So, in a very regular way, we need to apply the sprinkled blood to our consciences so our hearts can continue to be free. This is done through a very practical exercise: "If we *confess* our sins, He is faithful and just to forgive us our sins and to cleanse us from all unrighteousness" (1 John 1:9). By admitting to God our sins and weaknesses, the blood of Christ will cleanse our consciences and free our hearts from guilt, granting us *full* assurance of faith.

STRENGTHENING ASSURANCE—
BY PARTICIPATING IN OUR OWN SPIRITUAL DEVELOPMENT

The Bible portrays the Christian life as a dynamic, developing, growing, changing experience. It is not a passive affair, "happening to us" as though we were by-standers. Peter writes, "Add to your faith virtue, to virtue knowledge, to knowledge self-control, to self-control perseverance, to perseverance godliness, to godliness brotherly kindness, and to brotherly kindness, love" (2 Pet. 1:5-7). The operative word here is "add." God expects us to participate in our Christian lives by adding things to our faith. As He supplies the grace, the power, and the energy from within, we cooperate by adding.

Often the Lord enables us to add to our faith, but we refuse. Maybe we got lazy and started thinking that we didn't need self-control, knowledge, or virtue, and that faith was good enough. Yes, faith alone was good enough to save us. But a Christian who is hoping for spiritual development knows that it involves more than an initial faith in Christ.

Not adding anything to our faith results in spiritual poverty. That in turn leads to uncertainty about our standing before God. It is why Peter wrote, "He who *lacks* these things [virtue, knowledge, self-control, etc.] is short-sighted, even to blindness, and has *forgotten* that he was cleansed from his old sins" (2 Pet. 1:9). For someone to "forget" in that verse means that the certainty of forgiven sin is no longer at the forefront of his attention. He has forgotten the freshness, the power, and the assurance of it.

This condition plagues all who have not bothered to add anything to their faith. Since they have a habit of non-participation in their spiritual lives, the grace of Christ always seems very distant from them. When Christians finally get honest about their lackluster condition, then they tend to wrongly conclude that maybe they were never saved to begin with. That is exactly how inactivity can cause the assurance of salvation to deteriorate.

The Apostle Peter wrote, "Therefore brethren, be even more *diligent* to make your call and election *sure*" (2 Pet. 1:10). His command for diligence indicates that a new believer should never become passive and leave a vacuum in his life for old things to come back and fill. The Christian's diligence to interact with Christ will lead to the flourishing of virtues, knowledge, self-control, perseverance, godliness, brotherly kindness, and love. Under those circumstances, it will be much more difficult for him to dismiss his salvation as not being real. God's calling in his life will appear far more stable and sure.

We believers have been forgiven of our sins, and spared from the lake of fire. We have Jesus Christ living in us, the Holy Spirit flowing in us, eternal life deposited in us, and we now have a place as children of God. We have all this, *and we know it.* Such awareness has a revolutionary effect on the Christian life. It is like the difference between a man who *thinks* he has money in the bank and the man who *knows* that he does. Basically then, the assurance of salvation is just the certainty of ownership. Everything that is worthy of trust—the Bible, the Spirit, and various inward experiences—provides a united testimony to the fact that salvation is ours. Armed with those assurances, now we can go on with confidence into a glorious future.

10

HOW TO KNOW THAT YOU WILL BE SAVED FOREVER
(PART 1)

THE ULTIMATE RICHES-TO-RAGS STORY

They say you stand a better chance of being hit by lightning than of winning one of those multi-million dollar lotteries. So, when Jerry Stark managed to beat the odds it must have been a shock to his system. Suddenly, his 16 million-dollar payoff moved him to "easy street," where it seemed he would never need to worry again. But almost immediately he and his wealth were in jeopardy. Jerry's ex-girlfriend (as well as others) sued him for a sizeable share of his new fortune. In a bizarre twist, his own brother arranged to have him killed, apparently hoping to inherit the money. Jerry himself had no idea how to manage the millions that had fallen into his lap. He poured investment dollars into many schemes and ill-advised ventures, all of which failed. As a result, only one year past the time of his instant wealth, Jerry was living on foodstamps and was one million dollars *in debt*. His fortune had been completely wiped out due to his own poor judgment and the greed of others.

The whole sad story was, no doubt, a taste of what the Bible calls "uncertain riches" (1 Tim. 6:17). The wealth of this world is notorious for being here today and gone tomorrow. The question of the moment is whether or not the spiritual riches of salvation are also "uncertain." Having received "the unsearchable riches of Christ" (Eph. 3:8), could we by mistake or neglect, *lose* them? This is a matter of critical importance. If we became unsearchably rich when we received Jesus, then if we lost Him, we would become unsearchably bankrupt. Suddenly our sins would rematerialize before God. We would once more find ourselves aboard a spiritual Titanic whose destination was hell. The Holy Spirit would vacate our bodies, which had been His temple, and Christ would cease living in us. Eternal life would be taken away from us and we would become the aborted children of God. Losing salvation would be catastrophic—the ultimate "riches-to-rags" story.

Could we suffer this kind of loss? As with all the other questions related to salvation, the answer can only reliably come from the Bible. No appeal to opinion will do. Yet, even with an opened Bible, Christians don't arrive at the same conclusions. Some believers come away from the scriptures convinced that salvation can be lost. Others feel that it cannot be. If the two parties are together in a room and the subject comes up, there is liable to be a firestorm of debate. You can also bet that each side will be quoting the Bible to bolster their position. That is why, as we approach the subject of keeping or losing salvation, we must work our way through the biblical data with careful discretion.

ETERNAL SECURITY — A CONTROVERSIAL ISSUE

"Eternal security" refers to a Christian keeping his salvation forever, no matter what. Few people understand how problematic and challenging that belief can really be. For instance, if you believe that John Doe, a devoted Christian, loving father, and faithful husband will always be saved, then that might not be so hard to agree with. But once you believe it for all Christians, that same agreeable doctrine becomes controversial.

Christians have cases that are not pretty. There is Randy, a long-time believer, who shocked his family and friends when he revealed his secret life as a homosexual. Not only did he admit to numerous affairs with other men, but announced his intention to continue pursuing that lifestyle. Shortly afterwards, he abandoned his wife and children. Is Randy still born again? Then there is Sara, who was raised in a Christian home, saved at a young age, and participated in ministry work. She met a Muslim man and fell in love with him. She also found his religion, Islam, intriguing and decided to convert to it. Now she must believe that Jesus is only a human prophet and every day of her life must deny that He is the Son of God. Is she still saved?

In either Randy's or Sara's particular situation, you might find it difficult to agree that they remain saved. If so, you should know that they are only two cases out of thousands that involve believers who have gotten into drugs, witchcraft, adultery, heresy, and other evils. Perhaps you already disagree with eternal security, especially if you or someone you love has suffered at the hands of a sinning Christian. You may think that *bad* Christians cannot keep their salvation, or at least bad Christians who are not sorry for being bad. But if our beliefs are to have any consistency to them, then the conditions we set for others must apply to ourselves as well. If you say that salvation can be lost, then yours could be lost, too. That would mean the foundation you are currently standing on is a lot like a block of Swiss cheese—full of holes. And since you are not perfect it will only be so long before you fall into one of them.

SALVATION IS A GIFT—
BUT WHAT IF WE DON'T DESERVE TO KEEP IT?

Let's take a look at a number of ways—*holes*—through which we typically expect that salvation could be lost. The first is our mediocre success at living the Christian life after we have been born again. We are often sloppy with our spirituality, somewhat worldly, and at times, sinful. Eventually, we think, God is likely to get sick of us and revoke our salvation. The hardy souls among us determine that such a terrible thing is not going to happen to them. So, they try very hard to be exemplary Christians and set out to prove that they deserve to remain saved.

This performance-based approach misses one of the most fundamental thoughts about salvation. The Bible says, "The *gift* of God is eternal life" (Rom. 6:23). Salvation is a matter of gift. That should immediately establish two principles: First, a gift is something that is typically not taken back. That is why we are told, "The gifts and the calling of God are *irrevocable*" (Rom. 11:29). Second, a true gift does not require payback. Once it is given, it remains the property of the recipient, even if nothing is offered in return.

This is the way things work, even in the world. We've all received gifts of assorted kinds. Some of them we appreciated and used a lot. Some we didn't get any use from and put in the garage. And, of course, there were those that we put in the garage *sale*. Regardless of the scenario however, once the gift was given, the giver had no further claims on it.

On the night I graduated high school, my parents gave me a pocket watch with my name engraved on the inside. Today it sits in a trinket box on my dresser—a gift not used once in all these years. Later, when I was married, they gave me some bedroom furniture. This gift I thoroughly used, and twenty years of moving around have left scratches, gouges, and nicks in the wood—proof that I'm not always careful with nice things. Still another gift was given to me recently by some friends—a clock that makes bird calls every hour on the hour. It drove me so crazy that I finally tore the batteries out of it—anything, so that I would never have to hear the Belted Kingfisher again (My apologies to birdlovers). It was a gift that in some sense, I didn't even like.

All three items—the watch, the furniture, and the clock—were gifts. That means they were items given with the understanding that they wouldn't be taken back, regardless of my disuse, abuse, or dislike of them. My parents have never threatened to repossess the damaged bedroom furniture. They never attempted to get that pocket watch back and give it to someone who could really use it. The friends who gave me the clock know that I disabled all the pretty bird calls, but they haven't tried to take it back and give it to someone who would appreciate it. No one tried to do these things because their understanding of *gift* would not let them do it.

Likewise, our salvation was truly given as a free gift, with no strings attached. If God were to inquire of our post-salvation living and "unsave" us when we were not doing well, then the gift of salvation would change into the *incentive* of salvation. An incentive is meant to motivate someone to excellence. If a person does poorly, then the incentive is taken away. If they recover and do well again, the incentive is returned. Some college students get incentives from their parents in the form of a new car. The car feels like a gift to them since it is paid for, but if grade point averages start to fall, they will quickly understand that the car was only an incentive. The car keys will disappear back into Dad's pocket. However, when the D on the school transcript disappears, the car keys will reappear. Eternal life does not work that way. It is not an incentive. It was given as a gift and remains ours free and clear, irrespective of what our "grades" are.

Grace means that no matter how hard we work, either before or after salvation, we will never deserve eternal life, so God has provided it for free. It would therefore be senseless to work for something that we already freely owned.

In any event, grace and works *cannot* be mixed without canceling each other out, as the Bible says, "If by grace, then it is no longer of works...if it is of works, it is no longer of grace" (Rom. 11:6). Salvation is not ours by both grace and works. Either it is a gift or it is not. It cannot be both conditionally and unconditionally given.

The Bible does tell us to "Walk worthily of the calling with which you were called" (Eph. 4:1). Should we fail, however, it does not threaten us with the loss of salvation. If we could be lost due to unworthy living, then the gospel would be telling us up front that salvation is free, while hiding the real cost until later. It would not be a gift; it would be a credit purchase. Of course, gift and credit are two different things. A novice consumer frequently finds this out the hard way when he begins using credit cards. He likes the way the card seems to get so many things without any cash in hand. It all seems so easy, even free, until a few weeks later when the first bills arrive, announcing the debt that has been incurred. Then he finds himself working a second job in order to pay off all the "free" stuff he got.

Christians very often see themselves as being on the salvation-by-credit-plan. When they first heard the gospel, it sounded like it was free of charge. But later they began to make "payments" in order to keep it. No free gift requires such a thing. Imagine what would happen if God told a sinner, "I will give you salvation right now for free, but you will need to pay it back in daily installments for the next eighty-seven years. And by the way...if you miss a payment, salvation will be repossessed immediately." Of course, in that context, the word "free" would be meaningless.

David asked, "What shall I render to the Lord, for all His benefits toward me?" (Ps. 116:12). Yet, if David had gone just one step farther than that, he might have started wondering "What shall I give to the Lord so that His benefits toward me will continue?" Unfortunately, this kind of question is very often in our own hearts. God has given us His Son, but how much does it cost to keep Him? What must we do to remain saved? Questions of that kind indicate a basic misunderstanding of grace.

Sometimes the very thought of a legalized repayment insults, even hurts the giver of a gift. In God's plan of salvation, the best, most lovely life ever lived on this earth was given up for you. What did you have in mind for recompense—a promise to stop losing your temper so much, or to stop smoking? Compared to Christ's death and resurrection for us, those things are nothing. Since salvation is of inestimable value, the price we place upon it, no matter what, will always be too low. We cannot afford to buy it, and we cannot even afford to rent it for a day.

Ultimately, David answered his own question concerning what he should render unto the Lord. He said, "I will take the cup of salvation and call upon the name of the Lord" (Ps. 116:13). Salvation does not revolve around our giving; it centers upon our taking. The best way to show our understanding of salvation's worth is not to barter with God, offering church attendance, mission work, and good behavior as repayment. It is to simply take the cup of salvation. Yes, we give our lives to Him, but that is out of our love and gratitude, not out of our desperation to keep Him from snatching the cup of salvation away from us.

Can We Lose the Gift of Salvation By Not Wanting It Anymore?

Occasionally, people try to give gifts back to the giver. There are all kinds of reasons for this. Maybe the gift seemed overly extravagant, like a sports car. Perhaps it was something not wanted like a bag of second-hand clothing. Or it could have been something that brought too much responsibility with it, like a very large pet. In most cases, givers will not receive their gifts back. "It's yours," they say, "do what you want with it."

What would God do if we grew so weak that we tried to give the gift of salvation back to Him? I have seen this happen. I knew a Muslim college student who believed in the gospel and received Jesus. His joy was strong and clear for a while until his Muslim friends began giving him trouble about his faith. Disheartened, he told me later, "I've changed my mind. I had better not be a Christian anymore." With as much sympathy as I could muster, I told him, "Sorry, it's too late. If you want Jesus to come into you, He does. Then if you want Him to leave, He won't." That was my way of letting him know that his "troublesome" gift from God could not be given back.

"The gifts and the calling of God are irrevocable" (Rom. 11:29), even if we decide that they're not worth the turmoil of having. This can be clearly seen in the history of the Jewish people. God had chosen them and spared them from his judgment through the blood of the Passover lamb. Then He led them out of Egypt through the Red Sea, beginning a long journey toward their glorious destiny in the land of Canaan. Once in the wilderness, however, Israel began to feel that it was just too much trouble to press forward. They said, "Would it not be better for us to return to Egypt? So they said to one another, 'Let us select a leader and return to Egypt'" (Num. 14:3b-4). Egypt represented their lives prior to salvation. Going back there literally meant returning God's gift of deliverance, and rejecting His leading, His care, and His promise of future glory. "Thanks, but no thanks," the people would be telling Him. "We tried out the gifts and the calling of God for a while, and they're just not for us."

But even with Israel wanting to reject His grace, God the giver would not receive it back. Instead, he disciplined His people for forty years, breaking down their disobedience until they learned to treasure his gifts and calling. In the midst of all His dealings, however, God would not allow them to return to Egypt, the place of the unsaved, even for five minutes. The gifts of God have a no-return policy.

Can Salvation Be Lost if We Stop Believing?

No Christian should allow his heart to dwell in unbelief. That limits the Lord's work, like it was written in the Gospel of Matthew, "He did not do many mighty works there because of their *unbelief*" (13:58). Unbelief prevents us from entering and enjoying many of God's promises, as with Israel and the land of Canaan—"We see that they could not enter in because of *unbelief*" (Heb. 3:19). For this reason, we Christians are left with a warning: "Beware brethren, lest there be in any of you an evil heart of *unbelief* in departing from the living God" (Heb. 3:12).

Unbelief negatively affects our condition as Christians, but what about our eternal salvation? Since salvation comes through faith, can it be lost through a loss of faith? Perhaps if we do not continuously believe every second, then in some awful moment, salvation might evaporate and leave us unforgiven, hell-bound, and void of eternal life. Such a thought seems to be supported by the Gospel of John, where the word "believe" is always used in the present tense. John 3:16, for instance, does not say that "Whoever *believed* in Him should not perish but have eternal life." It says, "Whoever *believes*." That might be taken to mean that whoever does not currently believe right now, at this very moment, does not have eternal life.

This kind of logic, however, is shaky. There are other present tense words in John's gospel that are *not* meant to portray continuous activity. In John 6:33 it says, "The bread of God is He who *comes* down from heaven and gives life to the world." That refers to the birth of Jesus 2,000 years ago. But it says *comes* down. Was the Lord's birth in Bethlehem a one-time act in the past, or was John trying to tell us that it is a continuous, moment-by-moment event? Obviously, it only happened once. But If we say that "comes" does not mean continuous activity in John 6:33, then we should not say "believes" necessarily refers to something continuous in John 3:16.

At any rate, it would be incredible if God arranged for our salvation to rest upon our own fragile ability to believe.

He understands very clearly our tendency for crises of faith. In fact, He identified it repeatedly in His disciples:

"O you of *little* faith, why did you doubt?" (Matt. 14:31)

"O foolish ones and *slow* of heart to believe." (Luke 24:25)

"Why do *doubts* arise in your hearts?" (Luke 24:38)

The Lord especially singled out faith fatigue in the greatest of His disciples. He told Peter, "I have prayed for you, that your faith should not fail; and when you have returned to Me, strengthen your brethren" (Luke 22:32). The phrase "your faith should *not* fail" looks very encouraging, but how about "when you have *returned* to Me"? That phrase indicates the Lord expected Peter to suffer a major setback. He knew that Peter was going to deny Him with a string of lies and profanity. "I have prayed for you that your faith would not fail," the Lord had told him. He had to *pray* for Peter's faith, otherwise the hapless disciple would have stayed in a depressed, listless state.

Our sputtering faith could not generate the power to keep us saved moment by moment for the rest of our lives. That is precisely why our standing before God depends upon a one-time act of faith, not a continuous, unbroken flow of it. The Lord Jesus said to a sinful woman, "Your faith *has* saved you. Go in peace" (Luke 7:50). All that she needed was one isolated act of faith to receive salvation. Nothing further or ongoing was required. Of course this doesn't diminish the importance of following Christ beyond initial belief in Him. If we want to grow as Christians, none of us should believe in Christ once and then live the rest of our lives with overthrown or shipwrecked faith (1 Tim. 1:19; 2 Tim. 2:18). But setting growth aside for the moment, it does indeed only take a single act of genuine belief in Christ to secure our salvation forever.

Eternal salvation is secured immediately and yet the Bible does tell us that "He who *endures* to the end shall be saved" (Matt. 24:13). How do we reconcile this apparent contradiction? It is simple. Salvation in the Matthew passage does not mean salvation from hell. Although the same Greek root word for salvation ("sozo") is always used, it carries a different sense in some verses than it does in others. This is detemined by its surrounding context. We find that sometimes salvation is mentioned in the past tense—"*has* saved us"—(2 Tim. 1:9), meaning the once-for-all initial phase related to our human spirit (John 3:3-6). That is what this book is primarily about. But when the Lord said, "He who endures to the end *shall be* saved," He was not speaking of the initial phase of our salvation. He was emphasizing the end of it, that is, salvation in the future tense. He was not referring to anything past, initial or once-for-all. "Saved" in Matthew 24:13 deals with the final stages of salvation that occurs when God fills our *souls*. This is typically referred to as "the *end* of your faith—the salvation of your *souls*" (1 Pet. 1:9).

We are eternally saved in our spirit through a moment of faith in the Lord Jesus. Our souls, however, consisting of our attitudes, thoughts, feelings, and decisions, may take fifty years or more to be saved. Eternal salvation only requires faith. Future salvation requires the endurance of faith, as we suffer various temptations and tribulations. Eternal salvation means we have been forgiven and spared from hell, have received Christ and the Holy Spirit, and have gotten eternal life and a position as a child of God. Future salvation refers to a time when those very things eventually fill not only our spirit, but our soul and body as well. The eternal salvation of the spirit guarantees that everyone who believes in Jesus has been saved and will not be lost. The future salvation of the soul results in rewards such as the crown of righteousness (2 Tim. 4:8), ruling and reigning together with Christ (Rev. 20:4), and being placed over all the Lord's possessions (Matt. 24:46-47). Without salvation in his spirit, that is, without ever receiving the Lord Jesus, a man will be sent to the lake of fire. Without salvation in his soul, that is, without enduring to the end, a Christian will not be lost, but he will suffer discipline (1 Cor. 3:15).

The endurance of faith is important to a Christian. It leads to a more advanced state of salvation and ends in rewards. But we should not become confused. Our eternal salvation was secured through an act of faith. It is not maintained by us or kept through our endurance.

CAN SINS ANNUL OUR SALVATION?

If salvation cannot be lost due to our failure in sustaining positive things like good works and faith, then what happens to it when we commit purposeful acts of evil? Surely, we think, if there is any way to be lost, then sin must be it.

Legions of new believers, determined to live a holy life, crash directly into the sin issue shortly after salvation. It can be terribly disillusioning. These Christians have told themselves that salvation is their second chance at doing right. But falling into sin once more, they begin to feel that they have also violated their second chance. They made a mess of the old life and now they've begun to do the same to the new one. Too many then abandon their faith in sorrow, like the rich young ruler who simply gave up and walked away from Christ (Matt. 19:22).

In these cases, a large part of the problem is the assumption that the cross of Christ only deals with sins committed *before* salvation. What deals with sins committed *after*? As long as this question goes unanswered, there is the potential for us to become confused and shaken because "we all stumble in many things" (James 3:2). This includes elder Christians who are relatively mature (1 Tim. 5:19-20), and even an apostle like Paul, who said (as a Christian), "Christ Jesus came into the world to save sinners, of whom I *am* chief" (1 Tim. 1:15).

What are we to think of post-salvation sins? Could some of them lead us back into damnation? The very thought is illogical, because, to begin with, "Christ died for the *ungodly*" (Rom. 5:6). In fact, "God demonstrates His own love toward us, in that while we were still *sinners,* Christ died for us" (Rom. 5:8). He loved us in so dramatic a way, even while our whole life was lived in wickedness. At a time when we couldn't have cared less about the Lord, He gave Himself up for us. If that was the case, then how does He feel toward us now that we are saved? Since the intensity of His love was so strong for us then, the Bible assures that it is far greater now: "He who did not spare His own Son, but delivered Him up for us all, how shall He not with Him also freely give us *all* things?" (Rom. 8:32).

As a saved person, the floodgates of blessing are opened upon you. Paul said to the believers, "All things are yours: whether Paul or Apollos or Cephas, or the world or life or death, or things present or things to come—all are yours" (1 Cor. 3:21b-22). Without limitation, anything that we might need for Christian growth is now freely ours.

Sometimes the saved—those highly favored people— dip down into sin. If God were to respond by withdrawing His salvation, He would be treating the saved *worse* than the unsaved. In effect, He would be making the statement that the death of Christ is effective for the sinning sinner, but not for the sinning saint.

The truth is "We have been sanctified through the offering of the Body of Jesus Christ *once for all*" (Heb. 10:10). "Once for all" means that the sin question has been settled once both on the far side *and* on this side of salvation. The book of Hebrews also tells us that "Once at the end of the ages, He has appeared to put away sin by the sacrifice of Himself" (9:26). If salvation could be lost because of sins we commit *after* believing in Christ, then that would mean some sins escaped the cross and were not put away. Consider what an upside-down situation that would create. It would make the most dangerous part of our human lives the time after we were born again. Sins would be there that had not been covered by the cross and would consequently be fatal if we committed them. The whole dilemma would be like discovering one thousand black widow spiders in your home. Panicking, you call the exterminator. He fumigates your house and kills nine hundred and eighty of them. The other twenty can't be located. Why are you still nervous? *Most* of them are gone. Shouldn't you feel at peace? The answer is that you may never again feel restful in your home, not when you stand the chance of being bitten in bed or in the bathroom or while eating breakfast.

If only the sins of our past were put away, plenty of them would be left in our present or future that could still destroy us. But thankfully, *all* our sins were in the future when the Lord died on the cross. There was no such thing as our past sins, present sins, or future sins. When He died long ago, the sins of your past were in the future. So were those that you will commit twenty years from now and those you might inadvertently commit on your deathbed. Because the Lord's death predated them, they were dealt with no matter where they occurred or will occur in your personal life history. No sin escaped the cross. All of them were taken away. Therefore, losing our eternal salvation because of sin is out of the question.

CAN WE LOSE OUR SALVATION TEMPORARILY UNTIL WE REPENT?

Human beings are simply not comfortable with unconditional forgiveness. We imagine that there must be something hidden in the fine print—perhaps a clause that still allows sin to somehow destroy us. One scenario has to do with the *temporary* loss of salvation. That is, believers who sin can lose their salvation and can only get it back when they repent. First John 1:9 is thought to support this idea: "If we confess our sins, He is faithful and just to forgive us our sins and to cleanse us from all unrighteousness." Naturally, the reverse is that those who do *not* confess will *not* be forgiven or cleansed. Such logic would mean that a weak man might be saved and lost ten times or more (maybe up to a hundred times) before he dies. This has been referred to as "elevator salvation." It means that today you are saved and on the top floor. Next week, because of a serious sin, you are unsaved and in the basement. If you want to come out of the basement once again, you must confess your sins in order to be forgiven and cleansed. If you procrastinate and do not repent and something tragic happens to you like a fatal car crash, then you will go to hell.

Unfortunately, this thought has developed out of misunderstanding the whole subject of 1 John. That book functions to show believers how to maintain their fellowship with God, not their eternal salvation. It demonstrates how they can have a quality relationship with the Lord and what they are to do if they damage it. Nowhere in this book do we find eternal loss as the penalty of a believer's unconfessed sin. Instead, we see consequences like walking in darkness (1 John 1:6; 2:9, 11), that is, living as a Christian in a depressed, low condition. And if we continue in that state, we will be shamed at the Lord's coming (1 John 2:28)— shamed but not *destroyed*. Darkness and shame are very unpleasant prospects for a true believer. So, we do not confess our sins because we have become unsaved and fear going to hell. We confess them because we are *saved* and hate losing our healthy fellowship with the Lord.

Can Salvation Be Lost Due to "Special Sins"?

The Bible mentions certain sins that will receive unique judgments. When Christians read about them, they get nervous because these "special sins" carry stiff penalties that can at least sound like eternal loss.

The Lord Jesus referred to one of them when He said, "Whoever denies Me before men, him I will also deny before My Father who is in heaven" (Matt. 10:33). For us to deny Christ means that we deny our relationship with Him either out of shame or fear of personal loss. This sin is in some sense "special" because it brings with it a judgment all its own—that Christ will deny the one who denies Him.

The question is whether salvation is being denied here. Some think so. Before I suggest otherwise, let's consider Peter's example. He had been warned about the seriousness of denying Christ (Matt. 10:33). He had even been told by the Lord, "Assuredly, I say to you that this night, before the rooster crows, you will deny me three times" (Matt. 26:34). Peter disagreed. He vowed, "Even if I have to die with you, I will not deny you!" (Matt. 26:35).

Alas, short of the pain of death, Peter's resolve crumbled. Just seeing His Master arrested, interrogated, and then sentenced, cooled the fire of his devotion. In his shaken state, he decided to hide any connection that he had with the Lord. To make matters worse, this was no passive concealment where Peter simply got quiet and didn't volunteer any information. When questioned, his first denial of Christ was a simple lie (Matt. 26:70), his second was accompanied "with an oath" (Matt. 26:72), and on his third, "he began to curse and swear" (Matt. 26:74)—no "accidental" denial, but one strengthened each time with new determination.

As soon as the awfulness of what he had done hit him, Peter "went out and wept bitterly" (Matt. 26:75). If denying Christ is a believer's death sentence, this should have been the end of Peter's story. From that point, the Lord should have only had ten disciples—the original twelve minus Judas Iscariot (who had never been true to begin with) and Peter (who had been true, but was lost).

However, after Christ resurrected, an angel was sent to Mary Magdalene, saying "Go, tell His disciples—*and Peter*—that He is going before you into Galilee; there you will see Him, as He said to you" (Mark 16:7). Notice how the angel singles out Peter. He does not do it to isolate Peter from the rest of the disciples, but to especially identify Peter together with them. This was no doubt a message to the guilt-ridden man. The mention of his name beside the general group of the disciples meant that he was still being counted as a disciple. His salvation had not been revoked.

Peter's example is a text-book case of "special sin" that received forgiveness. In His story, though, we see some small indication of his repentance in his tears. No doubt there must be many cases down through church history where true Christians denied Christ, but never repented. What will happen to them? We must believe that the Lord will be true to His solemn warning and execute the judgment of denying them before the Father. This action, however, does not involve denying the fallen Christian's eternal salvation.

The disavowal of a person can occur on several different levels. The most basic one is the complete denial of having ever known or had anything to do with him. This was how Peter denied Jesus and it was a total lie. Peter had known and followed Jesus for years. The Lord's denial of a believer would never occur at this level. For Him to say of any Christian, "I do not know the man," and mean it like Peter had meant it would not be true. The Lord knows very clearly the day, the hour, and the minute that any of us received Him. Having lived in us, He knows our thoughts and motives and has even struggled within us to change us. So, if He said of a believer "I do not know the man" or "I never knew him," it would simply be untrue.

If the Lord says, "I do not know him," it must mean something on another level, where the statement is actually true. For instance, He could say of a compromising and self-centered Christian, "I do not know this man as a follower or a disciple, and I have never known him as a servant." (See also Matt. 7:22-23.) In that case, the Lord's denial would be the truth. He would not be denying the unfaithful believer's eternal salvation, but addressing his poor condition. The consequences would then be the Lord's discipline and a subsequent loss of rewards. It would not, however, mean that the shamed Christian would lose eternal life.

Aside from denying Christ, suicide stands out among the "special sins" alleged to cause a Christian to be lost. It is often considered the surest way for a believer to lose his salvation because it is the one sin for which there is no repentance in this world. Saying "Lord, forgive me for what I am about to do" before committing suicide is no repentance at all. Repentance means "to think anew." Therefore whoever truly repents before suicide will think anew and not commit suicide. At any rate, since there is no repentance related to it, this sin is thought to be the only one a Christian can definitely take to the grave.

Although we see examples of suicide in various Bible passages, we cannot find specific teachings on the subject, much less judgments concerning it. This is surprising. Given the strength of some religious opinions about suicide, we would assume that the Bible is full of prohibitions against it, complete with threats of eternal loss. But that is not the case. The closest we come to a teaching that deals with suicide is one of the Ten Commandments, which says, "You shall not murder" (Ex. 20:13). By way of derivation, we might say that since suicide deals with taking one's own life, it might be a form of self-murder. It is very difficult to determine, as murder is primarily about immorally taking another person's life.

Even if it is correct to say suicide is murder, we still have nothing telling us that it annuls a man's salvation. First John 3:15 says, "you know that no murderer has eternal life abiding in him." But the word "abide" does not deal with our positional, once-for-all relationship with God. It describes our experiential daily relationship with Him. For life to abide in us means that it continues to exert a holy influence from within. It is the ongoing, healthy contact between God and us. If eternal life does not abide in a Christian, then that Christian's spiritual condition is sick. For instance, a believer who commits murder cannot say he was experiencing the positive healthy effects of eternal life when he did it. He was not led by the Lord to kill anyone, nor was he in any way influenced by God to do it. Something has gone terribly wrong in his experience. He is neither abiding in life, nor is life abiding in him. That does not mean, however, that he has *lost* eternal life.

Christians who commit suicide or self-murder will not lose their salvation, but they will trigger a series of negative effects. For one, God is robbed of the glory He would have gained in that person's life. Instead of saying "The Lord is my Shepherd, I shall not want" (Ps. 23:1), suicide testifies that "The Lord is my Shepherd and He has failed." Our lives should show everyone that "though I walk through the valley of the shadow of death, I will fear no evil" (Ps. 23:4). Instead, the self-terminated life says, "I walked through the valley of the shadow of death and there was only one way out..." For a Christian, suicide is glory-robbery. It testifies that neither God nor His salvation is so great after all. I realize that this issue is problematic, especially with all of today's concerns about the sufferings of terminally ill people. Still, the Christian who commits suicide runs a very real risk of standing before a displeased Lord and being called a "wicked and lazy servant"(Matt. 25:26). None of us should want to meet Jesus in that way. Penalties will result, such as being stripped of the redemptive gifts we should have used in His service (Matt. 25:28-29), and for a while, being excluded from His glory (Matt. 25:30). This is a very strong kind of discipline. Even so, the Bible does not say that suicide can cause eternal loss. The "unprofitable servant" may be cast into the outer darkness, but he is still called "servant."

There are a lot of other evil deeds that have at different times been considered "salvation killers." Some of them are so grotesque that it has been asked if a genuine Christian is even capable of committing them. The answer is yes. If a child of God fails to abide in Christ, he is capable of doing anything an unsaved person could do. The Lord said, "I am the vine, you are the branches. He who abides in Me, and I in Him, bears much fruit; for without Me you can do nothing" (John 15:5). The phrase "without me you can do nothing" is like a sentence with a blank punch-line. You could fill in that blank with a lot of things: "Without Me you can do nothing _holy_." "Without Me you can do nothing _that pleases God_." "Without Me you can do nothing _but live as though you were unsaved_."

Without the power of Christ, the tempers, lusts, and weaknesses that course through our hearts easily defeat us. Some of these feelings can become violent and given a certain disposition and certain circumstances they can even turn murderous. Peter knew this and told the early Christian community "let none of you suffer as a murderer, a thief, an evildoer, or as a busybody in other people's matters" (1 Pet. 4:15). That should be a warning to any of us who are under the delusion that Christians can't commit certain sins. Real believers are still capable of real evil. When Peter warned us against committing sinful acts, his concern was that a stain of dishonor might come upon the church. He was worried about the reputation of the gospel. But none of his concern had to do with a sinning Christian losing his place

285

in God's family.

In saying this, I do not wish in any way to minimize evil behavior. We must keep a healthy equal tension between the seriousness of sin and God's unconditional forgiveness. Otherwise, we are just as likely to err on the side of being careless. It is important for all of God's children to know that He does not need to inflict eternal destruction upon us in order to deal with sinful conduct. His judgment can come in many forms, and we should take them all as deterrents against evil conduct.

First, grossly sinning Christians can be penalized through human "governing authorities...appointed by God" (Rom. 13:1). The government is "God's minister to you for good. But if you do evil, be afraid; for he does not bear the sword in vain; for he is God's minister, an avenger to execute wrath on him who practices evil" (Rom. 13:4). The "wrath" of human government upon criminal evils might be anything from prison to the electric chair. All of these are God's judgment by way of human representation (see also Gen. 9:5-6). When a Christian is removed from society for committing barbaric acts, then that is one possible avenue of punishment upon him. It must be understood, though, that the strictest penalties of human justice can only go so far. They may inflict confinement, pain, or even death upon an erring believer, but they cannot touch his eternal salvation.

Another way that judgment comes upon a sinning believer is by the direct hand of God. Ananias and Sapphira were believers who died on the spot for lying to the Holy Spirit (Acts 5:1-11). Certain Corinthian believers grew sick and died because of their divisive attitudes towards the other believers (1 Cor. 11:27-30). David, although not a New Testament person, exemplifies the man of God who yields to his baser drives and then is made to suffer under God's punitive dealing. He was a man after God's own heart (1 Sam. 13:14), but he fell into adultery and then murder. In this case, human government did not prosecute David. It was the government of God that came in directly to deal with him. In many ways, the consequences were more terrible than the sentence of any worldly court. Because of

David's murderous act, God withdrew the blessing of peace from David's house (2 Sam. 12:10) and his family was plagued with violence. During fits of anger, his children later killed one another (2 Sam. 13:28-29) or died tragically (2 Sam. 18:14-15). Because of David's adultery, the Lord allowed his house to become riddled with sexual confusion (2 Sam. 12:11-12)—incest (2 Sam. 13:11-14) and gross fornication (1 Kings 11:1-3)—which later damaged the entire nation of Israel.

David spent many a sorrowful night weeping over the state of things. He might have interpreted such a mess to mean that the Lord had discarded him. Yet from the very beginning, *before* any discipline fell upon him, the prophet Nathan had said to him, "The Lord has...put away your sin" (2 Sam. 12:13). God refused to spare David from the painful correction that was due him, but He did save him from being *eliminated* as a man of God. David suffered, but securely kept his position as God's anointed.

There is one final form of judgment for sinning believers and this is when Christ returns: "We must *all* appear before the Judgment Seat of Christ, that each one may receive the things done in the body, according to what he has done, whether good, or bad" (2 Cor. 5:10). This is not the eternal judgment that results in the lake of fire. The Judgment Seat of Christ has nothing to do with determining salvation or damnation. It is for deciding what Christians ought to "receive" as a result of how they lived their lives. At that time, we will "receive the things done in the body." This indicates a recompense of some kind for the things we did while on the earth. Some of us will receive a recompense, or reward, for many good things. Others who committed cruel and filthy acts will also receive what is coming to them. For those, it will not be pleasant. Paul mentioned "The terror of the Lord" (2 Cor. 5:11), meaning that short of losing eternal salvation, things could get pretty bad for believers who commit evil acts. "He himself *will be saved*," Paul says, "yet so as through *fire*" (1 Cor. 3:15). The Lord is obliged to deal with His own children at some time and in some way when they commit unrighteous deeds. There is, however, a stopping point. He will not take His discipline to the extent that He demolishes their eternal salvation.

CAN OUR SALVATION BE LOST DUE TO REPEATED SINS?

What would have happened to the prodigal son of Luke 15, if, after being restored, he fell into the same sin again? No doubt, in the midst of the happy celebration, no one was entertaining that thought. As far as the son was concerned, his backsliding was just an ugly memory, somewhere he never intended to go again. But good intentions are not enough. We often catch ourselves revisiting the site of some past sin. In other cases, we fall under the power of a brand new one. The question remains—if a sin cannot cause us to lose our salvation, then what about the same sin *repeated*?

Repeated sin was the underling theme of Peter's great question, "Lord, *how often* shall my brother sin against me and I forgive him?" (Matt. 18:21). In Peter's mind, as in ours, forgiveness is one thing, but the frequency of it is another. He wanted to know when he could stop forgiving. Peter proposed a noble estimate—"up to seven times?" (Matt. 18:21). Then the Lord said, "I do not say to you up to seven times, but up to seventy times seven" (Matt. 18:22). Peter's proposed limit for forgiveness needed to go seventy times farther than what he'd been thinking. He had to understand that the average brother needed more than seven chances. The Lord Jesus knew this very clearly. In fact, when He said "seventy times seven" it was more than a command; it was actually a description of *His own* forgiveness. Peter might have been awed at such a standard. Forgiveness once is good. Forgiveness seven times is saintly. But "seventy times seven" is a fathomless grace into which all sins and weaknesses disappear. In this case, "490" was a figure never meant to be taken literally, but as an illustration to show the vast storehouse of forgiveness in Christ.

This is an arrangement that seems ill fated. If a person "sins against you seven times in a day, and seven times in a day returns to you, saying, 'I repent,' you shall forgive him" (Luke 17:4). Yet, forgiving so freely would all but guarantee abuse at the hands of unethical people. Although it might sound wonderful, it seems that unlimited forgiveness would simply not work if it were put into practice. People would take advantage of us on every side. We would finally "explode" in a frustrated rage on someone.

We suspect that God's reserves of grace must be as scarce as our own. That is exactly why, according to human reasoning, salvation ought to be taken away from a Christian who repeatedly sins. It makes sense to us that after a day or two of trouble from a weak believer, God should realize His forgiveness is being abused, and then withhold it. Yet that is a fallen human attitude; it does not describe the God of the Bible. It is what God would do if He were in *our* image. When the Lord Jesus tells us to forgive without limit, it is not a case of "Do what I say, and not what I do." It is a call for us to behave according to *His* image.

Although I don't claim to fully understand this kind of grace, looking back over several decades of the Christian life, I know that I have needed it. I'm glad that the Lord didn't agree with Peter's proposal to forgive "seven times." I would have run my tab up to the limit the first week I was saved.

Abused Forgiveness

If you see in all this a possibility for abuse, then you are not the first to notice. Jude spoke of those "who turn the grace of our God into lewdness" (v. 4). Apparently, as they pursued a life of moral filth, they used grace as a "get out of jail free card." "Live it up," they told themselves. "Let grace pay the tab." Paul also spoke of Christians who decided to "continue in sin that grace may abound" (Rom. 6:1). They actually thought that if a believer remained saved regardless of what he did, then he might as well cast off all restraint. If anything, living in the flesh would simply bring more grace. Paul confronted this thought by asking, "Shall we continue in sin that grace may abound? *Certainly not!...*" (Rom. 6:1-2a).

When Jesus forgave the adulterous woman, He said, "Sin no more" (John 8:11). He did not tell her, "Relax, if you sin more, I'll forgive it." His mission was to "save His people *from* their sins" (Matt. 1:21). He had no intention of providing us a way to continue in them.

The security of salvation should not be understood as the security of sin. God never meant for us to pursue a life of lustful indulgences while resting on eternal guarantees. Since sin drove Jesus to the cross, why would we let it continue to be our lord? As Paul says, "Do not let sin *reign* in your mortal body, that you should *obey* its lusts" (Rom. 6:12).

Still, some would say, "Why not? Either way, I'll still be forgiven." The Apostle Paul wouldn't have argued that point. Instead, he spoke from another angle—one that had nothing to do with forgiveness. He asked, "Do you not know that to whom you present yourselves slaves to obey, you are that one's slaves whom you obey?" (Rom. 6:16). In other words, yielding to sinful urges does not place us in danger of being unforgiven; it creates the possibility of *addiction.* Constantly saying "yes" to ungodly behavior reinforces its hold over certain parts of our lives—"You are that one's *slaves* whom you obey." The result is that Christ can no longer be the Lord of such believers. Instead, they become "slaves...of sin."

Believers who are careless with sin and say, "So what? I'll always be forgiven," fail to take into account the *quality* of their Christian lives. They may boast of being forgiven of the same sin one hundred times in a day, but forget that every time they sinned they also grieved the Holy Spirit (Eph. 4:30). This essentially means that their joy, though restored repeatedly, was riddled with spiritual grief. Having such a pattern in their lives, they may never know the undisturbed power of abiding in Christ.

As long as a Christian derives encouragement from God's grace to live an evil life, then he has missed the whole point of it. Real grace never condones wickedness, "for the grace of God that brings salvation has appeared to all men, teaching us that, *denying* ungodliness and worldly lusts, we should live soberly, righteously, and godly in the present age" (Titus 2:11-12). Where there is no such restraint in the life of an alleged believer, we must wonder if he is really saved at all.

It is possible that such a lawless "Christian" is actually just an unsaved person hiding under the doctrine of eternal security. If there is absolutely no inward teaching of self-denial, then there is probably no saving grace present within him, either.

Still, genuine believers can and do harden their hearts toward the Lord. This makes an awkward situation for them. They rest on the grace of eternal security while living contrary to God. This is bizarre in the same way as if, having been assured of endless parental love, a child reasoned with himself that he should now burn his parents' house down, steal their money, and beat them up. What's the harm anyway, since they promised to always love him! A situation like that one is almost too fantastic to entertain, yet Christians often manage to think along those lines:

> "Since the Father graciously chose me for salvation and will not change His mind about me, I can freely reject Him."

> "Since the Son of God loved me and gave Himself up for me, I am safe to live a life denying Him."

> "Since the Spirit has committed Himself to stay with me forever, I can grieve Him daily."

As long as God's salvation is guaranteed, they think, there is no harm in just leaping into sin and enjoying the adrenaline rush. This is exactly how Satan tempted the Lord Jesus.

> "He [Satan] brought Him [Jesus] to Jerusalem, set Him on the pinnacle of the temple, and said to Him 'If You are the Son of God throw yourself down from here. For it is written: He shall give His angels charge over You, to keep You; and, in their hands they shall bear You up, lest You dash your foot against a stone.'" (Luke 4:9-11)

In effect, Satan was saying, "You know that God's protection over You is total, so have some fun! Besides, what a testimony it would be for all the temple worshipers to see you fall and then be saved." Christ's answer was simple: "You shall not tempt the LORD your God" (Luke 4:12). He did not deny that the Father would save Him, but why needlessly, recklessly put Himself in a situation that would require deliverance?

Grace is for our need and not for our entertainment. James said, "We all stumble in many things" (James 3:2a). Do we really need to set out on a deliberate course of wickedness? Before we leave this earth, we will have fallen enough times to prove His grace without needing to cast ourselves down on purpose.

You can choose a life launching yourself off "the temple" over and over; the Father will save you each time. But is this really what you want—a life always falling, always trying to recover, always bearing the damaging effects of addictions in your body and shaking off bouts of spiritual death? Do you want a retarded spiritual growth and then when the Lord returns, to be "ashamed before Him at His coming"? (1 John 2:28).

Indeed, our attitude toward the forgiveness of God can greatly affect our Christian lives. Consider these two different views and their outcomes:

Karla is a believer who has a strong love for Christ, but is plagued with things from her non-Christian past. One of them is her affinity for marijuana. It seems that no matter how she prays, fellowships with others, and reads the Bible, the urge to get high still comes over her. During a rough workweek, she often finds herself relaxing with a "little smoke." The condemnation that follows is severe. Karla imagines that each backsliding episode causes the Lord to love her a little bit less. There are bouts of depression. She wonders whether it is worth it to even continue meeting with other Christians, especially since she may no longer be saved, anyway. Then Karla encounters the truth that she cannot make the Lord love her less and that forgiveness is for those who really *need* it, even those who need it repeatedly for the same thing. She learns to trust the Lord's forgiveness. In the meantime, where her marijuana habit is concerned, she seeks to "obtain mercy and find grace to help in time of need" (Heb. 4:16). This might come in the form of inner strength for denying herself any more drugs. Or, it might be the help she gets through participating in a special Christian support group. Either way, Karla knows that as she deals with her sinful behavior, God is for her, even if she experiences setbacks. Her understanding of eternal security has had a healthy outcome.

But then there is George. George is a zealous Christian who has a weakness for the ladies. Since he is young, handsome, and something of a flirt, he frequently finds himself drawn into sexual encounters. He is bothered by it, but can't stop. Opportunities are all around him, and they are just too exciting to pass by. George's conscience is troubled by his habits, and his Christian life grows desperately weak. Being miserable, he begins entertaining the hunch that maybe he has lost his salvation. Then he comes in contact with the teaching of eternal security. George is stunned to learn of God's great forgiveness. "Good!" he says, and begins throwing himself into one sexual liaison after another. Years of this cavalier lifestyle pass by. George can still say he is saved though he neither enjoys his salvation, nor is he affected by it. He has misused God's grace and becomes a full-time sinner, locking Christ into the depths of his being like a prisoner in a jail cell.

Though Karla and George cast themselves upon the grace of God and both still have their eternal salvation, one life grew healthy while the other became comatose. God's unlimited forgiveness is no doubt one of the most powerful provisions that exists for us Christians. Its abuse, however, can become one of our greatest detriments. Truly the Christian can end up taking one of two ways. The Lord's way is "Watch and pray lest you enter into temptation" (Matt. 26:41). Satan's way is to "Take it easy and do not worry about temptation." The Lord says, "Follow Me" (Matt. 4:19) and then promises to catch us if we fall. The devil says, "Follow *me* and God will catch you as you fall."

Ultimately, the Father's hand lies under each of those approaches—yes, including the wrong one. In either case, the child that falls will be caught.

The issue at hand is not whether we will be forgiven but how we will use God's forgiveness—as a haven for sin or as a means of entering deeper fellowship with Him. Either way, though, our eternal security is not in question. We no longer need to wonder whether God will cancel His forgiveness and then condemn us. His grace settled that matter the moment we believed in Christ.

OUR SALVATION IS SECURE BECAUSE WE HAVE RECEIVED ETERNAL LIFE

Our salvation is secure not only because God has taken away our sins, but because He has given us something— eternal life. When I say "given" I must qualify what that means. Giving life is different from giving other things. Parents could say that they gave life to their child, and they could also say that they gave him a pacifier as well. The two "givings" are not the same. The pacifier can be taken away when the parents decide it is no longer needed. The life of the child, though, is an organic gift that has been given but cannot be taken back. It is the *fabric* of the child's very being. If his life could be undone and his birth taken back, then it would be a most surrealistic event. Cellular division would need to go in reverse, defying every law of life and reproduction. That is simply an impossible event. No person who has been born becomes unborn.

I don't believe I am stretching the truth of God by comparing natural birth to our spiritual rebirth. After all, God was the first One to make that comparison. This is clear through the phraseology of the Bible, which tells us that we have received the divine seed (1 Pet. 1:23), a new birth (John 3:3), have become "partakers of the divine nature" (2 Pet. 1:4), and now have become His children (1 John 3:1). The wording of these verses makes it clear that

294

we have received eternal life through processes similar to what we see in our world.

God's life has become our permanent possession. When Job said, "The Lord gave and the Lord has taken away" (Job 1:21), he referred to wealth and children and home—objective blessings that could be moved in and out of his life. Eternal life is not an objective blessing to us. It has become our subjective possession, woven into the deepest part of our being. If it is moved, then we move with it.

Though similarities abound between physical birth and spiritual rebirth, there are also dissimilarities between them. Let's return to the example of a child. His birth cannot be undone but his life could still be lost. Disease or injury could end it. Are such weaknesses to be found with the second birth? Can something kill the new life within a believer? If so, that would make the universe a very dangerous place for us. "The devil walks about like a roaring lion, seeking whom he may *devour"* (1 Pet. 5:8), a very risky thing for us believers, since we are compared to sheep (John 10:27). Additionally, our high-pressure environment tends to compound the problem by being toxic toward any developing faith—"the cares of this world and the deceitfulness of riches *choke* the word" (Matt. 13:22). Then there is trouble to be found within our own selves, as we stumble into negative internal experiences: "If you live according to the flesh you will *die"* (Rom. 8:13) and "to be carnally minded is *death"* (Rom. 8:6).

Many things sound potentially fatal to a believer, but thankfully, John 3:16 does not promise us just any life. It specifies *eternal* life. Eternal, of course, means something not confined by time, something that has neither beginning nor ending. In that definition we find the answer to all the threats in the universe: *Eternal life has no end.* Regardless of what threats come along, it cannot be terminated. If anything could kill it, eternal life would not be eternal.

Jesus said, "Because I live, you shall live also" (John 14:19). The same life in Him is in us. If we want to know whether there is any credible danger to our new life, we must first find out if anything poses a threat to the life in the Lord Jesus. As long as something can destroy Him, then it can also destroy us. But in Revelation 1:18, the Lord said, "I am He who lives and was dead, and behold, I am alive *forevermore.*" This is a statement of indestructibility. It is not only true for the Lord Jesus but for us as well, since we share the same life.

Sheep are fragile, defenseless, and prone to wander. However, a deposit of eternal life turns these weak creatures into something more immovable than the greatest mountain. We are, for the most part, not conscious of this. We seem to be more aware of our "sheepness" than of our indestructibility. A little temptation or trouble can make us feel like our immovable salvation is being pushed off in a wheelbarrow.

Even at those times, we are more secure than we think. Bart's story is a case in point. For a while he was a sharp young Christian who was very serious about following Christ. Then he began to notice all the things in the world that he could have if he only tried hard enough to get them. It was too difficult for him to see so many glittering things pass him by, so he made a decision to grab as many as he could. After a few years of work, his business-savvy mind had enabled him to make millions. In the meantime, his care for the things of God dwindled. Working long hours left him without any time for spiritual pursuits. What precious spare moments he did have were spent with the coveted toys he had labored so hard to earn.

During those years of spiritual stagnation, Bart also found that a wealthy businessman could have a lot of "fun" traveling away from wife and family. Since his faith had become stunted, he saw no compelling reason to resist the temptations that led him into immoral conduct. His resultant life both inside and outside began looking like he had lost the salvation he once possessed.

Bart became a spiritual missing person, chalked up as dead by the Christian friends who hadn't seen him in decades. For all practical purposes, the devil had simply devoured him. That's why it came as a surprise the day he showed up again. He had lost his wife and family and experienced how the greedy have "pierced themselves through with many sorrows" (1 Tim. 6:10). I remember listening as Bart confessed his failures before a large group of Christians and then soberly warned them not to do what he did. He was back—battle-scarred, tired, and no doubt disciplined by the Lord—but *still* saved. The eternal life he had received as a young man had passed though a gauntlet of desecration, and when the dust settled…it had remained.

There are thousands of stories like Bart's that testify to eternal life's unbreakable strength. All of them typically arrive at the same conclusion that God's life cannot be dissolved through our mistreatment or neglect. And though the devil is much more powerful than we are, neither can he destroy it. Even if he devours a believer as he did Bart, it can only be temporary, like a lion swallowing a penny. If that happened, the coin would not digest, but pass through undamaged. In the same way, eternal life may be subjected to all kinds of indignities, but it will remain intact to the end of time.

The Lord said, "I give to them eternal life and they shall *never* perish" (John 10:28). Look at how the same verse appears when it is literally translated from the original Greek: "I give to them life eternal and *by no means* they perish." The devil, the world, and our sinful flesh are all "means" commonly thought to neutralize our salvation. But the phrase "by no means" indicates that there is no possible way by which that could happen.

Since the life of God is indestructible, whoever receives it also becomes indestructible. Life is not one thing and we another. By receiving it, we have become one with it. The strongest indication of this occurs in the book of Genesis. There, Adam had eaten from the wrong tree, the Tree of the Knowledge of Good and Evil. His punishment had to be death (Gen. 2:17), and nothing was to negate that sentence. So, God did something "to guard the way of the tree of life" (Gen. 3:24). Why did God find it so important to keep Adam away from the life tree? Because He knew Adam might "put out his hand and take also of the tree of life, and eat, and *live forever*" (Gen. 3:22).

The Tree of Life represented the very life of God. If Adam

had taken it into him, he would never have died. He would never have paid the penalty of death, for nothing could have killed him. God was well aware of this. He knew the impossibility of terminating His own eternal life. That was why He prevented it from entering the man.

Neither did God consider it an option to simply withdraw His life if it had gotten into Adam. Once life is inside a person, it enters a subjective union with him. If that had happened with Adam, even God would not have exercised the freedom to just take it away from him.

Today, we have received the eternal life that Adam was denied. Nothing can destroy it, and nothing can remove it from us. That is why God is supremely confident in leading us through the worst trials and sufferings. He understands the durability of His own life. As a result, what the Psalmist said is literally fulfilled in us today:

> "You, O God, have tested us; you have refined us as silver is refined. You brought us into the net; you laid affliction on our backs. You have caused men to ride over our heads; we went through fire and through water; but you have brought us out to rich fulfillment." (Ps. 66:10-12)

As believers living in this fallen world, "We are accounted as sheep for the slaughter" (Rom. 8:36). During the times that we are standing in a circumstantial slaughterhouse, it is tempting for us to think that all is lost. However God remains bold and assured. He knows that nothing will be lost. His trust is not due to any ability of those small trembling sheep, but in the life that he has given them.

The devil once complained that God had built a hedge around Job so that bad things could not happen to the man (Job 1:10). The Lord did not dispute the point. Since Job was righteous, he had indeed been blessed, prospered, and protected in a very special way. Perhaps concerning the New Testament believers, though, God would argue with the devil, saying, "Hedge? I don't need to build a hedge around them, nor do they need Me to do it. They have My life. That is their protection forever. They are eternally safe from you, from the circumstances of this world and even from themselves."

Our Salvation is Secure Because Of What We Have Become— *Children of God*

The Bible demonstrates from many different angles that the bond between God and us is truly secure. A further way of showing this is to speak of what salvation has caused us all to become. Eternal life has affected us by turning us into something new. This new identity is a large part of what guarantees that we will be saved forever.

For instance, the day eternal life entered our being, we were born again as children of God (John 1:12, 1 John 3:1). It seems that the Lord purposely compares His new birth to our physical birth so that we would learn about one by looking at the other. Part of what we learn is that as natural birth is an irreversible process, so is the second birth. No one can be *un*born again—once a child, always a child.

As I discussed earlier, though, there are dissimilarities between the old and new births. Infants sometimes tragically die because the life in them is too fragile to survive. We cannot conclude that the same thing could befall God's life in us. The new life is different. It cannot die and neither, from the spiritual standpoint, can the person it enters. As the Lord said, "I am the resurrection and the life. He who believes in Me, though he may die, he shall live" (John 11:25).

Our eternal security does not come from being giants, but from being children. This may not sound very reassuring. In terms of status, children are considered weak and insignificant. It is another story, however, when they have been born of indestructible seed. The child of God has a life that cannot be overthrown, even by the entire world, "for whatever is born of God overcomes the world"(1 John 5:4).

299

WE HAVE BECOME THE BODY OF CHRIST

Biblical truths from every angle remind us that our salvation is secure. This is strongly due to what salvation itself has made us. We are told, for instance, that when eternal life came into us, we became the very body of Christ. This is a greater matter than being a child of God, because children (conceptually speaking) are separate from their parents. They have the same life but they are separated by space. However, "We are members of His *Body*" (Eph. 5:30). The Lord's life within us has made us *part of Him*. This does not mean that you are Christ Himself in the sense of being an object of worship, or in the sense of possessing omnipresence, omnipotence, or omniscience. What it does mean is that short of those things you are part of Him— "Now you are the body of Christ, and members individually" (1 Cor. 12:27).

When the Lord confronted Saul on the road to Damascus, He said, "Saul, Saul, why are you persecuting *Me*?" (Acts 9:4). This was a strange question. Saul had never directly laid a hand on Jesus. Jesus had already ascended to heaven before Saul even appeared in the biblical narrative. In fact, Saul had been persecuting Christians, so, it might have made more sense for Jesus to ask, "Why are you persecuting My church" or "My followers" or "My children." Instead, He chose a word that indicated the most immediate closeness between Himself and His believers—*Me*. He said, "Why are you persecuting *Me*?" In a very real sense, He was saying "They are *Me*."

Let's consider eternal security in light of this truth. Don't think that a lost salvation would only be catastrophic to the believers. If we could be lost, then the Lord would lose arms, legs, and toes. If He were to "unsave" us, He would need to amputate His own members.

But the Lord Jesus does not view sinful believers as hopeless parts that ought to be chopped off. He sees them as being ill and in need of healing. As the limbs of a physical body can become sick, sometimes even in the body of Christ, there are sick members. When some Christians began soliciting prostitutes, Paul said to them, "Do you not know that your bodies are members of Christ? Shall I then take the members of Christ and make them members of a harlot? Certainly not!" (1 Cor. 6:15). No doubt, these believers had become sick, diseased members. Paul rebuked them, yet he did not tell them that they had lost their salvation and were no longer members of Christ. He did not tell them that they had been amputated from the Lord. A sick member needs care, not destruction, "for no one ever hated his own flesh, but nourishes and cherishes it, just as the Lord does the church" (Eph. 5:29).

Sometimes however, the care that a sick member requires causes pain. Ask anyone who has suffered an injury and then endured the agony of physical rehabilitation. In the worst situations, some limbs even become gangrenous and need to be removed. There are sometimes such cases in the body of Christ. Paul told the Corinthians, "It is actually reported that there is sexual immorality among you, and such sexual immorality as is not even named among the gentiles—that a man has his father's wife!" (1 Cor. 5:1). Then he said, "Put *away* from yourselves the evil person" (1 Cor. 5:13). This was clearly a serious case of moral and spiritual infection. The person who had it was to be cut off from physical contact with the church. Because he had wandered into such a public sin with no repentance, he was a member that needed to be treated with extreme measures. His physical, social interaction with the church had to be suspended because of the danger of his sin spreading to others. That was why Paul said, "Do you not know that a little leaven leavens the whole lump?" (1 Cor. 5:6).

This discipline, however, did not sever that sinful Christian's invisible, eternal union with Christ. Paul himself confirmed it when he said that even as the man's flesh suffered destruction, it was so that "his spirit may be saved in the day of the Lord Jesus" (1 Cor. 5:5). And, before we assume that the word "may" leaves any room to doubt the certainty of salvation, we must remember that Paul had, only two chaters before, said that such Christians definitely "will be saved" (1 Cor. 3:17, 15). Later, when the erring brother came to his senses and repented, Paul encouraged the Corinthians to forgive him (2 Cor. 2:5-7). The man's visible attachment to the church was restored, although his spiritual attachment to it had never been lost, even for a moment. Salvation has made us the body of Christ. That, in and of itself, is a guarantee that we will never perish. Since we are the Lord's very members, we will never get lost, accidentally fall away, or suffer spiritual amputation.

WE ARE STONES IN GOD'S HOUSE

Eternal life has also made us something indispensable to the Lord's *work*. At the very beginning of the New Testament period, Jesus said, "I will build My church" (Matt. 16:18). Since that time, for two thousand years He has been engaged in a work of construction. Today, we believers are critical components in that effort.

The day that eternal life got into us, it changed our core substance from dust to stone. Now the Bible tells us that "you...as living stones, are being *built up* a spiritual house" (1 Pet. 2:5).

But what if we "living stones" became dead and reverted back to our previous unsaved status of dust? The answer is that we would not be the only ones to suffer. If our salvation could be lost, then stones would disappear out of God's house. This may sound inconsequential at first, but think in terms of a secular building project. Suppose the contractor lays a foundation and begins to erect a framework. After a few months, he shows up at the construction site only to discover that one hundred square feet of the house's foundation is missing. A cubed chunk of it has simply disappeared. He is astounded. How could such a thing happen? With great difficulty, he finds a way to patch the hole and then resumes his work.

The next morning, however, he discovers that a great length of water pipe has vanished from beneath the ground. After costly replacements, the next day brings more surprises. Twenty feet of electrical wiring has gone missing from the midst of the wall. The bizarre scenario continues on a daily basis with parts of the house dematerializing as fast as repairs are made. Finally, the contractor gives up and leaves his project in a shambles.

As "the Lord added to the church daily those who were being saved" (Acts 2:47), He was, in effect, adding living stones to His building. But think of it—as God's house took shape one day, what if scores of stones vanished out of it the next? That is exactly what would happen if the believers could go back to their unsaved state. Their lost salvation would turn God's house into a perpetual pile of rubble.

Let's look at the personal story of one "living stone" and the challenges that faced him. At a pivotal point in Peter's life, he confessed of Jesus, "You are the Christ, the Son of the living God" (Matt. 16:16). This caused the Lord to respond, "And I also say to you that you are Peter" (Matt. 16:18a). The name Peter comes from the Greek word *petros*, meaning "a stone." It was a glorious thing for the Lord to call a man, because prior to that moment with Peter, all God could say to any person was "*Dust* you are and to dust you shall return" (Gen. 3:19). Finally, someone among the human race was being called "a stone."

But shortly after that glorious instant, the same man argued with the Lord and was then called "Satan" (Matt. 16:23). The dust that had become stone had seemed to turn into dust again. The situation grew still worse. Peter denied Christ three times—delivering multiple blows to his new identity. Just as it was beginning to look like this new stone was pulverized and had disappeared from God's house, Peter stood up on the day of Pentecost and brought three thousand people to Christ (Acts 2:14, 41). The dust seemed to have become stone again. But then later Peter backslid and was charged with hypocrisy (Gal. 2:11-13). Once more it looked as though the stone had crumbled. Yet, at the end of his life we find this same man shining again like a brilliant stone as he prepared himself to die for Christ—"Shortly I must put off my tent, just as our Lord Jesus showed me" (2 Pet. 1:14; see also John 21:18-19).

The truth is, Peter never lost his salvation, even during his most fragile moments. The stone never became unsaved mortal dust, although it certainly did sometimes become dusty. In that respect, Peter represents us all very well. Like him, we have believed and confessed that Jesus is "the Christ, the Son of the living God." This made the Lord call us "petros." The problem is that afterwards, we sometimes do things that make us look more like dirt than anything else. In the thick of those occasions, we may seriously wonder if we are still stones. Yet, after confessing our sins and having the dust washed off of us, we will find stone underneath.

God's way is through cleansing, not discarding. He washes us in the blood of Christ (1 John 1:9) and in the water by the Word (Eph. 5:26) because His precious stones are not expendable. After all, He paid a great deal for us. We are "the church of God, which He purchased with His own blood" (Acts 20:28). What would the owner of a diamond do if it were accidentally dropped into a vat of dirty motor oil? We wouldn't expect him to walk away saying, "Oh, well, I'll get another one tomorrow." No, He would wash it off. In fact, we would question the sanity of any person who, after paying a high price for a ruby or an emerald, would toss it in the trash because it was soiled. A blotch of mud on the Hope diamond cannot reduce its inherent worth by one cent. Neither could spiritual contaminants ever devalue a redeemed soul to the point that it has to be thrown away. The Lord will scrub and scour His precious stones, but He will not part with any of them.

Jesus declared His purpose when He said, "I will build My church" (Matt. 16:18), which is "the house of the living God" (1 Tim. 3:15), the "spiritual house" (1 Pet. 2:5) of the New Testament. Even the smallest, youngest believer is now indispensable to that work. For in the moment that God gave us eternal life, He made us living stones. Nothing could be more central to a building effort than the building materials that go into it. And yet we are more than just "materials." The price the Lord paid for us has also elevated our personal worth to an inestimable degree. The cost for our souls was "the precious blood of Christ" (1 Pet. 1:19), making each of the building stones in God's house priceless.

In light of the fact that we are integral to the Lord's purpose and highly treasured by Him, our salvation rests inviolate and secure forever.

WE ARE GIFTS

Part of the reason why our salvation is so firm lies in the fact that eternal life has made us something *special*. Admittedly, we Christians don't seem like much. The unadorned and unknown seem to swell our ranks, just like the Bible says—"not many wise according to the flesh, not many mighty, not many noble, are called" (1 Cor. 1:26).

This is the way it looks through the eyes of men. Through the eyes of God, it is another story. In Psalm 1:8, God the Father tells the Son, "Ask of Me and I will give You the nations for Your inheritance." This implies that the Father and the Son see all the typical, common people of this world as potential treasures. In fact, when you believed in Jesus you became one of those treasures—a valuable gift from the Father to the Son. As Jesus said, "All that the Father *gives* Me, will come to me" (John 6:37). Later He said to the Father, "I have manifested Your name to the men whom You have *given* Me out of the world" (John 17:6). From those statements it is evident that your coming to Christ strongly involved the Father's *giving*. It might have been your feet that carried you to Him, but it was the Father's giving that propelled them.

Now, suppose that after gloriously being given to Christ, we could lose our salvation. It would mean that the Father had given His Son worthless gifts—men that would be saved one day only to be lost the next. This is like a man telling his son, "I have a gift for you." Then he hands him a few snowflakes. Within seconds, they melt into wet spots on the palm of the boy's hand.

Are these the gifts that the Father gives the Son—men that "melt" shortly after they are presented to Him? We must say no. In the past, we human beings might have inadvertently given worthless gifts to people. We had no idea that what we gave was junk. In short, we were ignorant.

But God isn't. He is all-knowing. When He gives a gift, He is fully aware of its quality, including how long it will last. He knows for certain that those He gives to the Son will not liquefy in the heat of trial.

The Father is careful in His giving and the Son is just as careful in His receiving. He is not irresponsible with the Father's gifts. Naturally, human beings don't have very heightened powers of vigilance, so gifts given to them are typically lost, stolen, or damaged. That is not the way it is with Christ. He said triumphantly to the Father, "Those whom you gave Me I have *kept* and none of them is lost except the son of perdition [Judas Iscariot] that the scriptures might be fulfilled" (John 17:12).

The Lord preserved all of the Father's gifts intact without any of them perishing. Only Judas Iscariot was lost, because he had never been a gift from the Father to begin with.

But concerning all the authentic ones He declares, "Behold, I and the children whom God has *given* Me" (Heb. 2:13 NASB). If even one of us could lose our salvation, He would be forced to say, "Behold, I and *some* of the children God has given Me." Of course, losing a gift is one thing; losing someone's children is quite another. Imagine the wretched situation if a woman agreed to watch over her neighbor's children and at the end of the day said, "Here are two of your four children whom you gave to me. I'm very sorry. The other two were lost somewhere downtown." The Lord Jesus will never be in those shoes. All the children that the Father begets will be found safely with Him at the end of the age.

Jesus said, "This is the will of the Father who sent Me, that of all He has given Me, I should *lose nothing*, but should raise it up at the last day" (John 6:39). If any one of us lost our eternal salvation, it would mean that He would never again be able to say "I have not lost one." The gloomy report to the Father would sound more like, "I have lost thousands." But the Lord Jesus is strongly confident in His care for God's gifts. This is why He repeatedly asserts the certain future of those gifts:

"This is the will of Him who sent Me, that everyone who sees the Son and believes in Him may have everlasting life; and I *will* raise Him up at the last day." (John 6:40)

"No one can come to Me except the Father who sent Me draws Him; and I *will* raise him up at the last day." (John 6:44)

"Whoever eats my flesh and drinks My blood has eternal life, and I *will* raise him up at the last day." (John 6:54)

There is no equivocation in these statements, no shadow of doubt, and no unforeseen possibilities. The Son implicitly trusts His own unfailing vigilance over God's gifts.

We might think of ourselves as plain or mediocre people, but according to the Father and the Son, there are no such believers—only precious gifts. This divine appraisal is part of the guarantee of our being saved forever.

As long as we simply think of salvation as something given to us, it will not be hard to think that it could be taken back. That is why we must keep in mind that salvation has caused us to become the children of God, the body of Christ, precious stones in God's house, and gifts from the Father to the Son. This wholesale transformation carries with it eternal assurance, for one's possessions might be taken away, but his identity cannot be so easily revoked. Our salvation is secure because it is interwoven with the new things that God has made us.

11

HOW TO KNOW THAT YOU WILL BE SAVED FOREVER
(PART 2)

BECAUSE OF WHO GOD IS, WE CANNOT LOSE OUR SALVATION

If what we are guarantees our eternal security, then what God is guarantees it even more. God's very character is attached to our eternal standing. His traits of righteousness, love, and power are to our salvation what steel girders are to a bridge. If God chose to demolish the "bridge" He built between Himself and us, He would be violating crucial elements of His own personality.

GOD'S RIGHTEOUSNESS IS OUR SECURITY

The Bible tells us that "the LORD is known by the judgment

He executes" (Ps. 9:16). Whatever He condemns or approves says something about His personal standard of righteousness. His judgments, which are contained in His law, demonstrates that He does not play favorites, make exceptions, or grade on the curve. He is not loose in any detail, nor does He modify any of His standards for the sake of convenience. He will not tolerate one spot or blemish, but judges each and consigns them to destruction. In a very real sense, the lake of fire is the ultimate display of righteousness according to God's law, for it penalizes sin without mercy.

This all, of course, does not bode well for sinners, whose righteousness always falls short of the divine standard. Yet there is good news: "now the righteousness of God *apart from the law is revealed*" (Rom. 3:21). This is an astonishing statement. It means that apart from behavioral perfection, it is now possible to be counted righteous by God—"Even the righteousness of God *through faith in Jesus Christ* to all and on all who believe" (Rom. 3:22). Now God's righteousness can be shown and given to us who believe in Christ, irrespective of how well we have kept His law.

"We are *justified* freely by His grace" (Rom. 3:24). Justified means acquitted of all charges, declared righteous. How could God legally justify sinners? The verse goes on to say that it is "through the *redemption* that is in Christ Jesus" (Rom. 3:24b). The death of the Lord Jesus was redemptive, that is, it functioned as payment for our souls. We had broken God's law and could not afford to pay the penalty. But "Christ has *redeemed us from the curse of the law*, having become a curse for us" (Gal. 3:13).

Now when God looks at us, He does not see sin. He sees the *payment* for sin—"the blood of Jesus Christ His Son" (1 John 1:7), "the precious blood" (1 Pet. 1:19). And when God sees it upon us, His righteousness is satisfied. He sees payment. He sees justice served.

Now suppose a redeemed person goes out and sins. What should God do about it? With our former understanding, we would guess that since God is righteous, He ought to condemn that person. But it is precisely because God is righteous that He *cannot* condemn the believer (remember Rom. 3:21-22, 24). The erring Christian has already been paid for with the blood of Christ. If God said, "I know My Son has paid your way, but you must also pay," it would be demanding a double payment for sin. That would be unrighteous. Not even a piece of bubble gum must be paid for twice. Surely, God would not require His Son to pay for our sins on the cross and then make us also pay for them in hell. Justice forbids such a thought.

God wishes "to demonstrate at the present time His *righteousness*, that He might be just and the justifier of the one who has faith in Jesus" (Rom. 3:26). The security of our salvation does not come from God "fudging" His standard for our sake. On the contrary, we are secure because of His utter refusal to do anything unjust. Condemning a Christian would be a breach of God's perfectly just character, because demanding a double payment for sin is simply wrong. Thus, the same righteousness that strikes terror into the hearts of sinners can inspire confidence in those sinners when they believe the gospel.

GOD'S LOVE IS OUR SECURITY

Few of us trust in God's love as any grounds for eternal security. Maybe it is because of the cheap way people speak of falling in and out of love. We see relationships fail all the time because of fickle emotions. The loving husband and wife of today are barely recognizable years later, as they try to destroy one another in divorce court. If love fails to even support a marriage, do we dare to rest our eternal destiny upon it? The answer would have to be no—not if it is merely human.

But the Bible describes God's love for us as transcending any in the physical world. The Lord describes His love as traveling beyond the limits even of parental affections, which is why He said, "Can a woman forget her nursing child, and not have compassion on the son of her womb? Surely they may forget, yet I will not forget you" (Isa. 49:15).

The Christian often cheerfully accepts this truth, but then

doubts it later, when he falls into a personal crisis. He could feel the love of God burn brightly in his heart when he was successfully living a holy life. But now he has failed. The voice of disappointment begins echoing in him, "You blew it, didn't you? You had a great month, but now you've ruined everything..."

We all know what that little voice is trying to say—that God's love must be reduced according to the seriousness of the failure. And if the mistake is bad enough then maybe that love must disappear altogether. After He "loved Me and gave Himself up for me" (Gal. 2:20), now He will begin hating me.

These concerns seem so reasonable to us because human love, the love with which we are most accustomed, can be mortally wounded. And nothing seems more damaging to it than unpleasant, unexpected disclosures. Will we care for someone next year the same as we do today? Perhaps not, depending upon what we find out about them. When a bride and groom promise each other "to have and to hold til' death do us part," it is a vow made with an imperfect knowledge of one another. They are pledging a life-long commitment in spite of unpleasant traits they may later discover in one another. The whole interaction is very risky since their vows of love are surrounded with blind spots and ignorance.

Would the bride give her heart to the charming groom if she could prophetically view all his weaknesses? Would she say "til' death do us part" while seeing his hidden self-centeredness, short temper and disturbing habits? If these things could be projected like a movie on a screen, maybe as she watched it, her love for him would die right there. Even the strongest human affections wither when its object proves to be unworthy.

In contrast, God says, "I have loved you with an everlasting love" (Jer. 31:3). The striking thing about His love is that it is accompanied with omniscience. God knows everything about us *from the beginning*, yet loves us forever in spite of what He sees. He does not discover who and what we are with the passage of time. God fully knew what He was getting into when He saved us. That includes knowledge about any failures and backsliding events that would occur. He knew it all, but could still say, "I have loved you with an *everlasting* love." That is the same as saying, "You cannot stop Me from loving you by giving Me unpleasant surprises. I love while knowing *all* your weaknesses."

Indeed, the Lord is clearer about our frailties than we are. Take Peter's case as evidence of this. He had no intention of denying Jesus. It was not in his conscious thought at all. He had prepped himself to follow Christ to the death. But Jesus could see deeper into Peter than Peter could see into himself. One of the things He saw was a streak of weakness in the man that ran deep and would lead to multiple failures. Still, the Lord loved him.

We have no idea what kinds of deeds, habits, or attitudes may pop out of us next week, let alone ten years from now. Some of them have never even crossed our minds. When they eventually emerge, we might be startled and disappointed in ourselves. The Lord, however, knows about them and when they are going to become a problem, yet loves us anyway.

If God's love for a sinning believer did fail, not only would it fall short of "everlasting," but it would also suggest that there was a shaky relationship in the Trinity. The Son prayed to the Father, "You...have loved them (the disciples) *as* You have loved Me" (John 17:23). The Father loves the disciples just as He loves the Son. So, if His love for us could shrivel and turn to hatred, that would be a statement about the kind of love He has for His Son—one that is conditional, dependent upon circumstances. Instead, we see Jesus saying to God, "You loved Me *before* the foundation of the world" (John 17:24). He acknowledged that the divine love for Him had endured from eternity past up until that moment. And since the Father loves us just as He loves Christ, we can trust that neither will His affection toward us ever diminish.

It is true that Christ is sinless and has never provoked God with personal failures. We obviously cannot make such a claim for ourselves. Yet the Bible shows that it makes no difference. Nothing is powerful enough to sever us from

His divine favor—

> "Who shall separate us from the love of Christ? Shall
> tribulation, or distress, or persecution, or famine, or
> nakedness, or peril, or sword?...I am persuaded that
> neither death nor life, nor angels nor principalities
> nor powers, nor things present nor things to come,
> nor height nor death, nor any other created thing,
> shall be able to separate us from the love of God which
> is in Christ Jesus our Lord." (Rom. 8:35, 38-39)

In that short passage, Paul literally turned the universe
upside down and tried to shake out something that could
terminate God's love for us. He couldn't find anything.
Our salvation is secure because of a love that can weather
the onslaught of every negative force.

GOD'S POWER IS OUR SECURITY

Underneath those who are saved lies an immovable
object—a God of unlimited power. His divine might ensures
that His salvation will never collapse. That is exactly why
He can afford to choose all the seemingly worst people in
the world for salvation. Apparently, God has always favored
the "underdog." The Bible admits, "Not many wise according
to the flesh, not many mighty, not many noble, are called" (1
Cor. 1:26). Weaknesses do not bother Him because He has
never required anyone to be strong in the first place.

When God chose an Old Testament people, He
deliberately did not go to the Egyptians—that industrious
race celebrated for their pyramids and various cultural
advances. He did not call the Assyrians, Chaldeans, or any
other famous peoples who were noted for their intellectual
achievements and military prowess. Instead, He picked a
small, almost unknown race—the Hebrews. Soon their
weaknesses would become manifest as they became slaves
to others, absorbed the evils of the world around them, and
even rebelled against the very God who chose them. From
the human viewpoint, the Hebrews were simply not

a good choice. But fortunately for them, their calling did not rest upon any human strength. *"I* bore you on eagle's wings" (Ex. 19:4), God told them. Moses also reminded them, "You saw how the Lord your God *carried* you, as a man carries his son" (Deut. 1:31).

The vast majority of Christians do not seem to be much better than their Old Testament counterparts. Even the spiritually seasoned among us get caught in struggles and setbacks. Jesus said to the Father concerning us, "I do not pray that You should take them out of the world" (John 17:15). That sounds like a recipe for disaster. This depraved world is a great place for spiritually weak men to get into trouble, for "The whole world lies under the sway of the wicked one" (1 John 5:19). It would seem more sensible to transport us to heaven, out of temptation's reach. Yet God finds it acceptable to leave us in this world. He trusts in His own power to keep us.

In the Old Testament, three men of God were thrown into a giant furnace. The fire was so hot that even the executioners who threw them into it were killed (Dan. 3:22). In heat of that intensity, the three should have been instantly cremated. Yet, the surprised cry of those watching them was "They are not hurt" (Dan. 3:25). Then the Bible describes the three as "these men on whose bodies the fire had no power; the hair of their head was not singed nor were their garments affected, and the smell of fire was not on them" (Dan. 3:27). This remarkable feat was accomplished through the power of God. How? Consider what the king saw as he gazed at the three who were in the fire—"I see *four* men loose, walking in the midst of the fire...and the form of the fourth is like *the Son of God*" (Dan. 3:25). They were protected through the presence of God's Son who is "Christ the *power* of God" (1 Cor. 1:24).

In similar ways today, believers survive fiery trials of all kinds—including the ones that they themselves foolishly kindle. Their protection is also "Christ the power of God." Thus after eighty years, the Christian appears to be a phenomenon of grace. He can say, "I have become as a *wonder* to many" (Ps. 71:7a). The steadfastness of his salvation is

315

like a candle that somehow stays lit in the middle of a hurricane.

Though such miracles could never be accomplished through human efforts, we Christians still tend to place an illogical trust in our own will power. We find it hard to lose weight or to be on time or to cut down our coffee intake. Yet where we fail with those petty issues, for some strange reason, we think we will succeed in superhuman ones. That is why, armed with naïve confidence, many assume the burden of upholding their eternal salvation. They believe that it will be secure if only they hang on to it with an unrelenting kung-fu grip for the rest of their lives. Where they are concerned, growing faint or relaxing their hold for only a minute could spell certain doom.

This concept, however, does not match the various portrayals of salvation that we find in scripture. For instance, was Noah's salvation a matter of hanging on to the ark? God could have instructed him and his family to dig their fingernails into the sides of it and hold on for their lives. Instead, "The Lord said to Noah, 'Come *into* the ark, you and all your household'" (Gen. 7:1). God's plan of salvation was for the ark to hold them, not the other way around. As the world perished, the structural power of the great craft kept them perfectly secure. As a result, even the smallest field mouse inside the ark made it through the flood unscathed.

There is a similar point made in the Gospel of Matthew, with a storm-tossed boat full of disciples:

> "Now in the fourth watch of the night Jesus went out to them, walking on the sea. And when the disciples saw Him walking on the sea, they were troubled, saying, 'It is a ghost!' And they cried out for fear. But immediately Jesus spoke to them, saying, 'Be of good cheer! It is I; do not be afraid.' And Peter answered Him and said, 'Lord if it is you, command me to come to You on the water.' So He said, 'Come.' And when Peter had come down out of the boat, he walked on the water to go to Jesus. But when he saw that the

wind was boisterous, he was afraid; and beginning to sink, he cried out, saying, 'Lord, save Me!' And immediately Jesus stretched out His hand and caught him, and said to him, 'O you of little faith, why did you doubt?'" (Matt. 14:25-31)

Here, salvation was not dependent upon how long Peter's faith lasted or how firmly he could hold on to Jesus. It was ultimately a matter of how firmly Jesus could hold on to him.

In another case, a shepherd, representing Christ, locates a lost sheep, representing a sinner. Then, "he lays it on his shoulders, rejoicing" (Luke 15:5). Consider the power that holds the sheep upon those shoulders. It does not come from within the animal. If the sheep exerts any energy at all, it is to *escape* the shepherd, to wiggle off of his shoulders and get lost again. No, the holding power originates in the shepherd. The Lord Jesus has an unfailing strength that never relaxes His hold on us. "And when he comes home, he calls together his friends and neighbors, saying to them, 'Rejoice with me, for I have found my sheep which was lost!'" (Luke 15:6).

If it were the sheep's responsibility to remain found, then the Lord's invitation to his friends to "Rejoice with Me" would have been terribly premature. After all, the ignorant defenseless little animal could have been lost again the very next day and killed by wolves. Nonetheless, "there will be more joy in heaven over one sinner who repents than over ninety-nine just persons who need no repentance" (Luke 15:7). Heaven rejoices at the very moment a sinner repents. Why? Because when the Lord finds the sheep, they are found forever. Rejoicing can happen right then, without postponement. Heaven does not need to wait until the end of the age in order to make sure the sinner remains saved. It is assumed from the beginning that the holding power of Christ is sufficient to carry the newly found person into eternity.

Christ Himself had something to say about the power of His grip upon the believers: "Neither shall anyone snatch them out of my hand" (John 10:28). We are in the Son's hand, clenched so tightly that no one can remove us. I used to play a game with my little sister called "open the hand." I would take a penny, clench it in my fist, and tell her if she could force my hand open, she could have it. Since I was sixteen and she was only four, the odds were all in my favor. I had to let her win every time, otherwise she would not have been able to peel back one finger. Likewise, when we are saved, the Lord closes His hand around us so that no power in the universe can force even one of His fingers open.

He further portrayed this awesome grip by saying, "My Father, who has given them [the believers] to Me is greater than all; and no one is able to snatch them out of My Father's hand" (John 10:29). This seems to be the introduction of another hand beside the Son's, and the two are clasped together with us in the middle. Nothing can force these hands open; nothing can pry them apart. We are sandwiched inside, safe from anything that would try to snatch us away.

You may ask, "Okay, no one can snatch us out of the Father's hand or the Son's hand, but could *you* remove *yourself* from their hands?" If it were possible, that would mean the divine hand only protects us from other parties. It would not safeguard a Christian if he wanted to get out of God's hand and run away. What that scenario fails to take into account is that we would never want to leap out of the Lord's hands in the first place, if it were not for hostile parties like the devil. No one arbitrarily decides to abandon Christ. A believer's desire to leave God comes from the devil trying to lure him away with various temptations. That is a snatch attempt. The good news is that even if believers succumb to such temptations, all is not lost, for *"No one* is able to snatch them." Standing between us and eternal loss are the clasped hands of the Father and the Son. They not only guard against something from the outside trying to get in, but from something on the inside trying to get out. No one, including our own selves, can break God's grip and invalidate salvation. As the Lord Jesus said, "My Father is greater than all" (John 10:29).

The believer's eternal security is based upon God's personal perfection—things such as His righteousness, love, and power. If for whatever reason He overturned our salvation it would mean contradicting His own attributes. That could never happen, for "He cannot deny Himself" (2 Tim. 2:13). Our safety is guaranteed because of what He is and the fact that He is unchanging.

BECAUSE GOD'S WORK IS PERFECT, WE CANNOT LOSE OUR SALVATION

Because of who and what God is, whenever He acts it is truly spectacular. Think about it—if someone living in your neighborhood were perfect, all-knowing, all-loving, and all-powerful, whenever he did anything, no matter how small, it would make headline news. The Bible is filled with such "headlines" announcing God's work. Even more impressive, many of those headlining works are recorded as being directed toward you. Seamless, perfect deeds have been carried out with us as the beneficiaries. The entire divine Trinity—Father, Son, and Holy Spirit—has done things for us that neither our carelessness nor our laziness can undo. God's work is truly our security.

WE ARE ETERNALLY SECURE
BECAUSE THE FATHER HAS CHOSEN US

Oscar is the orange, tiger-striped cat who lives in my home. I'm sure that he has no idea how he came to be in the Myer house. He is totally unaware of the premeditation that led up to his sudden departure from the pound and his introduction to our living room. He knows nothing about our family decision to get a pet. Nor does he comprehend that some intelligence beyond his own chose him out of a pack of other cats.

It is common for believers to walk around in the same oblivion. If you ask them how they became Christians, their answers may sound like the whole process was one big lucky accident. They will describe a number of things that just seemed to come together. The right people crossed their paths. The right word was spoken. The circumstances of life just happened to be conducive. When fortune was at a high tide they made a decision for Christ. It is as though salvation came by "happenstance."

But according to Ephesians chapter one, prior to our decision for Christ, the Father had already chosen *us* "before the foundation of the world" (Eph. 1:4). Since this choice was made in eternity past and hidden from human sight, we wouldn't know about it in the least without the Bible's help. We would be totally unaware that salvation has a dimension that is independent of human will. However, there is such an overarching reality. Jesus referred to it when He said that those who are born again "were born, not of blood, nor of the will of the flesh, nor of the will of man, but of God" (John 1:13). He also told the disciples "You did not choose Me, but I chose you" (John 15:16). Thus we find that our new birth is grounded in a divine decision, not merely a human one.[1]

We did not accidentally trip over Jesus during life's journey in this world. Our meeting Him and receiving Him was the result of divine appointment. We are told, "As many as had been *appointed* to eternal life believed" (Acts 13:48). The night before I received Christ was a typical one. I listened to music, talked to friends, and went to bed. The morning of the day I got saved was just as unremarkable. If you had told me that by the time I went to bed that night, I was going to be changed forever by Christ, I would have laughed at you. There might have been personal struggles in my life, but I certainly had not intended to bring Jesus into any of them. Yet when nine-o'-clock rolled around, regardless of previous commitments, attitudes, or desires, I believed. It hadn't been anywhere on my list of

---

[1] For a brief further discussion of God's choice versus man's will, see Appendix 2.

things to do, but that didn't matter. My salvation was definitely on *someone's* agenda.

While I was ignorant that I had been appointed to eternal life, I thought of salvation as something that had drifted into me. I also wondered if it could just as easily drift back out again. This concept is very prevalent with new believers, although it is not in harmony with the Bible. For, as long as the scriptures show us that salvation does not ultimately depend upon our best choice, neither can we lose it through a foolish choice. And as long as the Bible informs us that salvation has become ours according to divine purpose, then that means it cannot be lost by human accident.

As long as the idea of losing eternal life is a possibility, we are forced to ask a question: If God appointed us to eternal life, could He have made mistakes? Could He have chosen some people only to discover later that they were the wrong choices?

Human beings try to use a great deal of discretion in their choices. Before we choose things like a school, a new car, a restaurant, or a doctor, we normally take care in doing it. We read consumer reports, check references, and ask advice. Despite all the caution, though, we still pick lemons. Such are the pitfalls of human selection. We do our best to be right but then find ourselves wrong.

The Father's method of choosing is the opposite of ours. He selects without any reference to track records and no consideration of performance. He chose us "before the foundation of the world" (Eph. 1:4). That is, *before* your birth, *before* recorded history, *before* the dinosaurs, and *before* the existence of the world itself. Since God's choosing occurred before anyone had been born, no one had yet done anything good or evil (Rom. 9:11). This was a statement to the universe that salvation would neither rest upon our strength nor be frustrated by our weaknesses. In essence, God could say, "I did not choose anyone based on what they could do. I chose this or that person simply because I *wanted* to choose them." As He says in Romans 9:15, "I will have mercy on whomever I will have mercy, and I will have compassion on whomever I will have compassion." The Father's choice is based on

Himself and not us. But if He withdrew our salvation due to some personal defect in us, He would be saying that the opposite is true—that His selection *was* based on our talents and abilities.

As it stands though, God's choice happened before anyone could move a finger so "election might stand, not of works but *of Him* who calls" (Rom. 9:11). Selection is not a *you* thing, it's a *God* thing. The divine choice is unaffected when you seem to make a mess of your Christian life because you were not chosen based on how well you could be a Christian, anyway.

The fact that God has chosen us is a great thing, but He has gone even farther than that. In addition, He "*predestined* us to adoption as sons" (Eph. 1:5). It is one thing to choose someone; it is another thing to predestine him. For example, a football coach chooses players for his team and hopes they will all become great. But suppose that through some type of miracle, the coach was able to *predestine* his players to greatness? What if he could predetermine the outcome of their careers and ensure that every one of them made it into the Hall of Fame—from the very start, *before* the first practice was even called?

This was what God did when He chose us. He predestined us to "be holy and without blame before Him" (Eph. 1:4). Since our destiny has been preset, this removes any possibility for an uncertain, open-ended future. There is no such thing for us believers as a fifty-fifty chance of either being saved or being lost. Because God has decided our ending from the very start, there is only one possible way for us to end up—"holy and blameless...sons."

Let's return to the football analogy for a minute. No doubt, if the players really believed in their predestination to the Hall of Fame, it would powerfully boost their morale. But imagine their frustration when, during practice, the quarterback can't manage to pass the ball any better than an eight-year-old girl. The defensive linemen are terribly afraid of being hurt. The center is too fat to bend over for the snap. Other players can't get out of bed. And the more they all try, the more they realize they just don't have it in them.

During these times of depression and defeat, they would have to remember that they did not choose or predestine themselves. Their coach did it. Somehow the secret to their future is in him.

New Christians would do well to remember the same thing. Our "coach" didn't just choose us, set a goal for us, and then sit around hoping that we could make it. He furnishes the unlimited resources to get us there. He fully intends that we would reach the destiny preset for us.

This thought is strengthened even more where it says, "Whom He predestined, these He also called; whom He called, these He also justified; and whom He justified, these He also glorified" (Rom. 8:30). This verse describes an unbreakable chain. One end of it lies in eternity past, where God predestined us. The other end lies somewhere in the future, in our glorified state. Between the two ends are links that unerringly lead from one to another.

After the first link of predestination, there is the next link of calling. If God has predestined you, He will definitely call you. Next, if God calls you, then you will positively respond in faith, so He justifies you. At this point in the verse, we must stop and pay special attention. If there were a possibility of the justified being lost, then there could be no *definite* future statements to follow. We should find nothing more than a dotted line after salvation, for who can know whether he will sin and then cease to be justified? However, the chain link of justification continues on to the final link of glorification. There are no allowances made for stopping short of glory. Neither backsliding, lapsed faith, or bad days can snap the chain.

Today, if we have been justified by faith in Jesus Christ, we are assured of something in both directions. Looking behind us to the past, we can know that God has predestined us. Looking before us to the future, we can know that we will be glorified. We can know because these items are all inseparably joined as one.

Also, take a closer look at Romans 8:30. Consider Paul's use of the word "glorified." Shouldn't he have said, "those whom He justified, these He also *will* glorify"? It seems strange that something in our future is described by using the past tense of the word. The reason for doing it is quite profound. Romans 8:30 represents God's view of our salvation, and in His estimation, it is *all* completed! Even the part that lies in the future for us—glorification—from God's standpoint, is already finished. The moment He predestined us in the eternal ages of the past, all His subsequent work of calling, justifying, and glorifying us was as good as done.

Today, we believers are moving toward glory, the next and final link in the unbreakable chain. Many things will happen to us on this journey, some good and some bad. In the midst of it all, though, our future is never in question. This makes the Christian life like a ship that sets sail from New York, bound for an oversea port. During the trip, numerous things happen to the passengers on board. A few get seasick. Some fall in love. Others rest or engage in business. Yet no matter what happens, none of them can alter the vessel's destination. It will continue on course until arriving at its port. In the same sense, regardless of the many details of life, we will arrive at our destiny of glory. Nothing we do can abort the journey.

That is exactly why Paul could say, "We shall *all* be changed—in a moment, in the twinkling of an eye, at the last trumpet. For the trumpet will sound, and the dead will be raised incorruptible, and we *shall be* changed. For this corruptible must put on incorruption, and this mortal must put on immortality" (1 Cor. 15:51b-53). Taking into account the people to whom this was written—the Corinthians—it is striking that Paul says we shall *all* be changed. These believers were fleshly (1 Cor. 3:1, 3-4). They had fallen into division (1 Cor. 1:10-12), sexual immorality (1 Cor. 5:1; 6:15), suing one another in court (1 Cor. 6:1-8), food and sex addictions (1 Cor. 6:12-13), confusion about marital issues (1 Cor. 7:2, 9-11), degrading public worship (1 Cor. 11:17-18, 20), misusing spiritual gifts (1 Cor. 13:1-2), and holding wrong teachings (1 Cor. 15:12). These were not juvenile offenses. Paul warned the offenders of stinging reprisals—divine discipline for them in both this age and the next.

Still, though some of the believers had fallen, Paul could say that *all* of them would be changed. This demonstrates that nothing can derail the Father's choosing and predestination. He cannot be wrong, and He cannot fail to finish what He has begun in a believer.

WE ARE ETERNALLY SECURE BECAUSE THE SON PRAYS FOR US

Since much has already been said about the death of Christ, I will move on to another aspect of the Son's work toward us.

Every time a person believes in the Lord Jesus, then the Lord Jesus Himself is literally put to the test. Wicked, evil people receive the gospel every day, and all without exception are assured that Christ is "able to save to the *uttermost* those who come to God through Him" (Heb. 7:25). "Uttermost" means the greatest magnitude, the furthest degree. The Lord only deals with a man in that way. He does not render partial salvation, that is, salvation for a little while until something interrupts it. If He were to terminate His work at any point in a Christian's stormy life, salvation would fall short of "the uttermost." Under those circumstances, though the Bible might say that He is able, the Lord would have to confess that He was *not* able to finish what He had started in that person. He would need to blame the believer for being too difficult to work with. Of course, that will never be the case.

The Lord Jesus takes His believers the entire distance because "He always lives to make *intercession* for them" (Heb. 7:25). Intercession is prayer, which may sound a little anticlimactic to you. Our ideas about prayer don't do much to inspire confidence. We are used to people saying (and maybe we have said), "I'll pray for you," in the same noncommittal way as saying, "I'll be thinking about you." It often means nothing. But where Christ is concerned, prayer is not a courteous religious thing that He offers to do for us. His attitude goes beyond putting in a good word for us with the Father. He "*lives* to make intercession" for us. This is commitment of a total nature.

Furthermore, His prayers for us are not begging sessions that God may or may not hear. He Himself said, "Father, I thank You that You have heard Me. And I know that You *always* hear Me" (John 11:41b-42a). He has no doubt that His prayer will be heard because He always perfectly prays according to the Father's will. Even His prayer in the garden that "this cup pass from Me" (Matt. 26:39a) was controlled by His overriding love for the will of God. "Not as I will, but as *You* will" (Matt. 26:39b), He added, and meant it. This is the type of prayer He makes on our behalf—the kind that matches the Father's mind, will, and desire. It is intercession that is heard and never ignored.

We are all familiar with prayer that does not seem to net immediate visible results, so we tend to treat it as the last resort—something that is tried when nothing else works. Yet to the Lord Jesus, prayer is the first resort. It is power. For Him, doing something is not the first thing. Telling the Father is the first thing. His prayer always moves the heart of God. In John 12:28 He prayed, "Father, glorify Your name.' Than a *voice* came from heaven, saying, 'I have both glorified it and will glorify it again.'" Christ's request was short and simple, only four words long, but it moved the Father, making Him break silence and speak directly out of heaven. Today the Lord Jesus prays just as effectively on our behalf, and God responds just as powerfully.

The Gospel of Luke gives us a window into His potent prayer ministry toward us. At one point, the devil had noticed Peter and taken a personal interest in destroying him. The Lord warned His clueless disciple, "Satan has asked for you, that he may sift you as wheat" (Luke 22:31). Of course, Peter could do nothing about that. The devil is an invisible enemy, much more powerful and intelligent than mortal men. So, the Lord told Peter, "I have *prayed* for you that your faith should not fail" (Luke 22:32). No other promises were given. The Lord Jesus felt that His prayer could guarantee sufficient protection. Nothing else needed to be done.

The contest between Peter, a scared, compromising disciple, and Satan, the strongest of all the fallen angels, should have resulted in total ruination for the man. Yet later, though considerably weakened under satanic pressure, Peter's faith never completely failed. Something had interfered on his behalf—prayers from One whom God always hears and always answers.

The Lord expected that this satanic attack was not going to be an isolated incident, either. He said, "I do not pray for these alone [the twelve], but also for those who *will* believe in Me through their word" (John 17:20). Apparently, He could foresee many moments down through the centuries when the devil would try to isolate and destroy the believers. But having come to Christ, we are now the focus of His powerful ministry of intercession. The result is guaranteed to be salvation to the uttermost.

WE ARE ETERNALLY SECURE BECAUSE THE SPIRIT HAS SEALED US

When we heard and believed the gospel, we were *"sealed with the Holy Spirit of Promise"* (Eph. 1:13). A seal is a personal stamp of sorts. In ancient times, it was usually a ring or a clay ornament that was dabbed in ink and then pressed on a surface to leave some mark of ownership.

Since we believers have the Spirit, we now have the divine seal. We may not be aware of it, but this invisible imprint identifies us as God's property. It protects us from being lost, since the general idea is that possessions with names on them are less likely to go missing. But our experience in the secular world is that criminals can erase or alter marks of ownership. Serial numbers can be filed off of metal surfaces. Signatures can be digitally removed. On the low-tech side, an owner's name can simply be scratched out with a ballpoint pen.

Could we through sin or neglect obliterate God's seal? It is certainly possible for a believer to cultivate an outward lifestyle that makes it look like he belongs to Satan. The question is, can defeated believers deface *all* signs of God's ownership upon them, even to the core. The Bible answers by telling us that the Spirit is the One "in whom you were sealed, *for the day of redemption"* (Eph. 4:30). God's seal,

His mark of ownership, will be upon us all the way up to the day of redemption, that is, the day in which redemption's effect upon our lives is complete. Until then, no one can erase it, alter it, or scratch it off. The Lord said the Spirit was given "that He may abide with you *forever*" (John 14:16). As a mark of ownership, He is indelible.

In addition, the Spirit also acts as "the guarantee of our inheritance" (Eph. 1:14). His very presence promises us that we will one day receive the fullness of salvation—that we will continue to the end, regardless of how dark the days become.

This guarantee is so solemn that the third Person of the trinity—the Holy Spirit—has been given to us as a pledge that it will definitely be honored. When a living person acts as a down payment, we can be sure that the guarantor must truly intend to keep his word. In the Old Testament, Jacob's sons journeyed to Egypt and got into trouble there. They were allowed to go home, but they had to promise to return for further judgment. Their "pledge" to do so was their own brother, Simeon. He was to remain imprisoned in Egypt until his brothers came back (Gen. 42:19-24). Perhaps if they had posted bond with a bag of gold coins or a few head of cattle, they might have said to each other, "Egypt is too risky. Let's just forfeit the deposit and skip going back." However, the pledge was their own brother. Because of him, they could never seriously think of defaulting on their promise.

Today the pledge of our inheritance is also a Person, the Holy Spirit. He is the indwelling promise that our salvation will be successfully completed and we will be redeemed in every part of our being. He is God's very oath. As long as He is within (which is permanently), the believers have God's solemn assurance that they will inherit full salvation. The Spirit is the living, personal guarantee of our future. Because of Him, God would never think of defaulting on His promise.

The cumulative work of the Father, the Son, and the Holy Spirit guarantees that we will never be lost. Otherwise, the Father who has chosen and predestinated us would see His counsel overthrown. The Son who died for us and prays for us would find His labor quashed. The Holy Spirit who sealed us would suffer cancellation. Thus, the loss of only one believer would mean a disappointed Father, a defeated Son, and a voided Spirit. Of course, that would be impossible. No one can defeat the divine Trinity. His perfect work cannot be shaken and so neither can any force in the universe topple our salvation.

Doubts From the Bible

The Lord Jesus may have said that we "shall by no means perish," but we still imagine that there must be a means. Somewhere there has to be a loophole that allows for the saved to become the unsaved. Bible readers often suspect this as they come across verses that seem to contradict eternal security. They may begin to wonder if God is a Person who makes great promises out of one side of His mouth, while neutralizing them with opposite words from the other side. However, the Christian can rest assured that the Bible is not a book filled with assertions that eventually null each other out. Whether it is the word of Jesus directly or the word of the Holy Spirit through the apostles, the teaching of eternal security in the Bible is a consistent one. However, rather than ignoring questionable passages, we should pay close attention to what they say and why they say it. A brief survey of them will further clarify that believers do indeed keep their salvation forever.

Could a Brother Perish?

It's true that Paul was concerned about the possibility of a weak brother perishing (1 Cor. 8:11). But this verse only teaches the loss of salvation if we see the word "perish" and automatically assume that it means to be lost in hell. Biblical words can have different connotations depending upon how they are used. "Perish" is one of them. John 3:16 uses the word to mean eternal loss in the lake of fire. Luke 15:7 treats it differently. There the prodigal son says, "I *perish*

329

with hunger!" In that passage, physical starvation, not eternal loss, is the meaning intended.

Now, what does "perish" signify in 1 Corinthians 8? It describes damaged fellowship between a believer and God. This is why the chapter specifically mentions the believer's conscience (1 Cor. 8:7, 12). The conscience is the part of us that witnesses to the quality of our fellowship with the Lord. If our conscience is defiled (as with the perishing brother of 1 Cor. 8), then it immediately serves notice to us that our fellowship has also been defiled. In that condition we cease to spiritually thrive. We feel dull and dark within. If this condition is allowed to continue without repentance, then it will only get worse. At some point, we could become so deadened that we may not even desire to fellowship with the Lord anymore. Thus, this passage speaks about perishing as related to declining fellowship and not about the doom of lost salvation.

A similar thought occurs in James 5:19, where we find a brother wandering away from the truth. According to James 5:20, "He who turns a sinner [the wandering brother of verse 19] from the error of his way will save a soul from *death* and cover a multitude of sins." If the brother is not rescued from his error, it seems, his soul will be lost to the second death. James, however, is not attempting to teach anything here about the loss of salvation. The death he alludes to is not spiritual in nature. He had begun speaking of physical illness in verse 14, when he asked "Is anyone among you sick?" In verse 15 he gives the remedy—"the prayer of faith will save the sick, and the Lord will raise him up. And if he has committed sins, he will be forgiven. Confess your trespasses to one another, and pray for one another, that you may be healed."

The idea of physical life is clearly the issue here, and if we follow James's flow of thought, it continues down to verse 20. "To save a soul from death" in that verse is to help a man repent and confess his sins so that the Lord would not be forced to discipline him by taking his life. As I mentioned briefly in other parts of this book, that kind of judgment can occur if a believer offends the Lord

(1 Cor. 11:29-30; Acts 5:1-11), but it only touches the natural human life. Neither in James, nor in any those other "judgment" passages is there anything taught concerning the loss of spiritual life.

Was Paul Afraid of Losing His Own Salvation?

In 1 Corinthians 9:27 it seems that Paul is nervous concerning his own future: "I discipline my body and bring it into subjection, lest, when I have preached to others, I myself should become *disqualified.*" If the Apostle Paul himself was concerned about being lost, then certainly none of us "little potatoes" can rest upon any assurances.

The intended subject of that verse, though, had nothing to do with any alleged concerns that Paul had about his eternal salvation. Paul wrote within the framework of a metaphor. Just two verses prior, he had compared the Christian life to "those who run in a race" (1 Cor. 9:24). He also called the goal of the race "the prize" (1 Cor. 9:24).

These two phrases are hints that Paul was not speaking about being saved. He himself never saw the forgiveness of sins as being a race. On the contrary, he taught that it "is *not* of him who wills nor of him who *runs,* but of God who shows mercy" (Rom. 9:16). He also never referred to eternal life as a prize which must be won, but as a gift which is freely received (Rom. 6:23). The race of 1 Corinthians 9, therefore, does not deal with a great effort to keep the gift of salvation. The gift is kept by grace alone. This chapter deals with winning the prize—"an imperishable crown" (1 Cor. 9:25). That is a reward for those who faithfully follow the Lord in this world. It is possible to lose the crown, but not the gift.

We have all heard stories about athletes that cheated in order to win contests. They took steroids or engaged in other illegal shortcuts. As a result, they were "disqualified" (1 Cor. 9:27). They lost their crowns, but not their lives. They were penalized, but not executed. There is also a crucial difference for the believer between loss of prize and loss of eternal life. Paul was clearly concerned with the former. The latter he knew to be secure already.

331

WHY ARE SOME NAMES ERASED OUT OF THE BOOK OF LIFE?

In Revelation 3:5, the Lord makes a promise to certain Christians: "He who overcomes shall be clothed in white garments, and I will not *blot out his name from the Book of Life;* but I will confess his name before My Father and before His angels." The converse of the promise seems obvious. If the Christian does *not* overcome and is defeated instead, then he *will be* blotted out of the book of life. That takes us to the next logical step in Revelation 20:15: "Anyone not found written in the Book of Life was cast into the lake of fire." This simple two-step Bible study tells us that it is possible for Christians to be erased (lose their salvation) and to burn forever. The picture, though, becomes much less definite when we add in other pertinent details.

For one thing, when were our names written in the Book of Life? We would think that it was the day we received eternal life, that is, the day we believed in Jesus. But Revelation 17:8 says that we were "written in the Book of Life from the foundation of the world." This means our names were recorded before we were born, apart from anything we did. It was God's choice, God's will that put us there, not our own. As we have already seen, God's choice is always accompanied with His predestination to glory (Rom. 8:30). If God were to set a person's destiny and then abandon that person before it was fulfilled, then that would signify a divine failure. So, we must be careful when we assume that blotting out a name from the Book of Life necessarily means eternal loss.

What then, does it mean to be blotted out of the Book of Life? Let's follow the flow of thought in the actual passage where it is mentioned. There we find a message to the church in Sardis—"You have a name that you are alive, but you are *dead"* (Rev. 3:1). The Lord called this assembly of Christians "dead," meaning that their spiritual condition and experience from day to day was flat. There was no spiritual vitality with them. They might have been alive according to the second birth in their spirit, but dead every other way. Christians can fall into this condition by settling into low, base thoughts—"to be carnally minded is *death*" (Rom. 8:6) and by acting on those thought—"If you live according to the flesh you will *die*" (Rom. 8:13).

The believers in Sardis might have had a name, a reputation for being alive, but the Lord knew their true situation—that their works were "ready to *die*" (Rev. 3:2). He warned them that in their deadened spiritual state they would be ill-prepared for His return—"I will come upon you as a thief, and you will not know what hour I will come upon you" (Rev. 3:3).

Now, how could people in such a dead condition be recorded in the Book of Life? It is a dilemma. Fleshly, soulish, worldly Christians are not healthy representatives of eternal life. If God simply left their names intact, then that would falsely testify that they were living. Yet if God blotted them out of the Book, and withdrew their salvation, it would create an equally great controversy. He would have to admit that He could not bring them into glory.

The Lord's solution is similar to what is sometimes done in human affairs. Occasionally in an obituary, the surviving family of the deceased is listed—all, that is, except for one or two persons. The missing ones are not in good standing with the rest of the family or maybe even with the deceased, so their names were blotted out of the record. This erasure is meant to be a statement and a shaming. If you have ever been on the stinging end of this type of treatment, you probably remember the shame, the sorrow, or the outrage it produced in you. The feelings of an ostracized person can no doubt be severely affected. However, the genetic connection to his relatives is not severed. His name might be missing from the roster, yet he is still a part of that family.

God also blots names out of His record as a disciplinary measure. And though people have been unfairly erased from human registries, there is no such injustice with God. As He told the deadened believers in Sardis, "I *know*." That statement disallows any possibility of misunderstanding.

The most appropriate thing for God to do with believers who persist in spiritual death is to remove their names from the list of the living for a period of time. This will possibly occur during the one-thousand-year kingdom of Christ referred to in Revelation 20:4, where Christians are either rewarded or disciplined. After this period, the Book of Life will be consulted in the last judgment of Revelation 20:11-15. At that point, the names of *all* God's redeemed will be found intact.

WHY ARE SOME BRANCHES BURNED?

John chapter 15 contains some alarming imagery. There the Lord says, "I am the vine, you are the branches...If anyone does not abide in Me, he is cast out as a branch and is withered; and they gather them and throw them into the fire, and they are burned" (5a, 6). The phrases "cast out" and "they are burned" sound like eternal loss—that is, as long as the phrases remain isolated from their surrounding context. When we reinsert them into the passage where they are found, a thought very different from eternal loss begins to emerge.

As a whole, John 15 repeatedly emphasizes branches (the disciples) bearing fruit (John 15:2, 4-5, 8). Bearing fruit means that we visibly manifest the characteristics of the Spirit in our daily life (Gal. 5:22-23). It also means that we reproduce new believers through our work, words, and living (Col. 1:5-6).

The secret of doing this is to abide in Christ (John 15:4-7). Fruit will only come out of the Christian life if we experientially stay in contact with Him. If not, then we will be fruitless and will suffer side effects. First, "every branch in Me that does not bear fruit He takes *away*" (John 15:2). This describes a sense of separation and distance from Christ. Second, "if anyone does not abide in Me...he is *withered*" (John 15:6). This illustrates feebleness settling over a believer's spiritual condition. He is no longer fresh and full of vitality. Third, "they gather them [the branches] and throw them into the fire, and they are burned" (John 15:6)—referring to a Christian's sense of uselessness. He has failed to fulfill the purpose of a branch, which is to bear fruit and glorify the Father (John 15:8, 16).

His Christian life now seems a waste, a pointless endeavor.

The Lord chastises His wayward believers with all these inward sensations so that they will return to Him. These are lessons in *abiding*, not eternal salvation. In fact, at the beginning of His discourse in John 15, the Lord had confirmed "You are *already* clean because of the word I have spoken to you" (John 15:3). This meant that He had already settled eternal matters with them. They were clean. By telling them this, He wanted them to know that as He went on to speak of all the matters concerning the branches, He would not be addressing their eternal standing before God. He would be instructing them on the quality and productivity of their daily relationship with Him.

What Happens When a Righteous Man Turns to Evil Ways?

Most of us have known or at least heard of a committed Christian who left the path of righteousness. Maybe the break came from his being angry with God over a bitter personal disappointment. Or, perhaps he simply grew careless and found himself doing things he thought he would never do. Regardless, if we consult Ezekiel 18:24, the consequences seem to be clear:

> "When a righteous man turns away from his righteousness and commits iniquity, and does according to all the abominations that the wicked man does, shall he live? All the righteousness which he has done shall not be remembered; because of the unfaithfulness of which he is guilty and the sin which he has committed, because of them he shall die."

This verse appears to tell us that unrighteousness can erase righteousness. That would mean the righteous man can completely lose his standing before God. But if we look ahead to verse 27, we find that "When a wicked man turns away from the wickedness which he committed, and does what is lawful and right, he preserves himself alive."

In verse 24, a man can reverse his status before God from

righteous to unrighteous. In verse 27, he can change it from unrighteous to righteous. These passages give us a classic description of Old Testament righteousness, since in them, the standing of a man all depends upon what he can or cannot do. If he fails, he dooms himself; if he succeeds in changing his ways, he saves himself. For that reason, these verses do not address the salvation that is in Christ, for "a man is not justified by the works of the law but by faith in Jesus Christ" (Gal. 2:16). Old Testament verses like those in Ezekiel command human efforts for justification. They should therefore not be imported into the New Testament understanding of salvation. Ezekiel 18 does not speak of whether a Christian can lose his salvation; in fact, it is not meant for Christians at all.

WHAT IF WE SIN ON PURPOSE?

This is what I call a "five alarm" verse: "If we sin willfully after we have received the knowledge of the truth, there no longer remains a sacrifice for sins" (Heb. 10:26). The cause for concern is very clear—willful sin equals *no more sacrifice for sins*. That's a problem because the large majority of sins we commit involve premeditation. Our sins are willful. We plan them, even if it only involves thirty seconds of lead-time. if that were the case, of course, any sin would become fatal to a believer. However, if we plug Hebrews 10:26 back into the chapter surrounding it, it becomes clear that the willful sin the writer was talking about is not some random evil. The verse directly before it speaks of "not forsaking the assembling of ourselves together" (Heb. 10:25). *That* is the willful sin, not gambling or drinking or swearing.

Of course, stopping at this point, we would have an even shakier situation. Now you wouldn't have to go to the trouble of doing something evil in order to perish eternally. You would only need to "forsake" going to church meetings. But that is not what verses 25 and 26 are saying, either. The correct understanding lies in grasping the background of the book of Hebrews—that the Jewish believers were retreating into the old system of Judaism. They harbored a suspicion that perhaps they had made a mistake in leaving their religion to come to Christ. So, weakened in their Christian faith and thinking that there still might be unplumbed blessings in keeping Old Testament law, some had started a backward trek. That was the "willful sin" of which the writer spoke. It had to do with Jewish believers turning their backs on Christ and the New Covenant so they could return to their worship in the temple.

The Christians guilty of this sin thought there was still something of God's special blessing upon the Jewish temple and its system of animal sacrifices. But the writer of Hebrews protested that in going back, they would no longer find anything with real sacrificial power. No one would find a sacrifice for sins in the temple. Before the death of Christ, bulls and goats had been part of God's ordained way of dealing with sins. After His death, however, all of those sacrifices had been replaced, virtually rendered impotent— "He takes *away* the first that He may establish the second" (Heb. 10:9).

The Jewish believers were ignorantly going back to something obsolete. In Christ, they had already been forgiven of their sins. Returning to the temple would do nothing more than involve them with dead animals. They wouldn't find anything there that was special or blessed—only empty shells of God's past arrangement. This is exactly what was meant by "there no longer remains a sacrifice for sins" (Heb. 10:26).

Hebrews 10:25-26, then, simply says that it is a sin to turn away from Christ and His New Testament arrangement and that it is useless to re-embrace the Old Covenant. Nothing in those verses, however, says anything about Christians losing their salvation.

Could There Sometimes Be No Possibility of Repentance?

Hebrews 6:4-6 is often considered as the death sentence for fallen believers:

"It is impossible for those who were once enlightened,

and have tasted the heavenly gift, and become
partakers of the Holy Spirit, and have tasted the good
word of God and the powers of the age to come, if
they fall away, to renew them again to repentance."

Reduced to a bite-sized phrase, it says, "impossible...if
they fall away to renew them again to repentance." Thus
the Bible apparently confirms that there is such a thing as a
believer not being able to get up from a serious fall. At least
that's what it looks like until we go back to the beginning of
the chapter and follow the flow of thought from Hebrews
6:1:

"Therefore, leaving the discussion of the elementary
principles of Christ [the more simple, initial
teachings], let us be brought on to perfection [a state
of spiritual maturity], not laying again the foundation
of repentance from dead works and of faith toward
God."

Remember that the recipients of the book of Hebrews
were Christians who had stopped following the Lord and
were in a state of childish immaturity. That is why this
chapter begins with an appeal to continue growing—to leave
the elementary things of the Christian life and be brought
on to perfection. But what if the process gets interrupted
and believers stop growing? According to the writer, they
are not to lay again another foundation, but to simply be
brought on from where they had ceased.

This makes good sense. Think about it from the
perspective of a man building a house. Suppose after laying
his foundation he gets distracted and squanders his
construction budget. A year later he realizes how foolish he
was and determines once again to finish the house. What
does he do first? If he has any sense at all, he will not start
with a brand new foundation. He will begin where he left
off, on top of the foundation already laid.

In terms of the Christian life, the initial stage is "the
foundation of repentance" (Heb. 6:1), when we first believed

in the Lord and were saved. It is impossible for us to repeat that experience, that is, to "renew...*again* to repentance" (Heb. 6:6). No provision is made in the Bible for being born again *again*. Hebrews 6:6b tells us that this kind of attempted restart would be to "crucify again...the Son of God"—something entirely unnecessary. For the Bible says, "This man, after He had offered one sacrifice for sins *forever,* sat down on the right hand of God" (Heb. 10:12). Attempting to duplicate the crucifixion is a serious thing. It means we are suggesting that the Lord's death was not sufficient. He might have sat down after the cross, but we must ask Him to get up and revisit the cross all over again. That would be to "put Him to an open shame" (Heb. 6:6b). The best way to honor the Lord after we fall away is to accept His death as eternally adequate and to simply get up and continue following Him.

This Hebrews passage goes on to compare Christians to cropland (Heb. 6:7). Because the Lord has worked so hard to give it "rain," it should yield some type of harvest. However, "If it bears thorns and briers, it is rejected and near to being cursed, whose end is to be burned" (Heb. 6:8). This parting thought once again signals disaster because of the words "rejected" and "burned." Will the Lord *destroy* a field (a believer) that does not grow a good crop?

In response, let me tell you a story. When I was eight, my family moved to a place in Pineville, Louisiana. It had three acres of pasture that we used for horses, ducks, and chickens. The side yard was sectioned off to be a garden, but it was in bad shape. Bunches of sharp-edged grass grew there in waves. Some weeds stood as tall as a man. Others were coated with thorns and had roots like copper plumbing. But there was not one edible thing to be found. As far as a garden was concerned, that piece of ground was a *reject*. It was not even a good place to play. We avoided it as something cursed—but it was only *nearly* cursed. You see, my dad had no intention of giving up on that patch of ground until it produced something suitable for the dinner table.

His starting point was to eliminate the jungle that had grown up in it. The growth was too thick to reasonably handle, even with a swingblade, so he *burned* all of it to the ground. After the fire eliminated the offensive growth, then he worked it with a rotiller. In time, that garden became more fruitful than any of us could have ever imagined. It gave us corn and turnips and collard greens and eggplants and tomatoes. You would never have known that it was at one time rejected and near a curse.

Some believers are not much different than that garden in its unruly state. They let everything obnoxious grow in them. One day at the Lord's return though, they will discover that "weeds" are all they have to show for their Christian lives. The Lord will tell them, "This is not right. I gave you the rain of grace to grow healthy things." Then He will discipline them, burning away all the unwanted growth.

The fire of Hebrews 6:8 alludes to God's disciplinary action clearing but not destroying the ground. Like all the rest of the book of Hebrews and the New Testament, these types of verses show God dealing with Christians who have failed to live like Christians. Yet, the outcome is discipline unto fruitfulness, not destruction.

WHAT IF WE FALL FROM **GRACE**?

God's grace is there for us any time we fall, but what happens when "you have fallen from *grace*"? (Gal. 5:4). That has a very serious ring of finality to it. It sounds like the point of no return. We wonder what heinous act a person has to commit in order to get into that kind of trouble. The cause is revealed in Galatians 5:4, where the fallen believer is "you who attempt to be justified by law." Amazingly, it is not evil works that jeopardize our standing in grace, but *good* ones. Those who attempt to be justified by law try to do good things that match the law of God, deeds that are noble, decent, and especially religious.

Whenever we attempt to keep the law in order to maintain our position before God, then the inevitable result is that we fall from grace. The reason is simple: grace and law cannot coexist. Either something is free or it's not. Sometimes Christians receive the free gift of salvation but turn and began trying to pay for it. As described in the book of Galatians, this strange reversal always produces ill effects in the Christian life. One of them is that joy disappears—*"Where* then is that sense of blessing you had?"* (Gal. 4:14-15 NASB). Another ill effect is a stifling sense of religious slavery—"Stand fast therefore in the *liberty* by which Christ has made us free and do not be entangled again with a yoke of *slavery"* (Gal. 5:1). As long as a Christian seeks to be justified by law, he will feel heavy, a prisoner of performance, not the glad recipient of a free gift. The harder he works, the farther Jesus seems to be from him. Paul called it "estranged from Christ" (Gal. 5:4a).

That is what it means to fall from grace—not that you fall into hell, but that you fall into an alienation from the Lord, a coldness toward Him, and an oppressive weight of obligation. It is not a loss of grace in total, but a loss of the experience of it. Paul's word was a rebuke to the Galatians concerning their poor condition. However, he had no intention of telling them that they had been lost.

As I've pointed out in this brief survey of verses, it is very easy to misunderstand the thought of a passage. Sometimes only the more dramatic elements in them claim our attention, thus confusing the issue. It is like yelling to someone across a crowded beach that your favorite food is shark fin soup. There will always be a person who only hears "...*shark fin...*" Then the panic starts. If we approach the Bible with such partial hearing, doubts and fears will continue to surface about eternal security. However, if we pay attention to what a questionable passage is actually saying, its context, and its background, difficulties will tend to be solved.

DOUBTS FROM REAL LIFE

The truth of eternal security looks beautiful on paper. The inevitable challenge to it, though, comes from real life. One night at a home-group meeting, a young woman named Pam asked me a question. There was more than a little irritation in her voice. "John," she said, "My sister got saved a year ago, but not long after that she got back into the nightclub scene with all the booze and different men. She *couldn't* still be saved, could she?" The group took a brief intermission in place while I explained eternal security to Pam. I also told her that although saved people keep their salvation there are rewards for the faithful and discipline for the unfaithful. As I took her to some verses, she nodded politely, but as soon as I shut the Bible, she started talking about her sister again. After fifteen additional minutes of telling our group "My sister did this" and "My sister did that" Pam came back around full circle and said, "She *couldn't* still be saved." As far as Pam was concerned, the case was closed. She had passed a final judgment based on her human observations, regardless of what the scriptures had to say. For her, as for many of us, more weight was given to appearances than to the Word of God.

Yet, even in the Bible we can find problematic biographies. At face value, they involve people who appear to have lost their salvation. For instance, in the Old Testament the Spirit came upon certain persons (see 1 Sam. 10:6, 10; Judges 14:6, 19; 15:14) and then left them when their living became less than godly (1 Sam. 16:14). These are the recorded experiences of actual people. None of these ancient cases, however, can tell us much about the security of New Testament salvation. At most they can only demonstrate the operating principle of the Spirit in Old Testament times. There, the Spirit's visitation to men was never a permanent arrangement. He could come and go freely as if He were a dove settled upon a shoulder. Sometimes He would leave His "perch," because His man of choice would do things to disturb Him. Therefore, the relationship was temporary, transient, and subject to change. Even David knew this when he prayed "Do not take your Holy Spirit from Me" (Ps. 51:11).

While the continuity of the Spirit with anyone in the Old Testament was not guaranteed, the experience of New Testament people is much different. First Corinthians 6:17

says, "He that is joined to the Lord is *one* spirit with Him." This indicates the intensity and depth of the believer's attachment to the Lord—the Holy Spirit and his spirit are now "one spirit." Truly, the dove has done more than light upon us; He has attached Himself to our deepest part in an inseparable union. This is why the Lord Jesus told the disciples that the Spirit would "abide with you *forever*" (John 14:16-17). In the New Testament, men are no longer like revolving doors. The Spirit comes and stays in them.

Getting an authoritative word on eternal security from the experience of Old Testament characters can be tricky, if not misleading—at least from the standpoint of keeping or losing the Spirit.

Looking in the New Testament, we will find cases that are closer to home. These are people who directly followed Jesus or believed the gospel and yet were apparently lost. Judas Iscariot was one of them. In some sense, he believed in Jesus along with the other disciples (John 2:11). Peter said, "he was numbered with us and obtained a part in this ministry" (Acts 1:17). Regardless, Judas was never anything but lost. Even when he was included in the general group of disciples who believed in Christ, he must have managed a kind of "movement belief," that is, he was carried along in the pro-Christ momentum of others. Just as the Lord Jesus said to those who followed Him, "'there are some of *you* who do not believe.' For Jesus knew from the beginning who they were who did not believe, and who would betray Him" (John 6:64). He went on to say, "Did I not choose you, the twelve, and one of you is a devil?" (John 6:70). Judas's status was made even clearer when Jesus told the disciples, "You are clean, but not all of you. For He knew who would betray Him; therefore He said, 'You are not all clean'" (John 13:10-11).

The story of Judas was not a commentary on the life of a saved person. Actually, the Bible singles him out as unique, even among lost souls. We find, for instance, many people recorded in scripture who were possessed by evil spirits, but only of Judas is it specifically said that "Satan entered him" (John 13:27). In addition, the destruction of Judas was specifically foretold in the Old Testament, as the Lord mentioned in His prayer—"...I kept them in Your name. Those whom You gave Me I have kept; and none of them is lost except the son of perdition, *that the scripture might be fulfilled*" (John 17:12). Thus, we find strong evidence that Judas was not a genuine believer, even for a moment. His was not the case of a saved person who was lost, but only that of a lost person who was lost.

Other New Testament examples involve Aninias and Sapphira, the Christian couple who lied to the Holy Spirit (Acts 5:3). Though both of them died instantly (Acts 5:5, 10), nothing was said about whether they lost their salvation. Their story emphasizes a disciplinary measure of God, not eternal loss. This is most likely also the case with Hymaneus and Alexander. First Timothy 1:19-20a tells us of those who "concerning the faith have suffered shipwreck, of whom are Hymaneus and Alexander." These two men were probably believers since, in the first place, they had faith that could be shipwrecked. Because of their evil words, Paul delivered both of them to Satan "that they may *learn* not to blaspheme" (1 Tim. 1:20). Paul had not damned them, but expected that the two seriously wayward believers would *learn* to respect holy things. This indicates correction unto rehabilitation, not eternal loss. Those who perish in the lake of fire never learn anything. They are only punished. Thus, Hymaneus and Alexander were Christians who were going to learn a lesson through severe chastisement, but they were not to be eternally cast off.

Finally, there is the uncertain case of Demas. He was a coworker of the Apostle Paul, but Paul's last mention of him was "Demas has forsaken me, having loved this present world" (2 Tim. 4:10). Loving this present world is a sad parting note for the Christian life. Yet we are told nothing further about Demas. We do not find for instance that he "loved this present world *and was lost.*" No such footnote exists. We might see Demas forsaking Paul, but we never find the Lord forsaking Demas. His example, therefore, demonstrates a poor spiritual condition, not a lost salvation.

Eternal security is never contradicted in any life story, whether it is around us today or recorded in scripture. We ought to expect this. God does not teach us one way in doctrine while acting another way in real life. He does according to what He says. He is consistent. Since He has thoroughly demonstrated through teaching that salvation is ours forever, He will not fail to work it out even in the most difficult true-life sagas.

A tug-of-war begins whenever the Lord starts to bring a person into the truth concerning His salvation. It is as though we have a bias against being supremely blessed. First, through the gospel, the Lord reveals what He wants to give men. They respond with, "That sounds too good to be true!" Then God offers it all through faith, to which they say, "That sounds too easy!" God provides proof so that they can know they have salvation *now*, but men say, "We can only know *then*." Finally, He promises that what they have received will never be taken back, to which they reply, "That's crazy!"

From start to finish, salvation is a miracle of grace. It befuddles the human mind. But once we set aside our opinions and surrender to "the wisdom that is from above" (James 3:17), we will find ourselves solid—standing on the rock which neither wind nor wave can ever destroy.

THE TRINITY

Many who have attempted to define the Holy Trinity with scientific precision have crashed on the rocks of theological error. I am always suspicious when someone claims to be clear about the Trinity so as to remove every difficulty related to understanding it. The truth is, even with the comprehensive scriptural truth God has given us, the Trinity remains the greatest mystery in the universe.

Therefore, we can only proceed to understand it with what the Bible tells us and, based upon that, whatever imperfect examples that we can invent. For the sake of those who are very new to the subject, I will present a few abbreviated thoughts concerning the trinity. The rest I will leave to other books.

As an encapsulated guideline, it is good for us to remember that Christians only have one God, not three

(Mark 12:29; 1 Cor. 8:6; Eph. 4:6). But it is also true that our God is a Trinity of Father, Son, and Spirit (Matt. 28:19; 2 Cor. 13:14), all three of which are fully God and exist together eternally. The three are *distinct,* but not *separate.* That is why some Christians call God the "triune God"— "Tri" referring to three and "une" referring to one. That term is used in order to preserve the two sides of God's truth about Himself—that He is never so three that He is no longer one and that He is never so one that He is no longer three.

Examples of the Trinity abound, but it is difficult to cite one that is truly comprehensive. When my daughter was nine years old, she decided that since Daddy served God, it meant he should be able to somehow explain God. I had read many books, studied theology, taught workshops and given public messages with the Trinity at the heart of the subject or at least in view. But it was not until my little girl was standing there waiting for an explanation of how the three could be one and yet still be three, that I knew none of my past experience was necessarily going to help me. I realized, for instance, that she would probably not respond to the language of deep theology. I wouldn't be able to impress her with terminology like "co-exist" or "co-inhere" or even "triune." So I took her by the hand and went outside in the yard where I hoped to locate a ready example of the triune God.

We found a silver maple. This tree often grows up in clusters of trunks. Some are composed of three main sections that are all very distinct from one another, but at the ground level, share a common base. It is one tree, not a grove of them. Yet, in that one tree are trunks so distinct that they sometimes perform different tasks. For instance, one trunk might hang over in just such a fashion and with just enough foliage that it provides shade to a backyard. Another trunk may have grown in such a way that its flat, leafy platforms make it easy for squirrels to build nests there. The third trunk might have developed a slightly thicker diameter, so kids have attached a tire swing to it. Thus, it is one tree with three distinct (but not separate) sections and functions, a rather imperfect but functional example of the Trinity.

My daughter felt satisfied with this front-yard model of the Father, the Son, and the Holy Spirit. Although it is far from academically profound, I use it here because sometimes an example that works for a child will work just as well for adults. And since, because of space, this book cannot possibly explore all the truth related to the Trinity, my few referenced verses and the silver maple will have to suffice for the moment.

APPENDIX 2

GOD'S CHOICE OR MAN'S?

In the matter of salvation, is it God who primarily chooses us or is it we who primarily choose Him? The Lord seems to settle the matter with His own words: "You did not choose Me but I chose you and appointed you" (John 15:16). With that statement divine prerogative gets the nod, without human choice anywhere on the horizon. But Acts 17:30 says, "God...now commands all men everywhere to repent." If human choice were unimportant, then why would the Lord bother to issue such a call? It would be needless, even cruel. God would be telling people to repent when He knew that some of them *could not* do it.

God's choice apparently does not exist by itself to the point that man's free will ceases to exist. Yet somehow divine selection remains undiluted alongside human choice. The Lord

Jesus was "delivered by the determined purpose and foreknowledge of God" (Acts 2:23). Every detail of His redemptive death was divinely planned in advance. He was carried along by what had been predetermined. Yet Jesus Himself testified, "I lay down My life that I may take it again. No one takes it from Me, but I lay it down *of Myself*" (John 10:170-18a). In our limited estimation, it must be either divine choice or human choice. The two are at odds. Yet in the Bible, there does not seem to be any tension between the two.

Concerning who gets saved, Paul says, "it is not of him who wills nor of him who runs, but of God who shows mercy" (Rom. 9:16). But we find in Revelation 22:17, "*Whoever desires*, let him take the water of life freely." One verse stresses the will of God, the other, the will of man.

The Lord made a decision to save us and then later in time, we made a decision to be saved in accordance with His decision. All of this occurred without any violation of human free will or anything superceding the sovereign will of God. If this sounds incongruent, let me once again appeal to the mysteries of the divine counsel: "The secret things belong to the Lord our God, but those things which are revealed belong to us and our children forever..." (Deut. 29:29).

Where is the convergence between God's complete sovereignty and the free will of man? How are we to reconcile the two? The Bible does not reveal it, therefore it does not belong to us. However, the necessity of God's choice and our choice *is* revealed. These two items belong to us and should be held equally precious by "us and our children forever."

Men can attempt to grasp what only omniscience can understand but confusion will result. God's "secret things" are not a playground for finite minds. Rather than try to unravel the mysteries of predestination versus free will, even Paul surrendered. Faced with the unknowable, he broke into praise, not questionings: "O the depth of the riches both of the wisdom and knowledge of God! How unsearchable are His judgments and His ways past finding out!" (Rom. 11:33).

The truth of God's choosing-predestinating was never

given to confuse us or to lead us into questioning Him. It was given for our praise of God and our joyful knowledge of the security of salvation. It is sufficient to say that God's choice as well as our own is necessary for salvation. The Bible shows us that both are required. However, it is God's choice alone that makes our salvation *secure*.

SMALL GROUP DISCUSSION QUESTIONS

REMEMBER!

Answering quickly and simply is not the point here. The real purpose of these exercises is to stimulate group discussion. Most of the questions can only be answered through deeper thought and group considerations.

1. Before meeting Christ, many people attempted to build a relationship with God based upon His law. Others, on their own terms, attempted to simply be spiritual and connect with their Creator. Did you ever do either one of these things? What was the outcome and how did it

contribute to your coming to Christ? (Reference pages 19-20).

2. Sometimes people say that Christians are too narrow minded because they think that only Jesus can save people. From the biblical viewpoint, how would you answer this? (Reference pages 20-25).

3. Before being exposed to the truth of the Bible, what did you think of world religions and their leaders? Do you perceive a cultural pressure to "build a tabernacle" for each of them? Where do you think this comes from?

4. In your estimation, what offends people about saying Jesus is the only way to God? Is it the statement itself or particular kinds of attitudes that go along with that statement? What do you think?

1. Before becoming a Christian, did you ever hear Christians use the words "saved" or "salvation"? If so, what did you think they meant? (Reference "Saved from what?" pages 27-28).

2. Contrast what society defines as sin with what it is according to God. (Reference "What is a sin?/Why God hates sin" pages 29-34).

3. "Sinner" is considered a derogatory term by many today. What should those reacting to such a term realize before they become offended? What should we as Christians understand as we use that word? (Reference "Who is a sinner? Surely not me!/Surely not them" pages 35-39).

4. What does the Lord's way of dealing with sin tell you about His values and His personality? (Reference "Why God doesn't just forgive and forget/God on death row" pages 40-45).

5. It is typical to hear people speak of being angry with the Lord because He didn't do certain things for them. After surveying His work on the cross, though, how do you feel about such sentiments? (Reference "Paid in full" pages 45-48).

6. After the Lord has paid our way and offered a receipt as proof that He has done so, are there any legitimate hurdles left that keep people from gladly accepting that payment? (Reference "How *the* payment becomes *your* payment" pages 48-51).

3

1. What are some of the issues that people must face in light of the Bible's warning about future judgment? (Reference "The certainty of judgment/Sin's ultimate penalty" pages 53-57).

2. In order to give themselves and others comfort, sinners often down play the more graphic biblical descriptions of hell. How would doing such a thing be a cheating and a disservice to people in general? (Reference "Hell is more than a metaphor/The incredible wrath of God" pages 57-64).

3. The lake of fire typically strikes fear and loathing into the hearts of sinners. In more ways than pointed out in the text, how can it provide a measure of relief to the people of God and deal with "unfinished business?" (Reference "Why hell is necessary" pages 64-68).

4. How would you answer someone who asked, "Why would a good God send people to hell? (Reference "The way out" pages 69-71).

5. Why study such an apparently morbid topic as hell? (Reference "Getting off the Titanic" pages 71-73).

1. Often people who claim to have "tried" Jesus in the past are disillusioned with Him. Do you know someone who is in this category? What were his/her complaints? How would a more accurate biblical perspective help? (Reference "What should we do with Jesus?" pages 75-78).

2. Receiving Christ can be a matter that is conceptually difficult to grasp. That is why even the idea of receiving must be given a "handle." How does the Bible do this and how does it simplify what we previously thought about receiving Christ? (Reference "How to receive Christ" pages 78-79).

3. Christians commonly speak of Christ being in them, but from an objective standpoint, why would this tend to sound incredible? (Reference "Christ in you—how is it possible?" pages 79-80).

4. Many religious systems heavily rely on physical things to stimulate faith. How does having an invisible Christ accomplish this much more effectively? (Reference "Christ being in you is better for you" pages 80-83).

5. If you wanted to ask a loved one if he/she had Christ in them, how would you ask and how would you help them

understand your question? (Reference "Christ is not standard equipment/What it means for Christ to live in you" pages 83-86).

6. As a believer, how is your condition better than you think? Offer personal examples and insight (Reference "The blessings of Christ being in you/You are greatly beloved/ You were greatly saved" pages 88-90).

7. Answer question number 6 in light of "You have been greatly enriched by the Lord's humanity/divinity/You now have hope" pages 90-103.

5

1. How could knowing the Spirit's identity change our attitudes concerning Him? (Reference "Who and what is the Spirit?" pages 105-108).

2. In a certain way, the Spirit's coming to us was Jesus' coming to us. How could this be? (Reference "How many persons do you need to receive?/Jesus going and the Spirit coming" pages 108-111).

3. Have you recently required strong help from the Holy Spirit? If so, in this question and in the next, share some experiences related to how you needed the Spirit's "emergency roadside assistance" (Reference "God's practical help for us/What the Spirit does" pages 111-116).

4. Continue the above question in reference to "The Spirit shows Jesus as He is/The Spirit solves the problem of the antique Jesus" pages 116-119.

5. Sometimes Christians wander from the Lord, even if it is only for a short time. How does the Spirit provide help during these times? If this has been your experience, share it with the group (Reference "The Spirit is God's mark of ownership/The Spirit guarantees the fullness of salvation" pages 119-121).

6. Crisis points develop when it is difficult for us to know how to progress as Christians. If you have passed through any of these places (or if you are currently in one) share your experience (you may want to keep some details private, just between yourself and the Lord). Take time to have some group prayer for those who desire it (Reference "The Spirit helps us to know how to pray/ Shows us how to continue following Christ" pages 121-126).

7. What cardinal point would a person miss while looking for big, visible proofs that he/she has the Spirit? (Reference "How does a person get the Holy Spirit?" pages 126-127).

8. How can we know that we have received "God's best"? (Reference "The glorious outcome of the Spirit in you/ The best that the Father and the Son can give us" pages 127-129).

1. There are fine distinctions between sin and death. How might spiritual death be worse than mere sin? (Reference "The living dead/Spiritual death and where it takes you" pages 131-135).

2. What are the most serious differences between the Bible's definition of eternal life and that of society's in

general? (Reference "What is eternal life?" pages 135-140).

3. The gospel we typically preach includes the death of Christ on the cross for our sins. Based on this section, though, how would you explain the cross of Christ to someone in a more complete way? (Reference "A blueprint for giving life" pages 140-143).

4. How would the literal understanding of John 3:16 not only change a person's outlook on his future, but his present as well? (Reference "How to receive eternal life" pages 143-144).

5. In some cases, "born again" has become a label attached to everything from political ideology to religious hatred. Would Jesus agree with that labeling? Why or why not? (Reference "A new life for a new birth" pages 144-149).

6. Receiving eternal life triggers the second birth, a very comprehensive new beginning. What are some of your own experiences related to this new start? (Reference "It renews and enlivens your human spirit/The second birth brings us into resurrection" pages 149-152).

7. Answer the above question in light of referencing "The second birth grants a new, soft heart/The second birth brings the nature and life-law of God into us" pages 153-158).

8. Some people believe that no one can really know God. In what way is this true and how could it be remedied? (Reference "Knowing God by His life" pages 158-160).

7

1. Does the phrase "children of the devil" have a shocking or abrasive effect upon you? Why? When you thought of that phrase in the past, what was the first thing that came to your mind? (Reference "A shocking fact/How men could be children of the devil" pages 161-164).

2. What implications about unsaved people can we draw from the example of Pinocchio? In simple but profound words, how would you help someone make the transition from a created child of God to an actual child of God? (Reference "How men become children of God/Real children, not metaphors" pages 164-167).

3. Many new believers unconsciously consider themselves as second-class children of God, or even worse, distant cousins. How does the truth of adoption address this misconception? (Reference "The most blessed place of all" pages 167-169).

4. Share some of your experiences as a child of God placed in the family of God (Reference "A place of extraordinary care/A place always watched over/A place of protection" pages 169-177).

5. Patience is definitely needed during the maturing process. Where do you feel yourself becoming impatient? How has God used trouble or pain to help your maturity? (Reference "Maturing in God's family/Growing pains among God's children" pages 178-184).

6. Consider carefully the future for which God is preparing you. Can you see where He has a lot more to do in your life? Share your impressions. (Reference "The future greatness of God's children" pages 185-188).

8

1. Describe in your own words how that a poorly understood beginning will lead to consequences down the road. Was grace a difficult concept for you to realize, trust and understand? Share your experiences (Reference "Beware of the Galatian trail/Grace—Not so easy to understand" pages 188-189).

2. Have you ever heard someone say, "I am trying to believe but I just can't"? From the biblical perspective, what does this statement indicate? (Reference "Receiving with your spiritual hands/Where does faith come from?" pages 195-197).

3. Can you see how a person might be too casual concerning belief in Christ and another person could make it too complicated? How? (Reference "What is true belief?/Don't make it complicated" pages 197-204).

4. Why do you think it is necessary to make the power of salvation clear to the reader? (Reference "The power of salvation" pages 204-208).

5. Before you were saved, did you have any experiences working for salvation? What were they? (Reference "Why faith and not works?" pages 208-214).

6. How could a misunderstanding of the law's purpose or the purpose of New Testament practices lead a person into the worse kind of confusion? (Reference "Why God gave the law/New Testament practices cannot bring salvation, either" pages 215-226).

7. Are good works worthless? Sort through the qualifications on this issue (Reference "The place of works" pages 226-228).

9

1. Do you know people who are assured of their salvation based on the faulty premises of page 230? How would you tactfully speak in a way that would awaken genuine concern in them for their salvation? On the other end of the spectrum, how would you deal with someone who thinks no one can know whether they are saved? (Reference "A legitimate concern/You can know that you are saved" pages 229-224).

2. Can you relate a story about how a manual or a map provided direction for you when your feelings were confusing an issue? Relate your example to the way that the Bible clarifies matters of salvation. (Reference "How to know that you are saved—the Bible says so" pages 234-237).

3. The intuitive witness of the Spirit within us often defies human logic. Can you provide a personal secular example of how sensations such as hunger, hot, cold, etc., did not follow rules of reason? (Reference "How to know that you are saved—the Spirit says so" pages 237-239).

4. Experiences of peace, joy, and love can also be found in the lives of unsaved people. How do they differ from the peace, joy, and love which is in the life of a saved person? (Reference "How to know that you are saved—Your experience says so" pages 239-247).

5. As a new believer, have you already encountered a "heightened sense of righteousness?" Without divulging

too many personal details, share your experience (Reference "How to know that you are saved—you have a new family likeness" pages 247-248).

6. There are a few basic reasons why people doubt their salvation. Have you found yourself falling into one of them? If so, how did the text and the verses help you? (Reference "Answering doubts—That terrible thing in your non-Christian past/Sins after salvation/How much faith is enough faith?" pages 248-260).

7. Based on the positive recommendations in the text, what life changes should you make, and how do you propose to carry them out? (Reference "Strengthening the assurance of our salvation/By living a life in the light and dealing with our failures/By participating in our own spiritual development" pages 260-265).

10

1. Have you ever been faced with circumstances in your own life or in the life of others that made you doubt eternal security or at least made you wonder if it was "fair?" If so, share them with your group. (Reference "Eternal Security—a controversial issue" pages 269-270).

2. Sometimes Christians make a decision to stop following Christ. It may only be an unconscious determination but they begin distancing themselves from fellowship with other believers and from healthy spiritual habits. In those circumstances, how does the principle of "gift" protect the ignorant and straying? Have you learned any lessons related to the principle of salvation as a gift? Without divulging too many sensitive details, describe how that you were personally encouraged or enlightened through it. (Reference "What if we don't deserve to keep

salvation?/Don't want it anymore?" pages 270-274).

3. If salvation cannot be lost due to loss of faith, then where exactly does "faith fatigue" pose a real problem to the Christian life? (Reference "Can our salvation be lost if we stop believing?" pages 275-278).

4. What are the chief differences between loss of fellowship with the Lord and loss of salvation? How can God deal with a sinful believer without recalling his salvation? (Reference "Can sins annul our salvation?/Can we lose our salvation temporarily until we repent?/Can salvation be lost due to special sins/repeated sins/Abused forgiveness" pages 278-295).

5. There can be slumps of all sizes for Christians. Some only last a few hours. Others can last for weeks or even years. Why are such backsliding events not able to destroy eternal life? If eternal life is indestructible, then why worry about being away from the Lord? What harm could it do? (Reference "Our salvation is secure because we have received eternal life" pages 294-299).

6. It might come as a surprise that your own identity guarantees your eternal security. Review why, as a saved person, you are now so important to God and how your new status prevents you from being lost. (Reference "Our salvation is secure because of what we have become" pages 299-307).

11

1. Due to certain misconceptions of God, we may come to the conclusion that our salvation is not secure. What are some of these misconceptions? From the standpoint of God's righteousness, love, and power, how could we

address them? (Reference "Because of who God is, we cannot lose our salvation" pages 309-319).

2. From a humorous angle, consider the way you choose things, pray for people, and make promises. Compare it to the way the Father chooses, Jesus prays, and the Spirit seals. Discuss how that only God's work could provide any security for our salvation (Reference "Because God's work is perfect, we cannot lose our salvation" pages 319-329).

3. In some places the scriptures seem to suggest that salvation can be lost. Why do you think some new readers of the Bible might understand these verses that way? If the concern of the verses in question is not loss of salvation, then what is it? (Reference "Doubts from the Bible" pages 329-341).

4. Did you ever know someone who fit the description of Pam's sister? Did he or she make you feel the way Pam felt? If you could talk to the straying sister, how would you encourage her and how would you warn her? (Reference "Doubts from real life" pages 341-345).

SELECT VERSES
SCRIPTURE INDEX

TOPICAL INDEX